Personal Finance on the Web

Personal Finance on the Web: The Interactive Guide

Jonathan Michaels

John Wiley & Sons, Inc.
New York • Chichester • Weinheim • Brisbane • Singapore • Toronto

To my wife Inger and my two
munchkins, Tyler & Tiana.
On every page, in every breath.

To my mother,
for the inspiration that she is.

To James Goodchild,
for his tireless assistance.

And to Bari Zahn, Esq.
for giving me the chance.

Death and Taxes

Credit

Big, warm, gushy thank-yous go out to Andrew, Britta, Dad, Dale, Dawn and Eden Gaetz, Flash, Glorieux Dougherty, Grandma Arizona, Grandma and Grandpa Florida, Hannelore, Kiki, Stephen, my clients and business associates at Active Matrix Software, and friends and family too numerous to mention by name but too important to be forgotten.

More than just making it possible, you make it all worthwhile.

Special thanks to my managing editor on this project, Michael Detweiler, for his outstanding effort, and to Mr. James Goodchild, head of research, Internet troubleshooter, PageMaker advisor, and general, all-around, good guy.

Everything is changing. Maybe you didn't see it coming, but here it is. And how we conduct the business of our lives will never be the same.

"Internet," "Web," "Information Superhighway," "Cyberspace"; words and concepts that barely registered as a blip on the radars of our need-to-know awareness just a couple of short years ago now blink back at us, big and bold, across everything we do.

The Net has exploded onto the scene to become one of the most conspicuous facets of everyday life. Turn on the TV and you're greeted by an ad for a soft drink or a minivan or a <u>Floss-O-Matic™ Plax Smacker</u>, all sporting a shiny new Web address, the voice-over carefully enunciating every colon, every dot com (H. T. T. P. Colon. Forwardslash. Forwardslash. Something. Dot. Something. Dot. Com).

The hype is unmistakable, it's nearly epidemic. Yet to dismiss the extraordinary changes that surround us as *just* hype is to risk being left behind in the electronic dust of this brave new world.

Nobody can say for sure how many of us there are crawling around on the Web right now. 30 million? 40? 50? The numbers cited are as varied as they are astounding, but the bottom line is clear; tens of millions of us have heeded the call, and millions more will join us on the Net in the months and years to come.

Of course, you know all about the rush to explore this new frontier firsthand or you wouldn't bother reading the introduction to yet another Internet book. You have already equipped yourself with the requisite gear and have set out to join the cyber-swarm on the Web.

So, what did you find when you got there? The following is a list, supplied by one of the World Wide Web's most popular starting points, of the ten most accessed Internet links as of the day this introduction was written:

      1.)   <u>Regarding Sex</u>
      2.)   <u>Alt.Sex</u>
      3.)   <u>America's Job Bank</u>
      4.)   <u>Index of Companies with Job Listings</u>
      5.)   <u>Urban Desires</u>
      6.)   <u>Leslie's World O'Chicks</u>
      7.)   <u>The Web Voyeur</u>
      8.)   <u>JobHunt Meta-list</u>
      9.)   <u>Internet Public Library</u>
     10.)   <u>Screen Savers For Windows</u>

Now, I have nothing personal against screen savers or the un- and underemployed. And as far as sex goes, I think it's fair to say that without it, I wouldn't be who I am today. But surely, there must be more to all the Net noise than just this.

As we collectively begin to extend beyond our physical boundaries and explore the greater reaches of accumulated human knowledge, wisdom and insight we can do better than what the above list implies. Or can we? Raise your hand if you believe that <u>Leslie's World O'Chicks</u> represents the pinnacle of the human experience. Uh-huh. Pretty much what I figured. You. In the bookstore, with your hand in the air. Yes, you. Put this book back on the shelf. The magazine section is over in the corner, behind the gardening aisle. As for the rest of you, let's get down to business.

Somewhere, deep in the heart of Germany, there is probably a small wooden privy with a plaque on it that reads (auf Deutsch, of course) "In this outhouse, c. 1451, Johann Gutenberg proofread the first printed edition of the Vulgate Bible."

Books have changed little since that illustrious moment in history, and otherwise decent enough people, like yourself, have been hauling how-to's with them into the can ever since. This book, however, is a little different, and unless you are truly hard-core about your lavatory literature, you probably won't want to go through the trouble of installing a phone-line in your private sanctuary or the expense of purchasing a porcelain coordinated laptop. This book is "interactive", a widely overused term that simply means that after 545 some odd years of publishing, the printed word has at long last joined the electronic age. Here, I'll show you how it works:

This is a picture of a page from this book: This is a picture of a Web page from this book's on-line counterpart:

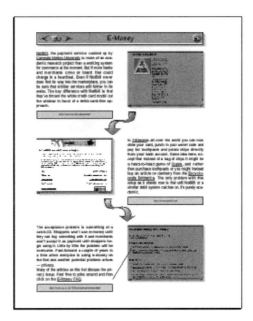

Notice any similarities?

As you can see, the printed book has an identical counterpart on the World Wide Web. Page 158 of the paper and ink version of the book (for one very random example) is reproduced faithfully on page 158 of the on-line version. The two versions work together so that you can get the most out of both the guide and the vast resources of the Web. With the printed book in front of you, you can easily see exactly where in Cyberspace you want to go and what the next step will be once you get there. With the electronic version of the book up on your computer screen, you can easily jump to any of the sites covered with a single click of your mouse.

Let's go in for a closer look ...

Before you can use the electronic version of the book there are a few things that you need to do. The first of which is to get there.

The http:// address for our Home page is **www.wiley.com/PRT/pfw** (the "/PRT" part does need to be capitalized). You can type this address directly into the space provided near the top of your browser's window. You would type it in like so and press the "Enter" key on your keyboard.

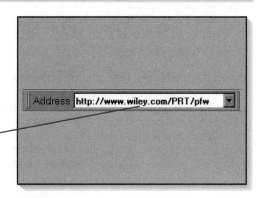

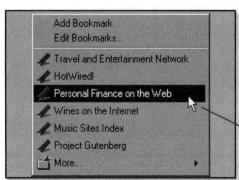

If you intend to use this site regularly, you will probably want to bookmark the Web page by choosing "Bookmark" (or "Favorites," or whatever variation on that theme that your particular browser uses) from your browser's menu and selecting "Add Bookmark" (or "Add Favorite") from the drop-down list.

Once added to your list of bookmarks, you can choose the site from your bookmarked list by name without having to type in the full address.

The on-line version of Personal Finance on the Web is both easy to use and faithful to the original paperbound version you have before you. To accomplish this feat, we use a clever little program called Adobe Acrobat. Once installed on your system, Acrobat enhances your Web browser to take advantage of it's features.

If you don't have Adobe Acrobat on your computer yet, you can click on the "Get Acrobat Reader" button from our Home page. Follow the instructions to install it and you're ready to go.

On our Home page you will notice two different versions of the guide.

Since you already own the printed book, all of the interactive features of Personal Finance on the Web are available to you.

Clicking on the button labelled "Interactive" takes you to the next step.

You will be prompted to supply a supersecret password before you can access the "Interactive" version of the book. And here it is:

GOTIT

Type this in to the space provided and click on the OK button to proceed.

Once inside the electronic pages of the book, navigating your way around is simple. At the top of each screen you will find the same forward and backward arrows that you see at the top of this page. Click on the appropriate arrow to move through the guide one page at a time.

Clicking on the page number between the arrows brings you to the Table of Contents. From there you can jump to any section in the book.

Further choices await you at the start of each topic. There you will find a menu listing all of the areas within that topic and buttons for each of the six main categories in the book.

Clicking on any of the items automatically takes you to that spot in the electronic guide. It's a quick and simple way of getting wherever you want to go.

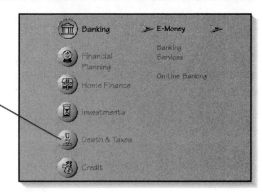

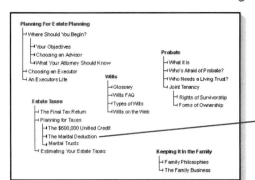

At the beginning of each section of the book you will find a graphical road map to all of the sites visited in the section's subsequent lessons.

Like everything else in the on-line version of the guide, the map is interactive; you can click on the name of any destination on the map to steer yourself to that specific spot on the Infobahn.

Throughout the book you will see screen captures of the Web sites being discussed. These pictures act as links to the Web page in the picture. Clicking on the picture to go to that site and use the printed version for guidance and instructions.

Don't be alarmed if the Web page looks different than the one pictured in the book, Web designers like to tinker, tweak and generally putz around with their sites. Such is the price of progress on the Web.

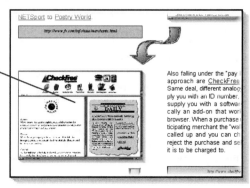

The blue, underlined text that you will come across throughout the book also works as a link to somewhere else on the Net. Clicking on one of these text links might bring you to the site being discussed, a different page within the book or somewhere completely strange and altogether wacky.

The Web is nothing if not a new world to explore. If you see a link that looks promising, click on it. You never know where you might end up.

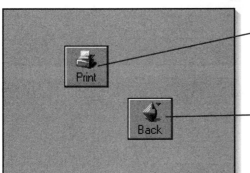

Remember, no matter where you go on the Web you can always use the Back button at the top of your browser's window to get back to where you left off.

And if you happen to chance upon some little personal finance gem in your travels, you can click on your browser's Print button and take it with you.

Flip through the guide and follow along with the interactive lessons on your computer. When you're ready to set off on your own, you can turn to the color-coordinated yellow pages located ever so conveniently at the back of the book and explore some more.

A world of personal finance resources awaits you on the Web. Poke around, learn, and most of all, enjoy.

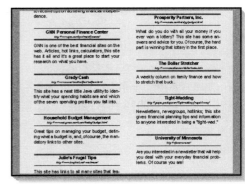

Click on the Page Number to
jump to the Table of Contents.

Use Arrows to move
forward and backward
one page at a time.

Use the Menu to navigate
between chapters and areas
of interest.

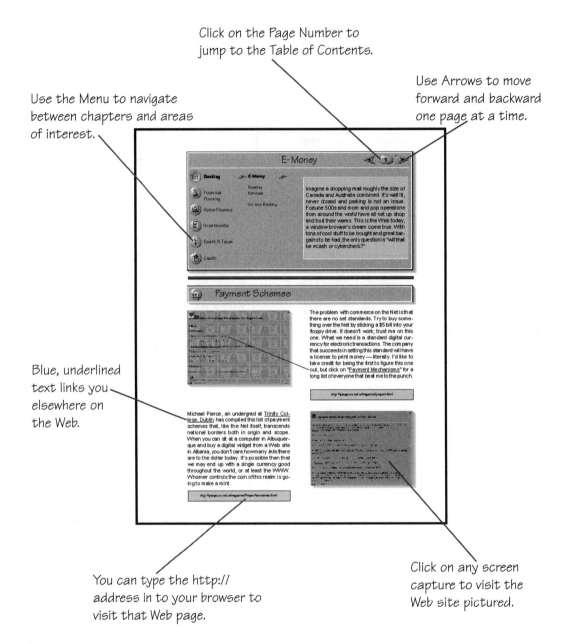

Blue, underlined
text links you
elsewhere on
the Web.

You can type the http://
address in to your browser to
visit that Web page.

Click on any screen
capture to visit the
Web site pictured.

E-Money

Payment Schemes

⊣ Network Payment Mechanisms and Digital Cash

    ⊣ First Virtual

    ⊣ CheckFree

    ⊣ NetBill

    ⊣ E-Money FAQ

    ⊣ DigiCash

⊣ Stuff You Can Buy

    ⊣ CD-Now

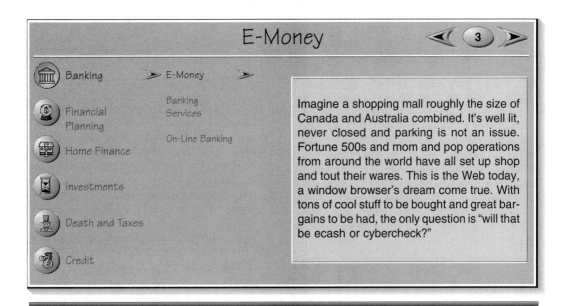

Banking

E-Money

Financial Planning

Banking Services

Home Finance

On-Line Banking

Investments

Death and Taxes

Credit

Imagine a shopping mall roughly the size of Canada and Australia combined. It's well lit, never closed and parking is not an issue. Fortune 500s and mom and pop operations from around the world have all set up shop and tout their wares. This is the Web today, a window browser's dream come true. With tons of cool stuff to be bought and great bargains to be had, the only question is "will that be ecash or cybercheck?"

Payment Schemes

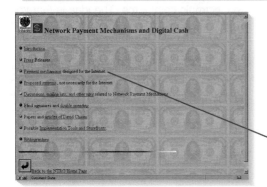

The problem with commerce on the Net is that there are no set standards. Try to buy something over the Net by sticking a $5 bill into your floppy drive. It doesn't work; trust me on this one. What we need is a standard digital currency for electronic transactions. The company that succeeds in setting this standard will have a license to print money—literally. I'd like to take credit for being the first to figure this one out, but click on "Payment Mechanisms" for a long list of everyone that beat me to the punch.

http://ganges.cs.tcd.ie/mepeirce/project.html

Michael Pierce, an undergrad at Trinity College, Dublin has compiled this list of payment schemes that, like the Net itself, transcends national borders both in origin and scope. When you can sit at a computer in Albuquerque and buy a digital widget from a Web site in Albania, you don't care how many *leks* there are to the dollar today. It's possible than that we may end up with a single currency good throughout the world, or at least the WWW. Whoever controls the coin of this realm is going to make a mint.

http://ganges.cs.tcd.ie/mepeirce/Project/oninternet.html

Payment mechanisms designed for the Internet

This is a collection of links and pointers to existing payment schemes that were designed for, or are in use on, the Internet. If you know of any more, please let me know. Now that I've finished my project, there is another one.
PayMe: Secure Payment for World Wide Web Services

- Anonymous Internet Mercantile Protocol
- BankNet offer an electronic cheque system in Sterling
- Brand's Cash. The PhD work of Stefan Brands on his Internet payment mechanisms
- CARI (Collect All Relevant Information), the Internet Voice Robot, uses virtual credit cards to provide secure transactions from the Web.
- Checkfree have plans for expanding the way commerce is conducted on the Internet.
- Clickshare is a publishing system to to track movements and settle charges for digital transactions.
- Commercenet are developing secure commerce on the Internet based on Secure HTTP
- CyberCash aims to offer secure credit card transactions, electronic checks and micro-transactions over the Internet. Currently they only have a credit card payment system. Here is the protocol specification. Later they will be migrating to SET for credit card payments. Also available are an abstract from a CyberCash paper presented at INET95 and a short presentation on CyberCash.

So, who's it going to be? Is Microsoft Money™ about to take on a whole new meaning? Is Chairman Bill's smiley face going to be on the face of your e-money anytime soon? Maybe. The software giant has thrown in their lot with Visa, but we have yet to see what these two will come up with. Meanwhile, the companies on this list have a head start. And though each one takes a slightly different approach, they all fall into one of three basic categories. Click on the link to First Virtual for an example.

http://ganges.cs.tcd.ie/mepeirce/Project/oninternet.html

First Virtual is one of several services that fall under the "pay later credit system" approach to electronic commerce. The idea is that you give these guys your credit card number and they give you an ID number. You then use this ID to purchase goods or services from participating merchants on the Net. The merchant passes your number back to First Virtual who proceeds to charge the amount, plus a small fee, to your credit card. In essence, the company acts as a clearinghouse for credit card transactions.

http://www.fv.com/

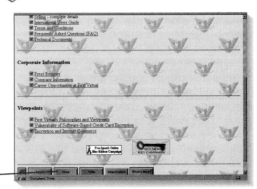

This saves you the trouble of having to whip out your plastic every time you want to make a purchase and, as an added bonus, all the merchant ever sees is your ID number. Your credit card number is protected and unless it's specifically asked for, so is your identity. It's probably no coincidence then that this approach is popular on "adult" (nudge, nudge, wink, wink) Web sites.

You can click the appropriate button to apply for an account, get additional information or click on Shop and see what you can buy.

http://www.fv.com/shop/index.html

Since Internet payment schemes are only as good as the sites that are set up to accept them, it's worth your while to take a look at where you can go and what you can buy before you apply for an account.

No payment plan has achieved anything close to universal acceptance yet, but with 2,200 merchants and counting, First Virtual is one of the more widely accepted. Sites that accept First Virtual as payment run the gamut from NETSport to Poetry World.

http://www.fv.com/shop/index.html

Also falling under the "pay later credit system" approach are CheckFree and Cybercheck. Same deal, different analogy. Rather than supply you with an ID number, these two services supply you with a software "wallet"—basically an add-on that works with your Web browser. When a purchase is made from a participating merchant the "wallet" is automatically called up and you can choose to accept or reject the purchase and select the credit card it is to be charged to.

http://www.checkfree.com/

Once again, the key benefit here is that your credit card information is not sent over the Internet, nor is it seen by any individual merchant. More than anything else, these systems boil down to an issue of security.

The problem arises when you don't want to purchase an item on your credit card. Or you can't. The idea of spending $.25 to have your cat's tarot cards read over the Net may not be *totally* ridiculous, but the idea of putting that $.25 reading on a credit card is. And if you don't have a credit card—tough.

http://www.checkfree.com/newcons.html

NetBill, the payment service cooked up by Carnegie Mellon University is more of an academic research project than a working system for commerce at the moment. But if more banks and merchants come on board that could change in a heartbeat. Even if NetBill never does find its way into the marketplace, you can be sure that similar services will follow in its wake. The key difference with NetBill is that they've thrown the whole credit card model out the window in favor of a debit-card-like approach.

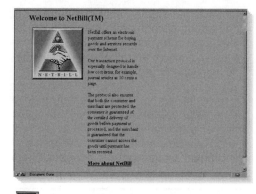

http://www.netbill.com

In 7-Elevens all over the world you can now slide your card, punch in your secret code and pay for toothpaste and potato chips directly from your bank account. Same idea here, except that instead of a bag of chips it might be a head-to-head game of Quake, and rather than purchase toothpaste you might instead buy an article on dentistry from the Encyclopedia Brittanica. The only problem with this setup as it stands now is that until NetBill or a similar debit system catches on, it's purely academic.

http://www.netbill.com/netbill/about.html

The acceptance problem is something of a catch-22; Shoppers won't use e-money until they can buy something with it and merchants won't accept it as payment until shoppers begin using it. Little by little the problem will be overcome. Fast-forward a couple of years to a time when everyone is using e-money on the Net and another potential problem arises—privacy.

Many of the articles on this list discuss the privacy issue. Feel free to poke around and then click on the E-Money FAQ.

http://www.ex.ac.uk/~RDavies/arian/emoney.html

Jim Miller, the author of the E-Money FAQ (frequently Asked Questions) splits digital dough into two basic food groups: identified e-money and anonymous e-money. All of the Internet Payment systems we've looked so far fall into the first category. When you buy something using one of those methods the money is fully traceable. You know exactly where your money's gone, the bank knows, the merchant knows, industrious marketing companies know, the IRS ...

http://www.ex.ac.uk/~RDavies/arian/emoneyfaq.html

E-money mini-FAQ (release 2.0)

Written by Jim Miller.

Comments to Jim_Miller@nsair.com
This Web page is maintained by Roy Davies. Comments to R.ey.Davies@exeter.ac.uk

- How is electronic money (e-money) possible?
- Are there different kinds of e-money?
- What is the double-spending problem?
- Where can I learn more about electronic money?

Q: How is electronic money (e-money) possible?

A: Public-key cryptography and digital signatures (both blind and non-blind signatures) make e-money possible. It would take too long to go into detail how public-key cryptography and digital signatures work. Put the basic gist is that banks and customers would have public-key encryption keys. Public-key encryption keys come in pairs. A private key known only to the owner, and a public key, made available to everyone. Whatever the private key encrypts, the public key can decrypt, and vice versa. Banks and customers use their keys to encrypt (for security) and sign (for identification) blocks of digital data that represent money orders. A bank "signs" money orders using its private key and customers and merchants verify the signed money orders using the bank's widely published public key. Customers sign deposits and withdrawals using their private key and the bank uses the customer's public key to verify the signed withdrawals and deposits.

Go to the top of this page.

Identified and anonymous systems both have their good and bad points. If anonymous currency takes off you'll still have to file your taxes every year. That's bad. If traceable e-money takes over you won't have to file your taxes, the IRS will just send you a bill. That's good— for the IRS anyway.

Take a look at what David Chaum, privacy crusader and founder of DigiCash Systems, had to say on the subject before the U.S. House of Representatives.

http://www.digicash.com/publish/pu_le.html

publications lecture transcriptions

- D. Chaum at Doors of Perception 2 Conference
- Testimony for US House of Representatives by D. Chaum

publications **digicash home**

Whether or not anonymous currency will be supported by government remains to be seen. The fear being that anonymity lends itself to illegal activity and money laundering. Dr. Chaum's testimony addresses that concern. Read it and decide for yourself how concerned we really ought to be.

Assuming that you're not a drug dealer, privacy, or lack thereof, is still an issue. When your every purchase can be monitored and your spending habits added to a database and sold, you can bet they will be.

http://www.digicash.com/publish/testimony.html

publications lecture transcriptions

David Chaum's testimony for US House of Representatives

Committee on Banking and Financial Services

Subcommittee on Domestic and International Monetary Policy

July 25, 1995

16 Chairman, Members of the Committee:

As an American who is regarded as the inventor of electronic cash, who has worked over the last dozen or so years to make the technology usable, and who is now CEO of a leading company pioneering in its commercialization, I am very pleased by the interest being shown here and to be here today.

We are being forced to decide between two very different kinds of electronic payment technology. The core values we as a nation have fought for, and continue to stand for, are at stake. As a consequence of choosing one of the two directions, these values will be profoundly eroded; by choosing the other direction, however, they will be preserved and likely extended. Wise decisions at this critical juncture may also allow us to avoid certain other pitfalls and to realize economic leadership and growth.

I think my limited time before you is best used to briefly explain the fundamentally different approaches to security, before coming to privacy, privacy technology, and its implications.

Use traceable e-money to look at the on-line Sports Illustrated Swimsuit issue and your name could be sold to Raunchies Smut Shack and added onto their mailing list. Download one too many creamy french recipes and your insurance premiums might mysteriously go up. These examples might sound far-fetched but use your imagination and the potential for abuse becomes obvious. With that in mind, click on the digicash home button at the bottom of the screen.

http://www.digicash.com/publish/testimony.html

DigiCash was one of the first companies to enter into the Internet currency fray. It remains one of the few to have embraced privacy as a central tenant in it's vision of the future. Based out of Amsterdam, DigiCash, the company, has had success with its smartcard and automatic road toll technology. Now they've turned their attention to the Net. The result is Ecash, an anonymous payment system for Cyberspace. Click on the Ecash button and on What is Ecash? on the next screen.

http://www.digicash.com/home.html

Essentially, Ecash is the digital equivalent of paper money. It works just like the money in your pocket with your computer's hard drive taking the place of a well-worn leather wallet. Like paper money, when you spend ecash you don't inadvertently leave behind personal information. The money simply changes hands (or hard drives, as the case may be).

To see how it works in action try clicking on the An Introduction to Ecash link at either the top or the bottom of the page.

http://www.digicash.com/ecash/about.html

You can't put money into your computer by dropping quarters into the floppy drive. Somewhere along the line you'll have to open up an account with a bank that supports ecash and withdraw spending money electronically from that account. The money is then put onto your hard drive. It's like visiting an ATM before going to the mall. You can also accept ecash from a friend who owes you or a (very hip) grandmother who wants you to buy yourself something nice for your birthday.

http://www.digicash.com/publish/ecash_intro/ecash_intro.html

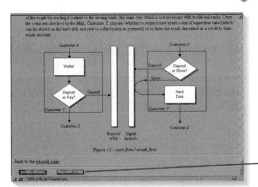

If granny is not only hip but generous as well, you can deposit the money back into your bank account. In almost every way, ecash acts just like paper money. Of course, that has its drawbacks too. Like cash, ecash can be lost or stolen. If your hard drive crashes, it's gone. If your laptop is stolen, so is the money stored on it.

The tutorial explains how it all works. Browse through it and when you're done, click the digicash home button.

http://www.digicash.com/publish/ecash_intro/ecash_intro.html

From the DigiCash home page, click on the Cybershops button and you will find yourself here. Again, you will need to open up an ecash account with a participating bank. Right now your choices are pretty slim. You can open up accounts either in Finnish Marks or U.S. dollars but there is currently only one U.S. bank to offer the service. Unless you want to see what a Finnish mark will buy you, click on the list of shops selling real objects for U.S. dollars link and jump to the Mark Twain Bank.

http://www.digicash.com/shops/cybershop.html

Don't despair, the speed at which the Net is evolving is nothing short of amazing. If ecash catches on more banks will begin to offer the service. At the time of this writing however, this is it. You can click on the "ecash" link at the bottom of the page and sign up for an account with the Mark Twain bank or click on any of the links at the top of the page for a list of on-line shops currently accepting ecash as a method of payment.

http://www.marktwain.com/shops.html

Like the other Internet payment schemes we've looked at in this chapter, the list of on-line stores accepting ecash is clearly in need of some expansion. At the moment, most of the stores that do accept electronic currency are small shops selling small items for small change. This too shall pass.

Try clicking on the link to the polished on-line music mega-store CD Now for a taste of things to come.

http://www.marktwain.com/shops/alpha.html

High-end stores like this one are popping up all over the World Wide Web. Few of them are set up to accept electronic currency at the moment, but it's hard to imagine that that can last. One way or another, e-money is coming to a computer near you. No one can yet say for sure which company will reach critical mass first but the Net is a big place built on a foundation of choice. Credit card clearinghouses, debit systems, and digital cash will all have their place, and their purpose, on the Net of tomorrow.

http://www.cdnow.com/

Banking Services

Financial Institutions
- Trusts
- Credit Unions
- Insurance

Savings Accounts
- Overview
- Passbook Savings Accounts
- Savings Clubs
- Money Market Accounts
- Cds

Checking Accounts
- Choosing a Checking Account
- Printing Your Own

ATMs
- Locating The Nearest ATM

Currency Conversion
- The Going Rate
- Historical Overview

Safeguarding Your Valuables in a New Age
- The Digital Bank Vault

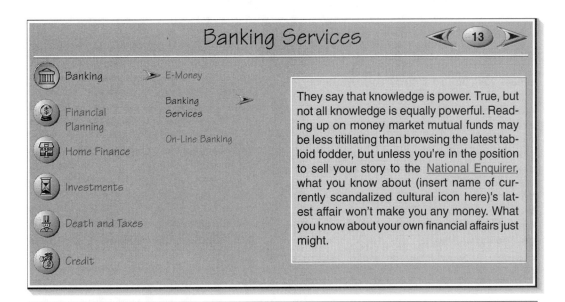

Banking

E-Money

Financial Planning

Banking Services

On-Line Banking

Home Finance

Investments

Death and Taxes

Credit

They say that knowledge is power. True, but not all knowledge is equally powerful. Reading up on money market mutual funds may be less titillating than browsing the latest tabloid fodder, but unless you're in the position to sell your story to the National Enquirer, what you know about (insert name of currently scandalized cultural icon here)'s latest affair won't make you any money. What you know about your own financial affairs just might.

Financial Institutions

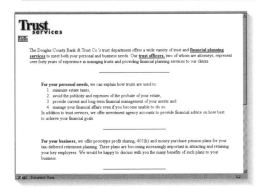

Banks, credit unions, and trust companies are usually lumped together in the public's mind, and not without reason either. Since they all offer most of the same day-to-day core services, it's the little distinctions that make up the difference. Distinctions like financial planning services and fiduciary responsibilities. Trust companies can offer these services. By law, banks can not. If the idea of one-stop financial services shopping appeals to you then banking at a trust company might be the way to go.

http://www.dcbt.com/trusts.html

Credit unions are another alternative to banks. As this Web page from the Boulder Community Network points out, credit unions are non-profit organizations. Unlike a bank owned by shareholders hoping to turn a profit, a credit union is owned solely by its own members. Any profits that the union makes is passed back to those members, usually in the form of lowered loan rates and enhanced services. It's a good deal if you can get in on it. The catch is that not everyone can.

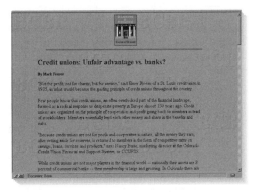

http://bcn.boulder.co.us/../business/BCBR/1995/oct/creditu2.html

Before you can join a credit union you must first be part of a company, community, church, or other group that sponsors one. There are over 1,200 credit unions in the U.S. and almost that many again north of the border, but since credit unions rarely advertise, finding them has traditionally meant searching through the yellow pages.

With links to virtually every credit union on the Web, the Credit Union National Association offers a high tech alternative to letting your fingers do the walking.

http://www05.web.binc.net:80/page4h.htm

No matter which of these "banks" you do your banking at, as long as your account is insured your money is protected. That's not to say that if you invest in pork futures through your bank you can't go belly up, but if some swine with a stocking over his head manages to make off with your money, your savings are secure. Through the FDIC, your checking, saving, CDs and retirement accounts are insured for up to $100,000. In Canada, the CDIC covers most accounts for up to $60,000. Lose more than that and you can kiss your assets good-bye.

http://www.fdic.gov/consumer/fdiciorn.html

Savings Accounts

Member ownership and investment services aside, all banks (and I'm using the lumpy sense of the word here) offer pretty much the same types of savings accounts. You've got your statement accounts, money market accounts, passbook accounts, and holiday/Christmas/vacation savings club accounts. The Tripod Web site does a fine job of describing them all. No one's sure how a subway token got mixed in with the pocket change, but click on it to learn more about the types of savings accounts.

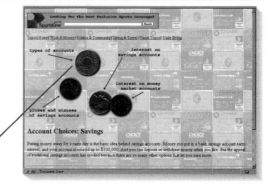

http://www.tripod.com/work/lightbulb/banking/bank3.html

Given the choice between having a savings account and being destitute, the savings account is always preferable. Given the choice between umteen different *types* of savings accounts though and the choice isn't quite so cut-and-dry anymore. Hopefully, this page can clear things up a bit. It describes the myriad of savings account options open to you, discusses the pluses and minuses of each, and, further down the page, delves into how the interest on those accounts will be calculated.

http://www.tripod.com/work/lightbulb/banking/bank3.html#types

Passbook accounts are your old fashioned walk-into-the-bank-with-your-passbook-wait-on-line-with-your-passbook-proceed-to-the-teller-with-your-passbook-have-the-teller-record-the-transaction-in-the-passbook-admire-the-new-balance-in-your-passbook-promptly-lose-your-passbook-have-to-pay-for-a-new-passbook type of savings accounts. Passbook accounts may not be good for the forgetful, but if you *can* manage to keep track of the booklet you'll always know where your balance stands.

http://www.fmmarinette.com/passbook.htm

Statement accounts are just like passbook accounts—without the passbook. Instead, you are mailed a statement of your account, usually monthly. Which you decide to go with is a matter of convenience more than anything else. The difference in fees tend to be nominal and the interest that you'll make on either is identical.

As more banks become Net savvy, you will be able to access your account statements online. Security First National Bank offers a vision of statements to come.

http://www.sfnb.com/demo/h_statement.html

Holiday Savings club accounts are used with a certain termination date in mind (like Christmas). A fixed-dollar amount is deposited into the account each week either by yourself, through direct deposits from other accounts, or through a payroll deduction. Come Christmas or vacation (or whatever) time, you should have accumulated enough to fill a few stockings or relax on a quiet beach.

Commonwealth Credit Union has a description of their saving clubs on-line.

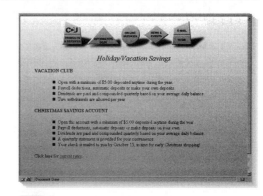

http://www.ccuky.org/prodserv/savings/holvac_savings.html

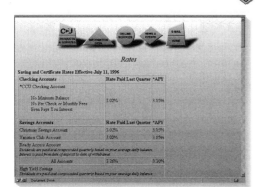

Interest is typically on par with savings accounts although some "clubs" pay little or no interest at all. More so than with any of the other types of savings accounts, putting your money here is a matter of convenience, not investment. They offer peace of mind and a higher interest rate than stashing your loot under a mattress, but even at their best, the money that you'll make in interest is often lost to inflation. That said, collecting a little interest on your savings is better than collecting little dust bunnies.

http://www.ccuky.org/prodserv/rates.html

Money Market accounts are savings accounts with a twist. They require that you keep a higher minimum balance than with other savings accounts but they also pay a slightly higher interest rate and offer perks that other savings accounts do not. Namely, with a money market account you can write a limited number of checks each month.

Prime Rate has an on-line program to search for the best interest rates based on your minimum balance. Select your projected balance and click on "Search ..."

http://www.primerate.com/scripts/dbml.exe?template=/menu/10mm.htm

Based on the minimum balance that you entered you will get a screen showing the best rates from the banks listed with Prime Rate. Repeat: the banks *listed with Prime Rate*. You will find good deals here, no doubt about that, but you should use the rates that you find here to compare with rates that you can get elsewhere.

Once you're satisfied that these rates are the best out there you can click on the "Go" button to the left of the bank's name and visit that bank's Home Page.

http://www.primerate.com/scripts/dbnl.exe?template=/menu/10mm.htm

By now you have a handle on savings accounts in all their various incarnations. A CD (certificate of deposit, that is, not the latest Hootie release) is a different way for you to invest through a bank. They pay higher interest than most savings accounts but carry the same negligible risks. The drawback with CDs is that your money remains locked up for a fixed period of time. Take your money out early and you will have to pay the penalty. Citizens Banks' CD offering is typical of what you can expect.

http://www.cnbe.com/ledocs/198sav.shtml

CD term lengths can be as short as one month or as long as 20+ years with six months and one year terms the most popular.

The interest you earn on CDs can be paid out through monthly checks or added back into the pile and compounded until maturity. To compare any two CDs that pay interest through monthly checks, look at the APR (or annual percentage rate) figures. With compounded CDs, you will want to compare the AAY (Annual Average Yield).

http://www.cnbe.com/ledocs/198sav.shtml

Limiting your CD shopping to banks in your geographical area is like only buying stock in local companies. Supporting your local bank is an admirable ambition but it won't always get you the best rates. CD brokers like Bank-CD Rate Scanner buy huge CDs from thousands of banks around the country and divide them up into easier to swallow pieces for the average investor. Since they buy in bulk, these brokers tend to get better rates than you or I could. Click on the List Of Top CD Rates in the USA.

http://vanbc.wimsey.com/~emandel/BankCD.html

APR (Annual Percentage Rate): interest rate with a monthly (or
    semi-annual) check being paid.
APY (Annual Percentage Yield): yield if compounded interest is
    calculated for one year only.
AAY (Annual Average Yield): yield if compounded interest is
    calculated until maturity.

+: higher amount available.
c: callable.
i: inverse variable.
s: semi-annual interest checks.
u: step-up.
v: variable.

This is our complete CD list as of today (CDs with lower amounts and/or different terms are not available); rates subject to change, no fees to pay (except for IRA's). If you are interested in any of the above CDs, please select the appropriate one and let us know by using our
CD-RATE QUOTE FORM.

Since you are buying only a piece of a much larger CD, brokers can often resell your CD before their term. Unlike banks, however, brokers often charge a fee for their services. Bank-CD Rate Scanner, in particular, does not. The rate you are quoted is the rate that you'll get.

To have them send you a quote based on your needs click on CD-RATE QUOTE FORM at the bottom of the page and fill out the form. Compare the quote that you receive with what you can get elsewhere.

http://vanbc.wimsey.com/~emandel/list.html

Checking Accounts

You're no fool. You know what a check is and you know how a checking account works. Not the little in and outs perhaps, but certainly enough to deposit your check every payday or pay for groceries at the supermarket. This is not rocket science we're talking about here. But pop back to the Web pages of Tripod and click on Choosing a Checking Account and you realize that what you don't know about checking accounts can fill a book. A very tiny book. More of a paragraph actually ...

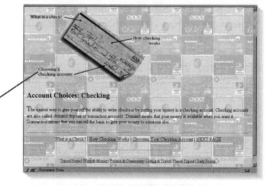

http://www.tripod.com/work/lightbulb/banking/bank2.html

Scroll up the page for a brief history lesson and a quick description of checks or read about bounced checks, overdraft protection, stop payments, and the like. Further down the page you'll find information on the many different checking account options. You've got your regular checking accounts, NOW accounts, money market, mutual fund, and asset management accounts. There are a lot of choices here. Choose the right one for your particular needs and you can end up saving money in the process.

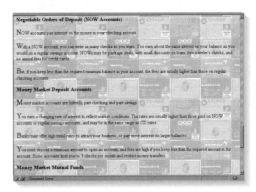

http://www.tripod.com/work/lightbulb/banking/bank2.html#how

In the brief history of checks on the previous site it was mentioned that checks used to be handwritten. I don't know how a handwritten check would go over today, but there's no reason why you can't print them yourselves. ChecksForFree is one company on the Net that gives you the software to do it. And, as the name implies, the software is free.

Click on the Download the free software link link to get the software (Windows only) or click on What's MICR ... to learn why the company is being so charitable.

http://www.checksforfree.com/

By supplying the software for free, the company *is* being generous. But they're not stupid. Anyone can print checks on a laser printer at home, but for the banks to be able to read those checks you need to use a special magnetic ink (or toner) and the paper that goes with it. ChecksForFree makes money by selling this paper and ink. Nothing in life is free, but it can still be a good deal. Besides being convenient, printing your own checks can save you up to 90 percent on the cost of preprinted checks.

http://www.checksforfree.com/whatmicr.htm

No matter how sophisticated home banking becomes, the personal computer will never take the place of an ATM stocked with cash and ready to dispense bills that you can hold in your hand, see, touch, smell, or taste. Not that anyone would *want* to taste their money, but it's nice to know that the option is always there if you need it.

There are over 100,000 ATMs in America. Almost every one of which supports either Visa, PLUS, or both. Click on Visa's Interactive maps link and find the nearest one.

http://www.visa.com/cgi-bin/vee/vw/products/atm/world.html?2+0

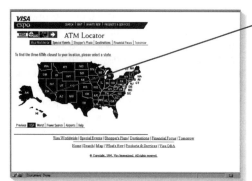

You can click on any state to begin your search for the three nearest ATMs.

Currently, Visa's ATM locator is limited to ATMs in the United States. With Visa cash machines in over 100 countries around the world it would seem that Visa truly is everywhere you want to be. Once you get there though, you're on your own. Visa will likely expand this service in the future. In the meanwhile, many Canadian banks offer a similar, albeit more partisan, feature.

http://visa.infonow.net/usa.html

Select the city and enter in a street address or the nearest intersection. If you happen to know the zip code, enter it too, it speeds things up a bit. When you're done click on the "Submit" button.

Chances are you already know where the closest ATMs are in your neighborhood, but if you're heading out on vacation or stepping outside of your usual stomping grounds, this can be handy. Of course, unless you take a laptop with a cellular Internet connection with you, you'll need to plan ahead.

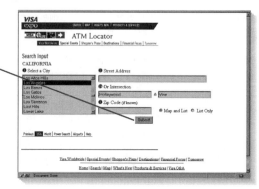

http://visa.infonow.net/usa.html

You can click on the ATM1, 2, or 3 buttons below the map to zoom in on a specific ATM or scroll down the page for the street address, hours of operation, and name of the bank that hosts the machine.

If nothing else, this is one cool little Internet toy. I have to admit that I entered the addresses of distant friends and family members, just to see where they live. Boys will be boys.

http://visa.infonow.net/usa.html

Currency Conversion

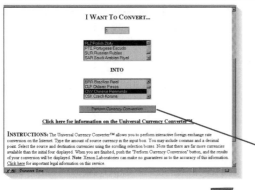

ATMs let you get your hands on money anywhere in the world. But how much local money will you get for your dollar? Banks used to be the first place to check the current exchange rates, but even banks can't offer the flexibility and convenience of Xenon Lab's Universal Currency Converter.

Pop in the amount that you want to convert, select the two currencies that you want to convert between (there are almost 60 to choose from) and click the "Perform Currency Conversion" button.

http://www.xe.net/currency/

It might interest you to know that on the day I checked it out, the going rate was 3.042 renmimbis to the zloty. Just in case you were wondering.

Also at the time of this writing, the exchange rates posted were taken from the morning paper with plans in the work to have the rates piped in in real time. Because you don't want to be taken by surprise when the zloty skyrockets, leaving you stuck with a wallet full of worthless renmimbis.

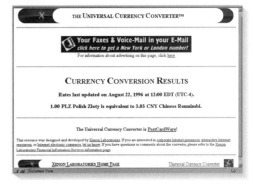

http://www.xe.net/cgi-bin/convert.new

The PACIFIC project from The University of British Columbia interacts with the data supplied by Xenon Laboratories and adds additional features and several new ways to manipulate the currency exchange rates. One of the more interesting things that PACIFIC allows you to do is plot historical exchange rates and display the results graphically. Choose the currencies that you want to plot, the time period to be shown and any other variable of interest then click the "Plot" button for the results.

http://pacific.commerce.ubc.ca/xr/plot.html

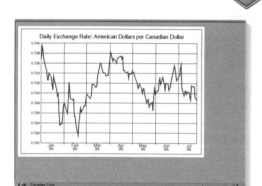

You get a graph showing how any given currency has fared against another over the specified period of time. If you go back to plot another set of numbers be sure to click the "Reload" button on your Web browser to ensure that you're not seeing the same graph again.

Die-hard investor types can display up to four years of data and plot currencies against precious metals. It's not a service that everyone will need, but for those that do, it can't be beat.

http://pacific.commerce.ubc.ca/cgi-bin/xrplot

Safeguarding Your Valuables in a New Age

Another function that banks commonly serve as is safekeeper of our valuables. And what better place to keep your jewelry, important papers, and dead fish than behind a bank vault (Just joking about the dead fish part. Don't want to give the rowdies amongst us any bad ideas).

Clyde Savings Bank offers a glimpse into the security features that banks employ to protect your valuables and some of the typical costs associated with renting a safety deposit box.

http://www.hometownbank.com/clyde/safebox.htm

As what we consider valuable broadens to include the intangible electronic documents that we live by, our ideas about safe storage has begun to change as well. Lifespanweb offers an electronic "safety deposit box" service designed to archive and protect your most precious data. You can't keep grandma's jewelry here, but you can store notarized images of your most important documents and copies of your most sensitive data, secure in the knowledge that your digital valuables are now safe.

http://www.twoscan.com/2scan/lifespanweb/sdb/

On-Line Banking

Banks of the World
- Comprehensive List of Banks on the Internet
- The Best Banks on the World Wide Web

Home Banking
- Proprietary Systems
- The Security Issue
- Taking a Test Drive
- Transferring Money
- Paying Bills
- Pay Anyone, Anywhere

Balancing Your Checkbook
- Doing it by Hand
- Software Assistance

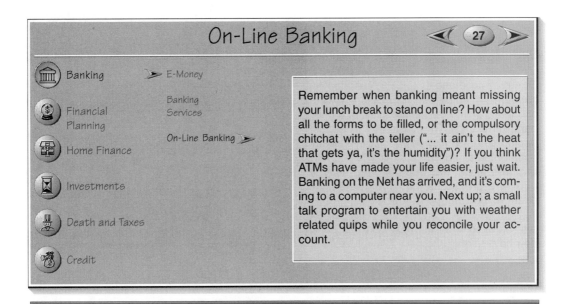

On-Line Banking

Remember when banking meant missing your lunch break to stand on line? How about all the forms to be filled, or the compulsory chitchat with the teller ("... it ain't the heat that gets ya, it's the humidity")? If you think ATMs have made your life easier, just wait. Banking on the Net has arrived, and it's coming to a computer near you. Next up; a small talk program to entertain you with weather related quips while you reconcile your account.

Banks of the World

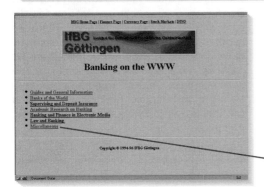

Just in case you needed proof that banking on the World Wide Web is indeed a world wide phenomenon, IfBG Göttingen brings us all one step closer to the corner branch.

IfBG Götwhataname lists a lot more banks than we can ever hope to cover here, so it might be a good idea for you to bookmark this page and come back later to visit more of the Banks of the World on your own. For the moment however, click on Miscellaneous.

http://wwpu20.wiso.gwdg.de/ifbg/banking.html

Tossed into the miscellaneous pile is a collection of banking odds and ends for you to sift through when you're looking for anything to do with banking on the Net other than the banks themselves. Help wanted postings, news of the day, tips, editorials... Everything about cyber-banking that you might possibly want to know. Unless, of course, all you want to know is how to pay your bills. In which case it's probably more than you need. So click on Banking on the Web and we're outta here.

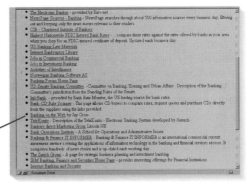

http://www.gwdg.de/~ifbg/bank_6.html

This Web page and its update illustrate what happened when the banking industry woke up and found themselves in the midst of a major paradigm change. Their customers were stampeding onto the Net and it quickly became apparent to all concerned that a radical new business model was in order. The result, to borrow a phrase, is that when paradigms change, shift happens. Click on Winners: Toronto Dominion and Wells Fargo for examples of some of the best shift that banks now have to offer.

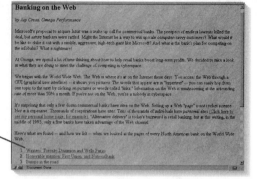

http://www.omega.sf.ca.us/bankweb.html

Home Banking

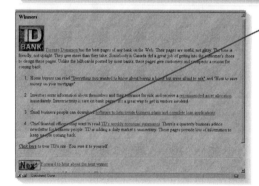

You are going to click the Click here link and take a tour of the Toronto Dominion Web site. Don't worry about whether or not you actually bank with TD, it's besides the point. There are hundreds of banks in North America alone, all of which either already have on-line banking services in place or will before too long. The particular layout of their Web pages, the buttons, graphics and links, are different with each site, but they all share the same basic features. And that is the point.

http://www.omega.sf.ca.us/winners.html

Rather than walk you step-by-step through the Web pages of a bank that you may never have heard of, let alone bank at, this chapter will instead highlight some of the best examples of the most common on-line banking services. These are the same services that you will likely find on the Web pages of your own bank, whatever bank that happens to be.

Try clicking on Preview TD Access for example.

http://www.tdbank.ca/tdbank/index.html

You are given the opportunity to learn about Toronto Dominion's "Access" software. The software does everything that you would expect from an on-line banking service. You can pay bills, transfer funds and so on, but what's so notable about TD's offering is less what it does than what it does not. Namely, it does not run over the Net.

This is one of the two directions at home banking seems to be heading in, and there's a good chance that this is where your bank will want you to go.

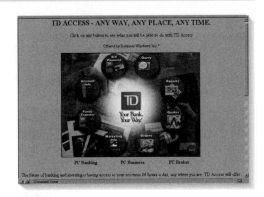

http://www.tdbank.ca/tdbank/tdaccess/index.html

There is nothing necessarily wrong with this no-Net approach, as long as you know what you're in for. Rather than managing your bank account over the Internet with a Web browser you would instead use the bank's propriety software to dial in to a local phone number. You can expect to pay an initial connection charge (TD charges $4.95) plus a monthly fee (in this case $3 a month) for the service. It would seem that banks are in business to make money after all. Imagine that.

http://www.tdbank.ca/tdbank/tdaccess/account.html

The issue of security on the Net has received a lot of attention in the press lately. The security issue *is* real and the concerns *are* valid, but despite the portrayal of pimply teenage super-hackers pounding away at their keyboards and siphoning millions from an unsuspecting public, no one has yet to lose even a single cent to these mythical cyberpunks. But then, no one wants to be the first either. Warranted or not, the upside to all of this attention has been tightened security and safer transactions.

http://www.qup.com/secur.htm

Canada Trust shows the same sort of security precautions that you can expect to see on your own bank's Web site. It takes advantage of the secure mode feature built into the current generation of Web browsers and requires a password before access to account information is allowed.

With these two safeguarding features in place it is reasonably safe to assume that you will lose more money renting bad movies about thieving cyberpunks than you will ever lose to the real thing.

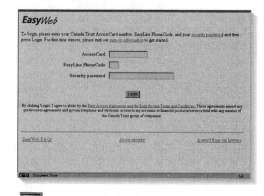

https://secure1.canadatrust.com/cgi-bin/web-bank

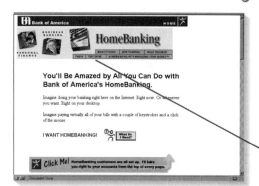

In contrast to the proprietary solutions that some banks have turned to, the Bank of America has gone the way of the Web. Kind of cool since (1) you can manage your finances over the Net and (2) it gives us something to talk about, this being an Internet book and all. Cooler still is that the Bank of America has invited all 30 million of us over to their site to play around with their new HomeBanking toy. You don't even have to be a customer, just click on the Test Drive button near the top of the page.

http://www.bankamerica.com/p-finance/homebanking/
homebanking.html

Ignore this page and click the "Continue" button. Actually, don't. Read this page and notice how B of A states, in no uncertain terms, that Netscape Navigator is *required* in order to use their HomeBanking service. Uh-uh. As long as your Web browser supports the industry standard SSL protocol and Java scripts (and because they are standard, pretty much all popular browsers do) you can let your personal preference dictate your choice in browsers, not your bank. *Now* you can click on "Continue."

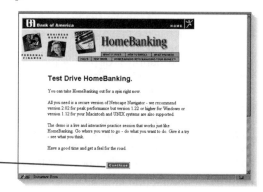

http://www.bankamerica.com/p-finance/homebanking/
hb_testdrive.html

See the key (or if you're using a different browser, it's equivalent)? It sits there in the corner of your browser's window to let you know when you've entered a secure area. Whenever you see it (or it's equivalent) you can rest assured that any private information that you supply will remain private.

If this was "real" you would have your own unique password and ID. But it's not, so just go with the supplied password and ID and click the "OK" button to continue.

http://www.bankamerica.com/p-finance/homebanking/
hb_testdrive.html

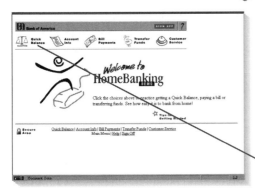

Like most other on-line banking services, Bank of America's HomeBanking lets you check your balance, pay bills and transfer funds from your computer. Also like most other on-line banking services, there is a monthly charge for the convenience. A more unusual feature of B of A's service is that it is integrated with a popular home finance program, in this case, Managing Your Money™. Expect to see more software/bank alliances like this one as the industry matures.
Try clicking on "Quick Balance."

http://www.bankamerica.com/p-finance/homebanking/
hb_testdrive.html

You are given a summary of your checking, saving and, credit card accounts. You can then burrow down into these accounts and view transactions by specified date ranges and activities. For example, you can set your criteria and get a nearly instantaneous rundown of all service charges on your checking account for the last two months or quickly track down a deposit posted to your savings account eons ago. See how long that takes you with a fistful of bank statements and a paper deposit book.

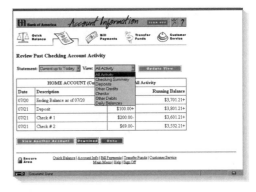

http://www.bankamerica.com/p-finance/homebanking/
hb_testdrive.html

The ability to transfer money between accounts is a common on-line banking feature. It's a quick and easy way to shuffle funds between any two accounts that you have at the same bank. You can, for example, pay a credit card bill from your checking account without having to visit a branch.

From the Britton & Koontz Electronic Banking Center you can click on Transfer Money Between Accounts and give it a try.

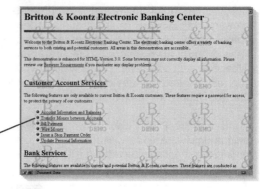

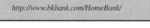
http://www.bkbank.com/HomeBank/

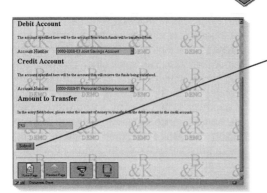

Simple stuff. All you have to do is select the two accounts your transferring between, specify the amount and click the button. See, simple stuff. Good thing too, especially if you lead a complicated financial life and you find yourself juggling funds between accounts regularly. It also makes taking out cash advances on a credit card a breeze. Click-click-click, the bill is tacked on to your credit card, the interest meter starts running and you're done. On second thought, maybe it's a little too easy.

http://www.bkbank.com/HomeBank/

Transferring funds between accounts is great, but it doesn't pay the bills. Alright, it does pay *some* bills. You can pay a credit card bill, but only if you happen to have an account with the bank that issued the card. But what if you don't? And what about paying the baby-sitter? Sitters work hard too you know. They deserve to be paid. Do you think that childcare is somehow less important than a stinkin' credit card company? No. I didn't think so. So click on test drive Web banking and pay the poor sitter already.

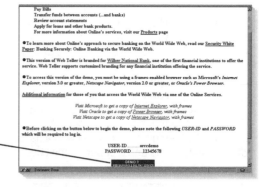

http://www.orcc.com/web_demo.htm

Now take a look at this site developed by a company named <u>Online Resources & Communications</u>. The company that designed it isn't a bank. Instead, they develop services like this one to sell to banks with neither the interest nor the expertise to do it themselves. It's possible then that you might find this exact service available from the Home page of your bank.

To use the demo, type in "**orccdemo**" for the User ID and "**12345678**" for the password.

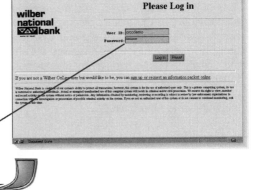

http://www.onlinebank.com/
donterase.formproc?ORCCGeneric+HREF+SignOnDemo

You won't be able to type in the http://... address and jump directly to the next few Web pages. You're going to have to go through the front door and <u>Log In</u>. This applies for any secure Web page that requires a password. Makes sense if you think about it. If bypassing security measures were that easy they wouldn't all that secure in the first place.

We're here to look at how the bill payment part of the service works, so click on the "BillPay" button at the top of the page.

http://www.onlinebank.com/
donterase.formproc?ORCCGeneric+HREF+SignOnDemo

Bills paid in this way are processed electronically. That is, the funds are transferred from your account directly into someone else's. This means that before you can pay anyone like this (the sitter for example. You didn't forget about the sitter, did you?) you'll need to find out their bank account number. It's an annoyance, but once it's set up, the information is recorded and you won't have to enter it again. With recurring payments it's even easier; you set it up once and the bank takes care of it forever more.

http://www.onlinebank.com/
donterase.formproc?ORCCGeneric+HREF+SignOnDemo

For each on-line transaction that you make you will be given a confirmation number. Make a note of it and write it down. You may need it someday if there is ever a discrepancy between what you know you did and what the bank says you did. Not that mistakes are any more likely to happen on-line than in person, but these things do happen. And if it ever happens to you, it's nice to know that you have this number to refer back to.

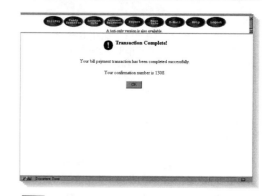

*http://www.onlinebank.com/
donterase.formproc?ORCCGeneric+HREF+SignOnDemo*

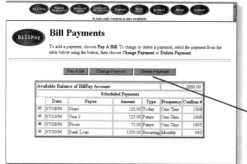

Scheduling payments in advance is a nice feature of on-line bill payment. It means that you can join one of those Cigar of the Month Clubs and have the money automatically debited from your account, saving you the trouble of visiting the post office as well as ye olde smoke shoppe. And just in case your significant other turns out to be allergic to those stogies, you can always change or delete the payments just as easily as you set them up in the first place.

*http://www.onlinebank.com/
donterase.formproc?ORCCGeneric+HREF+SignOnDemo*

Back in the heady days of the wild west, Wells Fargo was on the cutting edge of technology, delivering gold bullion by stage coach and dispatching the world's first electronic transaction by telegraph in 1864. The frontier has changed a lot since then but Wells Fargo still manages to deliver.

Remember the article at the beginning of this chapter that rated Wells Fargo as one of the best bank sites on the Net? Click on the computer icon for a demo and see why.

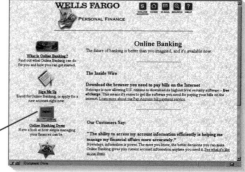

http://wellsfargo.com/nav/online1/

Wells Fargo offers a bill payment service called Pay Anyone. Unlike the other on-line banking services that we've looked at in this chapter, this one is not widely available. It may not be totally unique, but it's certainly rare. The basic gist of the Pay Anyone plan is that for $5 a month you can surf over to your bank, pop in a name, address, and amount and have the bank issue a check on your behalf to anyone, anywhere. It may not sound like much, but it sure beats the way we're all doing it now.

http://wellsfargo.com/per/online/demo/

You can schedule payments for a specific date or set up recurring payments. The bank tracks the payments, updates your balance, and sees to it that the checks are mailed out on time. And since there's no limit to the number of checks you can write, you might just make your five bucks back on postage alone. The idea is so simple that you have to wonder why no one thought of it sooner. Hopefully other banks will catch on. In the meanwhile, keep salivating. You're going to need that spit to lick stamps.

http://wellsfargo.com/per/online/demo/

Balancing Your Checkbook

If you are one of the unlucky ones whose bank hasn't yet opened up shop on the Web, tell them to get with it. As long as you're waiting anyway, you may as well check out this site from Deluxe Check Corporation. It show you how to balance you checkbook and reconcile your accounts the old fashioned way—slowly and carefully. It may not be as fashionable to do your banking by hand, but whoever said that bank statements has to be a fashion statement anyway?

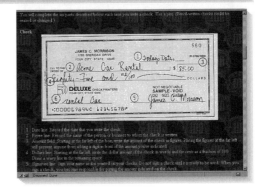

http://www.oba.com/public/chkmgmt.html

Or how about a little program that balances your checkbook for you. Well, it won't do it all by itself; the day when you can grab your computer and enter into a Vulcan mind-meld is still a ways away. Although I understand that they are working on it. Until Microsoft Mind-Meld™ hits the shelves though, I'm afraid you're going to have to enter in the numbers yourself. Even still, a program like Account Manager can sure automate an otherwise tedious procedure. Just click on the title and give it a go.

http://www.rtc-tallaght.ie/rtc_info/compdip/winfree.html

What You Have

Your Net Worth
└─ Calculating What You Have

Social Security
├─ Personal Earnings and Benefit Statement
├─ Social Security as an Investment
├─ The Social Security Crisis
└─ Are You at Risk?

Household Budgeting
├─ Budget? What's a Budget?
├─ Learning By Example
├─ Guidelines to Plan By
└─ Budgeting Software

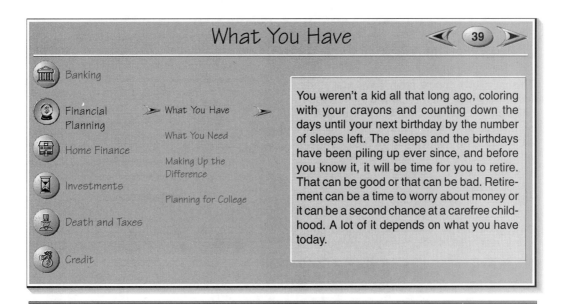

Banking

Financial Planning ➤ What You Have ➤

What You Need

Home Finance

Making Up the Difference

Investments

Planning for College

Death and Taxes

Credit

You weren't a kid all that long ago, coloring with your crayons and counting down the days until your next birthday by the number of sleeps left. The sleeps and the birthdays have been piling up ever since, and before you know it, it will be time for you to retire. That can be good or that can be bad. Retirement can be a time to worry about money or it can be a second chance at a carefree childhood. A lot of it depends on what you have today.

Your Net Worth

Before you can plan for the future, you have to know where you stand today, and if all you that know for sure is how much you have sitting in a savings account you are standing on unnecessarily shaky ground.

To determine your financial footing you have to add up everything that you own (your assets) and subtract everything that you owe (your liabilities). What you end up with is your current net worth. Altamira has a calculator to help with the process.

http://www.altamira.com/altamira/icat/toolbox/netcalc.html

The calculator consists of four parts; long- and short-term assets and long- and short-term liabilities. Fill in all of the applicable blanks to the best of your ability. If you don't know the exact value of something on either side of the equation you can guesstimate it and come back later when you have a more concrete figure.

When you're done, click on "Calculate Net Worth"

http://www.altamira.com/altamira/icat/toolbox/netcalc.html

This calculator should really have sound effects; a drumroll when you press the button to calculate the numbers, applause or boos depending on the results. What it has instead is a table showing you how your net worth stacks up against a moving target of age and income. Use these numbers as a plan of attack for the next time around. And since life doesn't stand still, there will be a next time.

It's a good idea to recalculate your net worth every year or so to help keep you on track.

			DETAILED ANALYSIS	
Type	Assets	Liabilities	Ratios of Assets to Liabilities	Analysis
Short-Term	$171000.00	$108100.00	$1.58 to $1.00	That's good. Your short-term assets are greater than your short-term liabilities.
Long-Term	$0.00	$0.00	Infinite	That's good. Your long-term assets are greater than your long-term liabilities.
Asset Mix	$171000.00	$108100.00	$1.58 to $1.00	Your assets are comprised of 100.00% short term assets, and 0.00% long term assets. See below for further analysis of your long-term asset mix.

You did not report any long-term assets, therefore no analysis is possible.

Return and adjust some results

Net Worth Tips:

- Caution should be taken to ensure that you have sufficient liquid assets to cover liabilities due in the next 12 months. In essence, an emergency fund should be set up to ensure that no shortfalls exist. A benchmark for an adequate level of short term funds is 3-6 months of employment income. If your employment is stable, and you do not expect large expenditures in the near future, this amount may be reduced.

http://www.altamira.com/altamira/icat/toolbox/netcalc.html

Social Security

 SOCIAL SECURITY Online

Welcome to Social Security Online, now starting our third year on the Web. Social Security Online is the official Web site of the Social Security Administration, and part of our Agency's commitment to the goal of providing World Class Service. Please use our feedback form to help us provide better service to you.

Check back often; information on this server is updated frequently. If you are not sure if you have the most up-to-date page, please RELOAD.

Request your PEBES - Personal Earnings and Benefit Estimate Statement—online. You must have secure browser software that supports SSL encryption. Our PEBES Home Page will further explain the security requirements. Before you start, you should have:

1. your name and social security number as they appear on your social security card;
2. last year's (1995) earnings; and
3. an estimate of future earnings.
   (Current and future earnings information is optional but will help us compute a more accurate benefit estimate for you.)

Not found on any net worth calculator is the equity that you've built up over the years by paying into the Social Security program. While it's a (really, really) bad idea to rely solely on Social Security for your retirement, it is something that you've been investing in since your first after school job and it's something that you'll keep paying into until they slip you a gold watch and ship you off to Florida. Visit Social Security Online, click on PEBES Home Page and see what all those SS payments adds up to.

http://www.ssa.gov/

The only group that likes acronyms more than the computer industry is the government. It is therefore with great pride that the SSA brings us PEBES—the Personal Earnings and Benefit Estimate Statement. This being the government, it should come as no surprise that even after three years on the Web, the Social Security Administration still hasn't managed to develop on-line response capabilities. You can fill out the form over the Net but the response will be sent to you by mail, in about a month or so.

http://s3abaca.ssa.gov/batch-pebes/bp-7004home.shtml

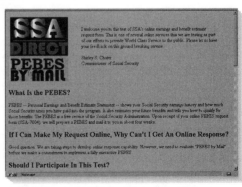

SSA DIRECT PEBES BY MAIL

I welcome you to the test of SSA's online earnings and benefit estimate request form. This is one of several online services that we are testing as part of our efforts to provide World Class Service to the public. Please let us have your feedback on this ground breaking service.

Shirley S. Chater
Commissioner of Social Security

What Is the PEBES?

PEBES -- Personal Earnings and Benefit Estimate Statement -- shows your Social Security earnings history and how much Social Security taxes you have paid into the program. It also estimates your future benefits and tells you how to qualify for those benefits. The PEBES is a free service of the Social Security Administration. Upon receipt of your online PEBES request form (SSA-7004); we will prepare a PEBES and mail it to you in about four weeks.

If I Can Make My Request Online, Why Can't I Get An Online Response?

Good question. We are taking steps to develop online response capability. However, we need to evaluate "PEBES by Mail" before we make a commitment to implement a fully interactive PEBES.

Should I Participate In This Test?

Scroll down the page and you should see a colorful logo stating that your browser is SSL compatible. If you don't, now would be a good time to upgrade to a new browser. You can include your current and estimated future earnings for a more accurate estimate, but at the very least you will need to supply your name and SS number. Having a secure browser will keep this information private. To begin filling out the form click on "Request a PEBES" and on then on "Continue" at the bottom of the next screen.

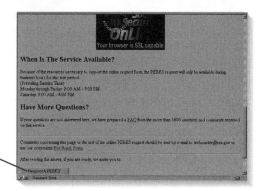

http://s3abaca.ssa.gov/batch-pebes/bp-7004home.shtml

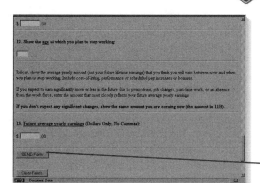

An unusual word of warning here; This form is guaranteed to work only during "business hours" (EST, Monday - Friday 8 a.m. - 9 p.m. and 9 a.m. - 4 p.m. Saturdays). It may work at other times, but there's no guarantee. Leave it to a government agency to put the Net on a time clock.

Check your watch, adjust for daylight savings time and fill in the form. Down at the bottom of the screen is the "Send Form" button. Click it and cross your fingers.

http://s3abaca.ssa.gov/batch-pebes/bp-7004home.shtml

Even after receiving your Personal Earnings and Benefit Estimate Statement back from the government you might still not understand where Social Security leaves you. You put 15.3 percent of your earnings into the system with every paycheck, but where's the payback?

You have questions, Portland State University has answers. Click on Will people retiring in 1995 get their money back from Social Security?

http://odin.cc.pdx.edu/~psu01435/ss95.html#Top

Social Security has the potential to be a good investment. Low-income workers retiring today can expect to see a full return of their contributions after just a few years. Those who earned the most (and therefore paid the most) will take the longest to recover their contributions with middle-class workers falling right where you would expect them; in the middle. All of this assumes that you're about to retire. Keep scrolling down the screen and see what happens to your Social Security income in the future.

http://odin.cc.pdx.edu/~psu01435/ss95.html#SS95

Payback for 1995 Retirees

Although soon-to-be-retirees who paid the maximum payroll tax over their careers may find themselves roughly breaking even, the majority of retirees are coming out comfortably ahead. Low-income earners will continue to do so, while some average-and high-income earners will see an erosion in what their money is worth by 2030 to the point where they may not break even.

For example, an indivvidual who retired in January 1995 at 65 after paying the maximum payroll tax would have paid in about $120,100, including interest. This retiree will get his or her money back in 10.5 years if only the retiree's payroll taxes are counted. But it will take 25.6 years if the employer's taxes are also considered. (If the retiree is married to a non-contributing spouse, the couple will get their money back in 15 years.)

Moderate earners will do much better. A 1995 retiree with average earnings would have paid in $67,536, plus interest, over 44 years; he or she will get this money back in 7.9 years if only the retiree's taxes are counted, 18.5 years if both emplyer and employee taxes are considered. (It will take just 11 years, however, if the retiree has a noncontributing spouse.) These rates of return

Payback for 2012 Retirees

Unquestionably, people retiring after 2012 will realize smaller returns than today's retirees, a development that's inevitable with the maturing of the system. Unmarried, maximum earners may actually get a negative return on their contributions. For example, a maximum-earning, single worker retiring at 66 in 2015 will need 47.1 years to get back his and his employer's taxes (compared to 25.3 years for a married retiree with a noncontributing spouse).

Moderate-income workers will do better. A single worker with average earnings retiring at 66 in 2015 will need 29 years to get back combined employee-employer taxes, while a couple with a noncontributing spouse retiring with average earnings will require 17.1 years.

Go to Social Security Questions Above

Questions or comments about Social Security can be directed to:
psu01435@odin.cc.pdx.edu

Revised: (December 22, 1995)by IG
Visitors reported by Mr. Web Counter = 11686

If you won't be retiring for a few years, Social Security is less of a bargain. For example, a single person retiring in the year 2015 who made maximum contributions will take over 47 years to recoup the full amount paid into the system. This means that if you retire at 65, you will need to live to the ripe old age of 112 just to break even. Average income earners fair better, they only have to live to 94. Once again, some major assumptions here, namely, that Social Security will even exist when you go to retire.

http://odin.cc.pdx.edu/~psu01435/ss95.html#SS2012

In the end, demographics may break the system. When baby boomers go to retire en masse in the coming years there will be fewer workers left to support a growing number of retirees. At around the year 2015 Social Security benefits will exceed the revenues (taxes) being taken in. By 2030, the well will have run completely dry.

Scroll down Scanlandia's Social Security Crisis Page for more fun facts.

http://www.panix.com/~stern/ss/socindex.html

The Social Security Crisis

Here's the problem: you're paying 15.3% of your paycheck into a black hole. More money is poured into Social Security each year than into the defense budget or the interest payment on the national debt. The government tries to hide the magnitude of the social security tax by charging it half from the employer, half from the employee, but it's 15.3% however you add it up.

The money paid into the social security system is not saved or invested. It is paid immediately to current retirees. That means that the more retirees there are, and the fewer workers, the more money each worker will have to pay into the system. This problem is made worse because politicians for decades increased the payments made to retirees whenever they wanted to buy some votes. (Annual increases are now mandated by law, which makes the problem worse). Demographic trends in the United States are such that, by 2030 or so, workers will be paying 40% of their income or more into Social Security.

This site presents facts, figures and discussions of the problem. Most significantly, I am creating a model of the Social Security trust fund that you can use to test the effects of changing policies and demographics on the state of the fund.

Social Security Fun Facts for 1996

- Social Security serves 46 million people who receive benefits and 141 million who are paying into the system.
- It takes, on average, 4.25 years for a retiree to receive back all of his or her Social Security contributions.

The crisis is compounded by the fact that members of the "Baby Boomer" generation, which will put such a strain on this system in its retirement, are not saving money themselves. A study published in July 1995 by the Rand Corporation reveals that the average American couple in its 50s, which is to say, about to retire, has just over $17,000 in financial assets. The average black or Latino couple in its 50s has close to $0 in savings. These people need social security to survive and, even with their regular checks, many of them will never be able to retire.

- The government explains Social Security benefits.

If you like bad news, you're in for a real treat. All of the articles here paint a bleak picture of Social Security in the future, each one more depressing than the last. On the bright side, 80 million starving boomer retirees screaming for food will make for one loud political voice. It's unlikely then that Social Security will disappear entirely. Something will be done because something will have to be done. But even if we do manage to salvage the Social Security net, many will fall through the holes.

http://www.panix.com/~stern/ss/socindex.html

This site presents facts, figures and discussions of the problem. Most significantly, I am creating a model of the Social Security trust fund that you can use to test the effects of changing policies and demographics on the state of the fund.

Social Security Fun Facts for 1996

- Social Security serves 46 million people who receive benefits and 141 million who are paying into the system.
- It takes, on average, 4 25 years for a retiree to receive back all of his or her Social Security contributions.

The crisis is compounded by the fact that members of the "Baby Boomer" generation, which will put such a strain on the system in its retirement, are not saving money themselves. A study published in July 1995 by the Rand Corporation reveals that the average American couple in its 50s, which is to say, about to retire, has just over $17,000 in financial assets. The average black or Latino couple in its 50s has close to $0 in savings. These people need social security to survive and, even with their regular checks, many of them will never be able to retire.

- The government explains Social Security benefits.
- The Atlantic Monthly discusses the coming crisis.
- Are we paying more than the law requires?
- Bob Kerry says that we face "insolvency by 2030."
- Review is inevitable, Dole says.
- Will Boomers go bust?
- Kerry and Simpson argue for their reform package.
- Others think the Kerry/Simpson package misses the point.
- Reform is good for all.
- The Wall Street Journal ran a list of wishy-washy alternatives.
- A plea for privatization.

Back to Sternlandia

Will Boomers Go Bust?

By Spencer Rich
Washington Post Staff Writer

And herein lies the problem with including Social Security in the *What Do You Have* chapter—with Social Security you don't really know what you have. You can get printouts from the government telling you what your estimated benefits will be, you can analyze Social Security as an investment, but you can't even be sure that it will be there for you when you need it or, if it is, that it will be enough. Consider Social Security a part of what you have for retirement, but please, don't make it the only thing that you have.

http://www.panix.com/~stern/ss/boomers_suck.html

According to Merrill Lynch's annual Baby Boom Retirement Index, an iffy Social Security check is all that many of us have to look forward to. Even being optimistic, the survey found that on average, boomers have to nearly triple the amount they're saving for retirement or risk putting their retirement plans on hold indefinitely and lowering their standards of living significantly.

Golf and sunshine may be the dream, but without the savings to back it up, a cold tin of cat food might be the reality.

http://www.plan.ml.com/personal/retire/bb_index.html

The 1996 Merrill Lynch Baby Boom Retirement Index

Prepared by Dr. B. Douglas Bernheim, Stanford University
Sponsored by Merrill Lynch & Co., Inc.

Index of Retirement Saving Adequacy Aggregated Categories				
Household Characteristics	Income		Pensions	All Households
	<$60,000	>$60,000	Traditional	Non-Traditional	
Index of Retirement Saving Adequacy	31.9%	42.9%	51.1%	30.7%	35.9%

Not only is a cat food brunch distasteful, but it's also high in cholesterol and saturated fats. You don't want to eat that stuff. Put your budget on a diet early enough and you won't have to.

If you have always lived hand-to-mouth the first thing you should do is check out <u>Harvey A. Dapeer</u>'s article on budgeting. Click on <u>What is a Household Budget?</u> and learn how you can keep yourself well stocked (and satisfyingly regular) with a lifetime supply of bran flakes and prune juice.

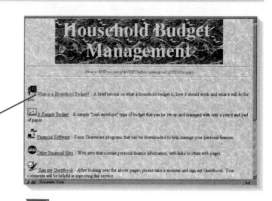

http://www.netxpress.com/users/hadap/budget.html

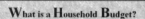

If you already know everything there is to know about budgets, great. This site isn't for you. It's for the millions of people who haven't begun saving for their retirement because they never have any money left to save. Sure, you can keep putting it off until you have more, but tomorrow won't wait around forever. If you don't have much right now, you just have to make the most of what you do have.

When you're done, go <u>back</u> to the previous screen and click on <u>A Sample Budget</u>.

http://www.netxpress.com/users/hadap/whatis.htm

See Dick. Dick makes $350 a week. See Jane. Jane makes $500 every two weeks. Together, Dick and Jane make $2,600 a month. See Dick and Jane's expenses. Dick and Jane need $2,255 a month to live. See the balance. Dick and Jane will put part of that balance into a tax-deferred annuity.

See Dick and Jane. They are older now. Dick and Jane are golfing.

See Fred. Fred is eating cat food.

http://www.netxpress.com/users/hadap/sample.htm

Now that you have the basics down it's time to take budgeting to the next level. Merrill Lynch has a form that you can print out and use to help you design you own budget. It's not interactive by any means, you're going to have to go at this one with a pencil and a calculator. What it does offer are some guidelines that you can refer to while creating a budget for yourself.

Merrill Lynch suggests setting aside 10% of after-tax income for investments. Sharpen up your pencil and see how close you get.

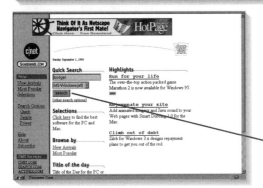

http://www.merrill-lynch.ml.com/investor/budgetprintform.html

Budgeting Software

Guidelines are good, but what's the use of having an expensive computer sitting there on your desk if you have to whip out a calculator, especially when Shareware.Com has plenty of free and low-cost home budgeting programs available for the asking.

Just select your platform (Windows, Mac, etc.), type the word "budget" in the search field (without the quotation marks) and click the "Search" button (no quotation marks here either).

http://www.shareware.com/

You should end up with a sizable collection of budget-related software programs for you to choose from. If you see something of interest click on the title and give it a spin. Heck, for the price of the download you may as well try out a few.

And remember, when you go to create your household budget try and think of it at short-term financial planning with long-term goals.

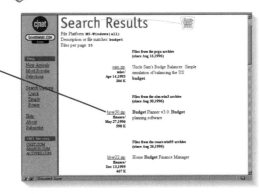

http://www.shareware.com/

What You Need

Life After the Money's Gone

⊣ Outliving Your Savings

⊣ The Longevity Game

⊣ When Will Your Money Run Out?

⊣ Planning Ahead

⊣ Some Helpful Advice

⊣ The Magic of Compound Interest

⊣ The "Rule of 72"

Where You Stand

⊣ Pop Quiz

⊣ What You'll Need Calculator

It's The Little Things

⊣ Inflation

⊣ Relocation

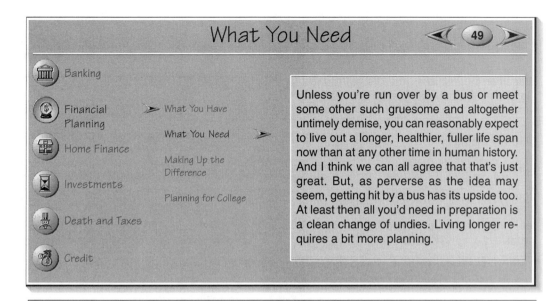

Banking

Financial Planning   ➤ What You Have

                        What You Need   ➤

                        Making Up the
                        Difference

Home Finance

                        Planning for College

Investments

Death and Taxes

Credit

Unless you're run over by a bus or meet some other such gruesome and altogether untimely demise, you can reasonably expect to live out a longer, healthier, fuller life span now than at any other time in human history. And I think we can all agree that that's just great. But, as perverse as the idea may seem, getting hit by a bus has its upside too. At least then all you'd need in preparation is a clean change of undies. Living longer requires a bit more planning.

Life After the Money's Gone

OUTLIVING YOUR SAVINGS

Americans seem to underestimate their staying power. Roughly 45 percent of people who plan to retire between ages 55 and 64 say they expect to enjoy 11 to 20 years of retirement, according to a study from the Employee Benefit Research Institute (EBRI). However, these people may actually spend between 17 and 24 years in retirement. That means they could easily outlive their retirement savings. Census statistics show that the percentage of Americans over 65 who live below the poverty line has risen to 12.9 percent.

To compound the problem, a recent EBRI public-opinion poll of 1,000 Americans found that most of the low-income people polled believe that Social Security benefits will increase in the future. EBRI president Dallas Salisbury calls the survey results alarming because low-income individuals are also less likely to have started saving to supplement Social Security.

Related poll results found that higher income individuals were more likely to believe that Social Security benefits would decrease. In fact, 69 percent said that they believe the level of benefits will either drop or be eliminated in the future.

STAGES Magazine, Fall 1994

Home | Index | Search | Comments | Help

© Copyright 1995-1996 FMR Corp. All Rights Reserved

Live fast, die young. Yesiree, that's my motto. I also like "he who dies with the most toys wins." And I do love my toys. I really have my heart set on a pair of $30,000 killer loudspeakers. Only problem is that I may not die young, and then where would I be, old, poor, and most likely deaf (after all, what's the point in having killer speakers if you don't crank them once in a while).

Outliving my money would really suck. But as this article from Stages Magazine points out, that's exactly what will happen to a lot of us.

http://www.fidelityatwork.com/publicsector/participants/AI/noutlive.htm

So, how long do you plan on sticking around? Northwestern Mutual Life has a twisted little longevity "game" you can "play" to calculate the probable age of your certain demise. Fill in the blanks and tick off the boxes to see how many years you have left amongst the living. Try some what-if scenarios and see how many years a serious drug problem will take off your life—just for fun.

When your done "playing", click the "Submit" button at the bottom of the screen.

http://www.northwesternmutual.com/games/longevity/longevity-main.html

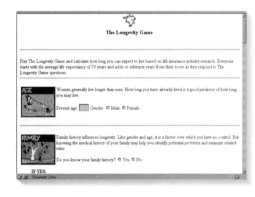

Based on the results pictured here, I see that James, my clean-living research assistant, has a statistically good chance of living to the age of 90. All those early mornings at the YMCA must be paying off.

And I'm sure that James isn't alone. Since the 1930s our life expectancy as a group has jumped up something like 30 percent. With our low-fat, high-fiber, aerobically-pumped lifestyles we will live longer. With our spend-it-all, future-be-damned attitudes, how well we will live is open to debate.

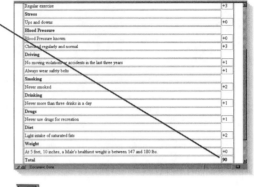

Regular exercise	+3
Stress	
Ups and downs	+0
Blood Pressure	
Blood Pressure known	+0
Checked regularly and normal	+3
Driving	
No moving violations or accidents in the last three years	+1
Always wear safety belts	+1
Smoking	
Never smoked	+2
Drinking	
Never more than three drinks in a day	+1
Drugs	
Never use drugs for recreation	+1
Diet	
Light intake of saturated fats	+2
Weight	
At 5 feet, 10 inches, a Male's healthiest weight is between 147 and 180 lbs.	+0
Total	90

http://www.northwesternmutual.com/games/longevity/longevity-main.html

http://www.profiles.com/money.htm

Financial Profiles, Inc. has a calculator that will determine how long your money will last. Compare the results with what you got from the longevity game and see if the money will last as long as you will.

You can put your own numbers in of course, but let's look at James's. Mr. Goodchild is 35. He plans to retire at age 70 and he's managed to sock away $300,000 (way to go James). He's assumed 4 percent for inflation, a 7 percent investment rate and he figures he'll need $2,000 a month to live on.

Looks pretty good. James started saving young, plans to retire late, he's conservative with his numbers and he's put away more than most. But when he clicks the "Calculate" button look at what he gets. According to this, his money is going to run out when he's 85 years old. Not bad, but based on his life expectancy calculations, that's five long, lean years before he kicks the bucket.

Looks like James is going to have to either save more or quite the Y and take up smoking as a hobby.

http://www.profiles.com/money.htm

The fact is, many people don't even begin thinking about retirement untill it's nearly upon them. And by that time saving for the future is no easy task.

Think of it as saving up for the vacation of a lifetime—literally. Not the sort of thing you want to start thinking about on your last ever day of work. Fleet Financial Group has a decent collection of retirement related articles on their site. Try clicking on Retirement Planning— Haven't Thought About it.

http://www.fleet.com/abtyou/retplan/

Well, think about it! ...A comfortable retirement takes planning.

Yes, you're just starting out and have lots of demands on your cash. But you can save for it all -- and still retire when you want. Here's how.

First Things First
Your retirement savings will grow more quickly if you invest for the long haul. You can't keep removing money for emergencies. If you have no savings, begin by stashing cash for surprise car repairs or unexpected visits home. If you want a house, put money aside for that, too. Then, you can confront the ultimate savings challenge -- your retirement nestegg.

A Little Savings Goes a Long Way
Experts say you'll need 75% or so of your pre-retirement income when you retire. Social Security will only get you part way there. Since you're young, getting the rest can be fairly simple -- even if you save in small amounts. The key is to make saving a habit, and to start your savings now. Let's say you put $150 a month in a tax-deferred investment program, beginning at age 25, and earn an 8% annual return that's compounded monthly. By the time you're 40, you'd have $51,906 in savings. If you'd waited even five years to start, your savings would be just $27,442. Take a look at the Retirement Planning Worksheet to see how much you should be saving.

Growth to the Max
Tax-deferred investment programs, like an individual retirement account (IRA) or a company 401(k) plan, are the best places to begin your retirement savings. Money you invest can grow more quickly because you delay taxes on what your money earns until you remove it. In most cases, you can also put off taxes on money that you put into savings.

Where should you invest? Because you have time to weather short-term losses, you can take more risk -- which can often mean higher returns. You can check your personal risk profile with the Investment Allocation Analyzer.

If you really haven't thought about it yet Fleet offers some very practical advice starting with "well, think about it!" First thing they say is to make saving a habit. You can't keep removing money for "emergencies." Killer loudspeakers are definitely out.

You'll need about 75 percent of your preretirement income to keep the same standard of living after you retire. Since Social Security will only cover part of that (if that) it's up to you to come up with the rest. Even if it's just a little at a time. The key is to start saving early.

http://www.fleet.com/abtyou/retplan/havtho.html

The reason why saving early is so important is that time is the special ingredient that lets the wonder of compound interest work its magic. Stephen DiRose has a compund interest calculator that shows this magic in action.

Put in a dollar amount that you can reasonably afford, say $120 a month. Put in the number of years you have left until retirement, assume an annual return of around 8 percent and click the "Calculate" button to see what compound interest has up its sleeve.

Continuous Deposit Investment, Annual Compound Interest Calculator

This calculator will *roughly* calculate compound interest on a continuous deposit investment 'Wealthy Barber' style. Fill in the form an press calculate.

Interest Rate	Number Years	Monthly Payment	Icrease Monthly Payment p/y	Years of Payment
8	30	120	None	30
Ex: 12	Ex: 30	Ex: 200	Ex: 10	Ex: 30

Calculate

dirose@cs.buffalo.edu
Last modified: Sat Jun 1 12:43:38 1996

http://www.cs.buffalo.edu/~dirose/ci_calculator.html

If you stick $30 a week under your mattress for the next 30 years and you'll end up with $46,800 and a bad back. Same amount of money, same amount of time but put into an investment that earns an 8 percent return and that $46,000 turns into $176,000. At that rate, even if you never add another cent, the money will continue to double every nine years or so. Conversely, waiting nine years to begin saving means that you're starting off with half as much to show for the same amount put in.

Year	Total Value	Average Monthly Payment	Total Invested
1	1555.20	120	1440
2	3234.82	120	2880
3	5048.30	120	4320
4	7007.91	120	5760
5	9123.74	120	7200
6	11402.84	120	8640
7	13876.74	120	10080
8	16542.03	120	11520
9	19420.65	120	12960
10	22529.50	120	14400
11	25887.06	120	15840
12	29519.23	120	17280
13	33429.49	120	18720
14	37659.04	120	20160
15	42226.97	120	21600
16	47160.32	120	23040
17	52485.35	120	24480
18	58242.62	120	25920
19	64457.23	120	27360
20	71169.01	120	28800

http://www.cs.buffalo.edu/~dirose/ci_calculator.html

Personal Finance 101: Rule of 72

How quickly your money will double in value at a given interest rate can be estimated by the Rule of 72. It works like this, if you have $1 and you're getting an interest rate of 1 percent per year on that dollar it will take 72 years for it to turn into $2, at which time you will be able to celebrate by blowing the whole wad on a piece of Bazooka bubble gum.

To determine how long that dollar will take to double at a higher interest rate, you would use the formula 72/ RATE = Years to Double.

http://www.datalife.com/mall/pages/examples/RULE_72.HTM

No big deal with a 1 percent interest rate on a buck, but higher amounts at higher rates will turn into something that you can retire on. Datalife has included some examples of the Rule of 72 in action.

Divide 72 by 10 percent (the historical return on common stocks) for example, and you can estimate that it will take roughly 7.2 years for your money to double, 14.4 years for it to quadruple, 21.8 to octuple, 29.6 years to ... is there a word for a 16-fold increase on your investment other than "cool?"

http://www.datalife.com/mall/pages/examples/RULE_72.HTM

Pop quiz! Put away your books and take out a pencil. The Vanguard Group, Inc. has an on-line quiz designed to help define your basic retirement plan.

There are ten quick questions here that will test your basic understanding of retirement investing. Answer the questions by clicking on the circle to the left of the answer. When you're done, click the "Calculate" button at the bottom of the screen for your results.

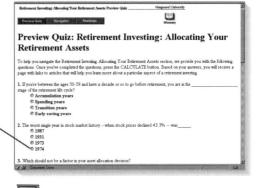

http://www.vanguard.com/cgi-bin/R3Quiz

So, how'd you do? At the time of this writing the average test score was 68 percent. The question that most people had trouble with was "If you are 35-years old and wish to save $100,000 by age 65, you would need to save approximately ___ per month: (assuming an 8 percent annual return). I won't spoil it for you by giving you the anwer, but only 1 in 3 got that one right.

If you do have an incorrect answer, the quiz gently points you to a relevant article that you can click on to bone up on the subject.

http://www.vanguard.com/cgi-bin/R3Quiz

In keeping with the sooner the better approach to retirement savings, what better time than the present to find out how much savings you'll need when you retire.

There are less complex retirement calculators on the Net that can give you a rough idea of what your savings goals should be, but this one from Fidelity Investments is far and away the most complete. Start by selecting your marital status and click the "Begin Questionaire" button. You'll then get a disclaimer page, click on "Continue."

http://personal.fidelity.com/fidbin/retire_image?00

Some of the questions may leave you scratching your head but help is at hand with a click on any underlined link.

Besides marriage, this calculator takes into account any investments you currently have, inflation, Social Security benifits, and life expectancy. The more accurate you are in your answers the more accurate the results will be. The whole thing should take about 15 minutes to complete. When you're done, click on the "Results" button and see what you get.

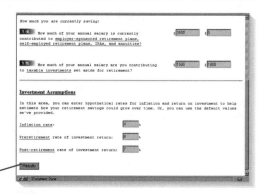

http://personal.fidelity.com/fidbin/retire_image?00

The results are broken up into four categories; how much you will need when you retire, how much you will have at retiremnt based on current savings, the surplus or (more likely) shortfall in savings and how much you need to be savings annually, monthly, and as a percentage of your income in order to make up for any shortfall and meet your goals.

Remember, all numbers are in today's dollars. You will need to increase your savings by the inlation rate each year.

http://www.fid-inv.com/fidbin/retire_image?00

It's the Little Things

The whole inflation thing can get confusing. If you calculate that you need say, $600,000, but you don't retire for another 35 years, that money will only have $68,000 worth of buying power when you go to spend it. With inflation averaging at about 6 percent your money is worth half as much every 12 years.
Use Corporate Image Software's Funky Inflation Calculator to see where it all goes. Just pop in a dollar amount, specifiy a time frame and *voila*, a half a million dollar surround sound speaker system.

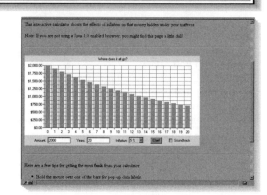

http://www.cisoft.com/cisweb/215e.htm

Remember when I mentioned that experts say that you will need around 75 percent of your preretirement income to keep the same standard of living after retirement? One reason that you need less money to keep the same standard is that many people relocate to warmer, less expensive climes when they retire. Homefair's Salary Calculator can help you see the effect relocating will make on your retirement expenses. Start by selecting your current location and destination and click on "Show Cities."

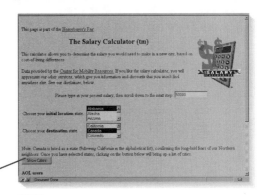

http://www.homefair.com/homefair/cmr/salcalc.html

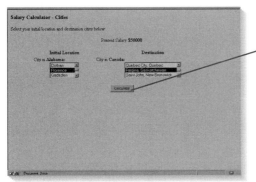

Now you can zoom in and select the specific cities that you're starting from and moving to and click on "Calculate".

I chose to calculate a move from Alabama, the Heart of Dixie, up to my present location in Saskatchewan, Canada where not only is it more expensive to live, but we get to enjoy those nine-month, 65-below-zero winters. It's not so bad really; it's a dry cold. Feels more like a balmy -35.

http://www.homefair.com/homefair/cmr/salcalc.html

Hopefully, you'll have better sense and pick a nice, warm, senior-oriented community somewhere in Arizona or Florida or something—somewhere where the cost of living is reasonable, the sunshine is plentiful and the locals won't look at you funny for wearing Bermuda shorts pulled up to your chest.

Remember, relocation is hardly a replacement for proper financial planning, but when there's less income coming in, how far you can stretch whatever you do have can be the difference between getting by and living well.

http://www.homefair.com/homefair/cmr/salcalc.html

Making Up The Difference

Pension Plan Basics

⊣ Pension Trends

⊣ Defined Benefit Plans

⊣ Defined Contribution Plans

The Pension Plan as an Investment

⊣ Using Age as a Guide

⊣ Qualified Plans

⊣ Non-Qualified Plans

⊣ The Advantage of Tax Deferred Plans

401(k)s, 403(b)s and 457s

⊣ More Than Just a Catchy Name

⊣ Calculating the Value of a 401(k)

SEPs and Keoughs

⊣ SEP IRAs

⊣ Determining Your SEP-IRA Contribution

⊣ SAR-SEPs

⊣ Keoughs

⊣ Comparing Your Choices

IRAs

⊣ Everything You Need To Know About IRAs

⊣ Contributions

⊣ Deductions

⊣ Withdrawals

⊣ IRAs and Taxes

⊣ IRA Calculator

RRSPs

⊣ RRSP Reference Library

⊣ Take the RRSP Challenge

⊣ RRSP Calculator

Annuities

⊣ Tax-Deferred Annuities

⊣ Fixed and Variable Annuities

⊣ Avoiding the Traps and Gimmicks

⊣ Annuity Calculator

Professional Advice

⊣ Finding a Financial Services Professional

Remember What It's All About

⊣ Bright Baggy Pants and Little White Balls (GolfWeb)

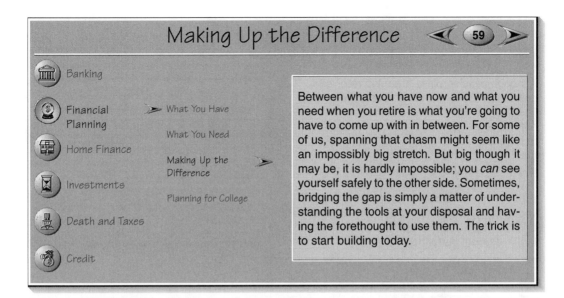

Banking

Financial Planning ➤ What You Have

What You Need

Home Finance

Making Up the Difference ➤

Investments

Planning for College

Death and Taxes

Credit

Between what you have now and what you need when you retire is what you're going to have to come up with in between. For some of us, spanning that chasm might seem like an impossibly big stretch. But big though it may be, it is hardly impossible; you *can* see yourself safely to the other side. Sometimes, bridging the gap is simply a matter of understanding the tools at your disposal and having the forethought to use them. The trick is to start building today.

Pension Plan Basics

personal financial planning
stages

Pension Trends Who's responsible for how much a worker will have to live on after retirement? Increasingly, the worker is. Defined-contribution benefit plans, in which employees manage their own money individually, are growing in relation to the number of traditional pension plans. Many companies do offer both types of plans. But according to the Internal Revenue Service, for every pension plan that was started in 1991, 27 more came to a halt. At the same time, the number of defined-contribution plans remained steady.

In a defined-contribution plan, such as a 401(k), employees can make tax-free contributions to their retirement account, where interest accumulates tax-free until the money is withdrawn. Companies often match those contributions. But the amount a worker has at retirement depends on how he or she has invested the money. By contrast, a company-managed pension plan provides a fixed level of benefits, usually based on salary and years of service.

One reason for the shift: Industries that tend to rely on pension programs, such as those that involve heavy manufacturing, have been growing more slowly than newer industries, such as high tech, which tend to offer defined-contribution plans, according to Celia Silverman of the Employee Benefit Research Institute, a nonprofit research organization. Also, she says, because job-hopping is more common now than in the past, employers are less likely to offer the same incentives to keep employees.

These changes mean that it's more important than ever for employees to learn how to plan for retirement and how to manage their money wisely. Says Silverman, "Participants in defined-contribution plans need to take more responsibility in choosing plans for investment."

STAGES magazine, Summer 1992

©Copyright 1995-1997 FMR Corp. All rights reserved. Important Legal Information

As a child you had parents that looked after you, clothed you, fed you, and put a roof over your head. Now that you're older you may find that it is you who will have to look after them. Government can supplement your retirement income but at best it will only provide for a portion of what you will need. And companies that used to provide pensions out of an obligation to lifelong employees tend not to feel so obliged anymore. As Fidelity Investments points out, the responsibility of saving for retirement is increasingly your own.

http://wps.fidelity.com/401k/pfp/stages/current/401ks7.htm

Thankfully, even when retirement savings *is* your responsibility you don't have to go it entirely alone. Many employers offer savings and investment assistance in the form of a pension plan. The government helps the process as well by seeing to it that these plans are tax deferred—in essence lending a hand by not sticking out their hand until later.

Pension Appraisers helps too, at least in defining the two general types of pension plans available with their guide to The Basics of Pension Plans.

http://www.pensionappraisers.com/penbasics.html

The
Basics of
Pension Plans

A PENSION PLAN is a tax deferred savings plan. Typically, during the years of employment, contributions are made by the employee or on behalf of the employee to a retirement plan. The contributions and earnings generated accumulate tax free until retirement. At which time, the employee receives a specific monthly income for life or a lump sum payment. There are two general types of retirement plans:

DEFINED BENEFIT PLAN

This type of plan promises that upon retirement the employee will receive a defined (known) monthly income for life. The yearly contributions necessary to provide the promised monthly benefit upon retirement are unknown and depend upon a number of variables, such as:

- the amount of the monthly benefit to be received upon retirement;
- the number of years left until retirement;
- the length of time benefits will be received;
- the amount of income that can be earned on yearly contributions;
- etc.

Although pension plans are often referred to collectively there are two distinct types—defined benefit and defined contribution. With a defined benefit plan your employer contributes to a pension fund for you and manages that fund to ensure that upon retirement you can count on x number of dollars a month for the rest of your life. With a defined contribution plan you invest a portion of your salary through your employer. What you end up with depends on how much you contributed and how well the investment performed.

http://wps.fidelity.com/401k/pfp/stages/current/401ks7.htm

---

personal financial planning

stages

Pension Trends Who's responsible for how much a worker will have to live on after retirement? Increasingly, the worker is. Defined-contribution benefit plans, in which employees manage their own money individually, are growing in relation to the number of traditional pension plans. Many companies do offer both types of plans. But according to the Internal Revenue Service, for every pension plan that was started in 1991, 27 more came to a halt. At the same time, the number of defined-contribution plans remained steady.

In a defined-contribution plan, such as a 401(k), employees can make tax-free contributions to their retirement account, where interest accumulates tax-free until the money is withdrawn. Companies often match those contributions. But the amount a worker has at retirement depends on how he or she has invested the money. By contrast, a company-managed pension plan provides a fixed level of benefits, usually based on salary and years of service.

One reason for the shift: Industries that tend to rely on pension programs, such as those that involve heavy manufacturing, have been growing more slowly than newer industries, such as high tech, which tend to offer defined-contribution plans, according to Celia Silverman of the Employee Benefit Research Institute, a nonprofit research organization. Also, she says, because job-hopping is more common now than in the past, employers are less likely to offer the same incentives to keep employees.

These changes mean that it's more important than ever for employees to learn how to plan for retirement and how to manage their money wisely. Says Silverman, "Participants in defined-contribution plans need to take more responsibility in choosing plans for investment."

STAGES magazine, Summer 1992

The Pension Plan as an Investment

Your Personal Financial Resources

Your financial situation will be the final factor that influences your asset allocation decision. If you feel that your financial situation is tenuous -- for example, your company has been experiencing layoffs -- you may want to reduce your investment risk. On the other hand, if your finances are on sound footing, you may be able to assume a higher level of investment risk. When evaluating your financial situation, you should consider factors such as:

- The stability of your job and career
- Current income relative to your income needs
- Your level of emergency savings
- Additional income sources that will be available to you during your retirement

As noted earlier, before you begin accumulating even one dollar in your long-term retirement investment program you should establish a short-term emergency reserve equal to at least three to six months' worth of living expenses. This emergency fund should be invested in some form of short-term reserves, such as a money market fund or a bank certificate of deposit (CD), or perhaps a short-term bond fund. These monies are meant to be immediately accessible, and therefore should not be invested in a tax-deferred retirement plan where they may be subject to premature withdrawal penalties.

Once your emergency reserve is in place, you can then turn your attention toward determining the appropriate asset allocation for your long-term retirement program. As a starting point, your initial portfolio allocation should be based on your position in the retirement life cycle, which encompasses four stages:

1. The accumulation years (ages 20-49)
2. The transition years (ages 50-59)
3. The early retirement years (ages 60-74)
4. The late retirement years (age 75+)

Think of a pension plan as a tax-deferred, employer-sponsored framework for an investment rather than an investment itself. Once the money is placed into the pension framework you still have a decision to make as to where that money would be best invested. Once you've taken part in a 401(k) plan, for example, you still have to decide if that 401(k) money should go into stocks, bonds, or what have you. There's no single right answer for everybody but Vanguard suggests that age should help guide your decision.

http://www.vanguard.com/educ/retire3/r3_1_4.html

Vanguard breaks investments into four distinct stages; The Accumulation Years (age 20–49), The Transition Years (50–59), The Early Retirement Years (60–74) and The Later Retirement Years (75+). Depending on where you are in this cycle you can gear your retirement decisions with an eye toward your investment horizon. Given the choice, it may be wise to put more money in higher risk, higher return stocks early on, switching to more conservative, guaranteed return investments later when you can ill afford a major setback.

http://www.vanguard.com/educ/retire3/r3_3_1.html

Accumulation Years (Age 20-49)

In your early and middle working years, when your investment horizon extends 40 years or more, your primary investment objective should be to accumulate capital for your retirement. At this point in your life, common stocks should be your dominant investment option, for two reasons:

1. Stocks have provided the highest long-term total returns of any major asset class.
2. While stocks also have had the highest volatility level of any asset class, the passage of time has a dampening effect on their short-term fluctuations.

Although a 100% stock portfolio may be appropriate for accumulation investors in the earliest stages of the investment life cycle, few investors possess the necessary fortitude to commit all of their savings to stocks. For most investors, it is probably wise to maintain a modest investment in bonds as well. The recommended allocation during the accumulation years is 80% stocks, 20% bonds.

How would this asset allocation have performed in the past? To calculate a historical return, the Standard & Poor's 500 Composite Stock Price Index can be used as a proxy for the returns on common stocks, and the long-term U.S. government bond can be used as a proxy for the returns on bonds. Of course, while historical returns are useful in assessing the past performance of particular investments, they do not represent the returns that will be achieved in the future. Financial markets are unpredictable, and all that can really be said about the future is that investment returns will fluctuate.

In any event, using these two benchmarks, the total return for the 80%/20% stock/bond allocation would have averaged +9.8% annually from 1926-1995 (before taxes and any investment expenses). But this long-term average performance figure conceals more than it reveals in terms of the actual risks to the investor. For instance, if you held an 80/20 stock/bond mix during this period, you would have experienced a loss in 19 of the 70 calendar years. That equates to a loss in one out of every four years. The losses in these years would have amounted to about -10% on average. In other words, during these 19 "down" years, your savings would have been an average of 10% lower at the end of the year than at the beginning. In 1931, during the

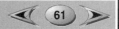

Some employers offer a small selection of investment options to choose from. Others leave the investment decisions entirely up to you. Few are willing or able to offer much advice, either because they don't know where you should invest your money any better than you do or because they fear that they'll be held liable if their advice doesn't pan out. Do your homework, because in the end, it's your retirement plan on the line, "plan" being the operative word here.

http://www.vanguard.com/educ/retire3/r3_4_1.html

Pension plans have to meet certain government imposed rules and regulations; who's eligible, how much can be contributed, when the money will become available ... If a pension plan meets the requirements they're considered "Qualified." What they qualify for is tax deferral. Neither the money deposited into the plan nor the income generated by it is taxed until years later when you go to cash in all your chips and head off into the sunset.

First New England Advisors, Inc. has more to say on the subject.

http://Execs.ActWin.Com:80/articles/docs/discret_rpF.html

If a plan doesn't meet these guidelines it is considered non-qualified. That's not necessarily a bad thing; it just means that while the income generated from the plan remains tax deferred, the original investment has to be paid for with after-tax dollars. This would be applicable if you've maxed out the annual contributions you're allowed for qualified plans but still want to contribute more and save on taxes. If you earn a solid income and make hefty contributions to a retirement plan, non-qualified plans might be worth consideration.

http://Execs.ActWin.Com:80/articles/docs/discret_rpF.html

The advantage of putting your money in a tax deferred retirement plan is easy enough to understand; The more you put, in the lower your taxable salary. The less you have to pay in taxes, the faster your investment can grow. Unfortunately, tax deferred means just that. You *will* have to pay taxes on the money eventually, but by investing it now instead of handing it over to the IRS your tax money has a chance to make you money. And as this graph from ITT Hartford Group clearly shows, that can make a big difference over the long haul.

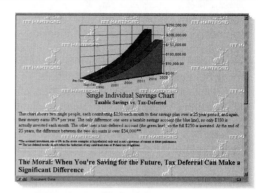

http://www.itthartford.com/retire/taxdef_cht.html

401(k)s, 403(b)s and 457s

Of all the employer sponsored retirement plans out there the most widely known is the 401(k). And what better way to learn more about 401(k)s than with Snoopy and the MetLife gang?

Perhaps the 401(k) is so popular because you get to choose how much you want to contribute and where you would like to invest it (within IRS guidelines, of course). Maybe it's because 401(k)s are tax-deferred and employers will often match a percentage of your contributions. Maybe it's just the catchy name.

http://www.metlife.com/Lifeadvi/Brochures/Retire/Docs/retire2.html

Whatever the reason for their popularity, 401(k) and their next of kin 403(b)s (for employees of nonprofit organizations) and 457s (for state and municipal workers) are an all-around good deal.

Some employers offer one of the 400 family members in addition to a defined benefit plan while others offer them in lieu of a traditional pension making the choice 401(k) or nothing. Not a very difficult choice. The only way to really lose out with the program is by not taking advantage of it.

http://www.metlife.com/Lifeadvi/Brochures/Retire/Docs/retire3.html

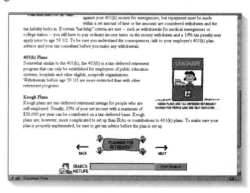

The biggest downside to 401(k) plans is that once you put your money in you can't get it back out again until you hit the precise age of 59 1/2. How they came up with that number is anyone's guess, but take your money out before then and your little nest egg will be subject to some heavy-duty penalties. Still, there's worse things than watching your money grow and you can use this 401(k) Calculator from Interface Technologies to estimate just how large your 401(k) fund will get. Fill in the numbers and click on "Calculate."

http://www.iftech.com/centers/finance/CompoundingCalc.htm

Current rules say that you (or you and your employer, if your employer is nice enough to pitch in) can contribute as much as 15 percent of your annual salary up to a maximum of $9,500 per year. But even if you put in half that amount it can really add up given enough time.

Remember to treat these numbers as the estimates they are. How close they get to the actual dollar amounts you will see 30 or 40 years down the road depends on how well your investments do between now and then.

http://www.iftech.com/classes/finance/CompoundingCalc.htm

SEPs and Keoughs

The 400 family and big business style pension plans don't work for everybody. If you own your own small business you probably can't afford the time, effort, and expense required to set up a large pension fund. And with a SEP-IRA you don't have to. SEP-IRA's ("SEP" standing for Simplified Employee Pension) are easier to set up, easier to administer, and still offer a lot of the same advantages that the big boys are getting. Interested? Scroll down the page to learn more from Strong Capital Management.

http://www.strong-funds.com/strong/Retirement/sep-iras.htm

A bit further down you'll find Strong's <u>SEP contribution calculator</u>. The laws change every year, but as of the time of this writing the maximum you can contribute to a SEP-IRA is a generous 15 percent of your compensation or $22,500, whichever is less.

To find out what your maximum contribution would be just fill in the percentage of your salary you would like to contribute, your total net earnings, and your self-employment tax then click on "Calculate Now" for the results.

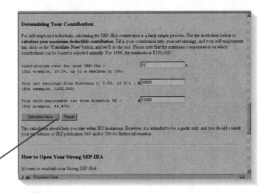

http://www.strong-funds.com/strong/Retirement/sep-iras.htm

Salary Reduction SEP's (SAR SEP)

Simplified employee pension plans are commonly referred to as SEP's. SEP's are excellent vehicles for retirement savings. Instead of making payments to the company pension plan, the company makes payments to your IRA. The employee's salary deferrals (you would have that money if it wasn't placed in your IRA), are made directly to the IRA. Contributions are not currently taxed and accumulated earnings are tax deferred. If you're self employed or a partner in a small business, you can also use SEP's. Keep in mind that the salary reductions are subject to FICA (Social security) and FUCA (Federal unemployment) taxes.

For 1995, the maximum annual elective deferral (the most that can go into your SEP - IRA) is $9,240. This amount is indexed in all future years for inflation. The employer has until his tax return is do to make his final contribution for the year to your SEP - IRA. The participant/employee has until December 31st to make the final contribution to the plan.

The plan may be invested in stocks, mutual funds, and bonds. The fund may not invest in life insurance or collectibles (except for U.S. gold and silver coins). The participant decides where the assets will be invested.

Again, withdrawals made prior to age 59-1/2 are subject to a 10% penalty tax. The government has come up with a nice word for it. They call it an excise tax. Nevertheless, 10% is 10%. The exceptions to this are death or disability, or if the owner of the IRA decides to use it as an annuity, and the distributions are made similar to an annuity which disperses the funds evenly over the life expectancy of the owner. If the owner of the IRA - SEP chooses the annuity option, no alteration can be made until the owner reaches the age of 59-1/2 or five (5) years pass.

With SEP-IRA's all of the money comes from the employer, like a pension. But a <u>SAR-SEP</u> (this one stands for Salary Reduction - SEP) is the small-company equivalent of a 401(k). Like 401(k)s, SAR-SEP are paid through your salary contributions, although employers may choose to match part of that contribution.
Even though SEP's were designed with simplicity in mind they're not exactly no-brainers. Before you run out and sign yourself up for a SAR-SEP you can check out all the little details first on the Web pages of <u>Equity Analytics</u>.

http://www.e-analytics.com/fp18.htm

If you're self-employed or earn money outside of your regular job another option open to you is a <u>Keogh</u>. And as <u>Fidelity Investments</u> explains it, the options don't end there. There are actually three distinct types Keoghs available, Profit Sharing, Money Purchase and Paired Plans. None of the above are as easy to administer as a SEP, but Keoghs enjoy some advantages that SEPs can't touch—namely the ability to make put in as much as 25 percent of earned income, up to $30,000 per year.

Keoghs: To Contribute More

If you'd like to contribute a higher percentage of your earned income to your retirement plan, you may want to consider a Keogh. While a Keogh generally requires more administrative work than a SEP-IRA, it does give you the opportunity to contribute a higher percentage of your earned income each year.

There are actually three different Keogh options: a Profit Sharing Plan, a Money Purchase Plan, and a Paired Plan. The three Keogh options are primarily distinguished by:

- How much you can contribute each year; and
- Whether or not you are required to make an annual contribution

As with SEP-IRA plans, you will need to contribute the same percentage of each eligible employee's earned income (W-2 wages) as you contribute for yourself.

Profit Sharing Plan

This type of Keogh offers you the most flexibility, but limits you to the lowest annual contribution of all Keogh options. In a Fidelity Profit Sharing Plan you can:

- Contribute from 0% to 15% of your earned income each year, up to $30,000 per year, per participant(1)(2); and
- Vary the percentage of earned income you contribute each year, or skip a year if you need to.

Money Purchase Plan

This Keogh option allows you to contribute the highest percentage of your earned income, thus offering you the potential for the largest tax deduction. With a Fidelity Money Purchase Plan:

http://www.fid-inv.com/planning/keogh/contribute_more.html

So which one's right for you? SEP plans have that whole simplicity thing going for them but Keoghs offer some pretty attractive investment opportunities to offer too. And if you're leaning towards a Keogh, which one? Ugh! It's no wonder that you need a book and the vast resources of the Net to make sense of it all. Enter T. Rowe Price Investment Services and their handy little side-by-side comparison chart. Use it to weigh all the pros and cons of each of your options before coming to any firm decisions.

Retirement
T.RowePrice

Comparing Your Choices

	SEP	Simplified Keogh - Profit Sharing	Simplified Keogh - Money Purchase	Simplified Keogh - Paired
Key Benefit	Simple and inexpensive to set-up and maintain	Amount and frequency of contributions is flexible	Allows for maximum contributions	Combines flexibility with greater savings potential
Annual Contributions				
Required?	No	No	Yes	Yes
Maximum (per participant)	15% of compensation* or $22,500, whichever is less	15% of compensation* or $22,500, whichever is less	25% of compensation* or $30,000, whichever is less	25% of compensation* or $30,000, whichever is less, between Profit Sharing and Money Purchase

http://www.troweprice.com/retirement/choiceschart.html

IRAs

INVESTOR Education
Library

About Vanguard · Education · Services · Planning Tools · Mutual Funds

Retirement Planning: FAQs about IRAs

An Individual Retirement Account (IRA) is a personal retirement plan that lets you save for retirement while at the same time reducing taxes on your current income. You can accumulate substantially greater savings through an IRA than through a conventional taxable savings program. This is because of the two important tax advantages offered under an IRA:

All dividends, interest, and capital gains accumulate in your IRA on a tax-deferred basis.
That means that your IRA earnings grow free from Federal income taxation until you actually start making withdrawals. Over time, the tax-deferral advantage can have a dramatic effect on your retirement funds, permitting them to increase at a more rapid rate. Although withdrawals from an IRA are generally taxable as ordinary income (with the exception that amounts attributable to any nondeductible IRA contributions are returned tax-free), even after paying taxes on your withdrawals, you will normally end up with substantially more money than you would through a conventional savings program.

Your contributions to an IRA may be tax-deductible for Federal income tax purposes.
As a result, if you are eligible to take a full or partial tax deduction, your current-year tax bill is reduced. For example, if you make $2,000 of deductible contributions to an IRA and you are in the 31% tax bracket, you will save $620 on current-year taxes. That is, you will have invested $2,000 at an after-tax cost of only $1,380!

Here are the answers to some frequently asked questions about IRAs.

Even if you're in line to receive a pension or contribute to a retirement plan through work (and especially if neither is the case) you'd be wise to consider setting up an IRA for your retirement. IRAs (Individual Retirement Accounts) were set up by the government to help people help themselves save for the inevitable.

The Vanguard Group, Inc. has set up an IRA FAQ (that's Frequently Asked Questions, don't you just love acronyms?) for you to learn everything you need to know about IRAs.

http://www.vanguard.com/educ/lib/retire/faqira.html

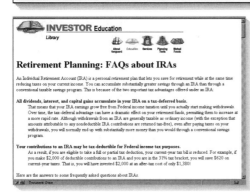

Not every employer provides a pension and/or sponsors a retirement plan. But everyone who works is entitled (make that *encouraged*) to start saving towards their retirement. Sometimes it's just a question of taking financial matters into your own hands with an Individual Retirement Account or IRA.

IRAs work in much the same way as some of the other plans discussed; they defer taxes on earnings, can reduce taxable income, and offer a host of investment options.

FAQs on Contributions

Q. Who is eligible to make IRA contributions?
A. Generally, anyone under age 70-1/2 who earns income from employment, including self-employment, may make annual contributions to an IRA.

Q. How much may I contribute to my IRA annually?
A. A maximum of $2,000 or 100% of your compensation, whichever is less, may be contributed to your IRA for each year.

Q. If my spouse is also employed, how much may be contributed to our IRAs?
A. Each employed spouse may open a separate IRA and contribute 100% of compensation, up to $2,000 a year. Thus, it's possible for a working couple to make total contributions of up to $4,000 annually to their IRAs.

Q. What if my spouse does not earn compensation?
A. If your spouse earns no compensation (or earns less than $250) for the year, you and your spouse may be eligible to increase your total IRA contribution as a couple by establishing an additional but separate "Spousal IRA" for your spouse. With a Spousal IRA, your maximum annual IRA contribution may be increased to $2,250, which may be split between the separate IRA accounts of you and your spouse in any manner you wish, so long as not more than $2,000 is contributed to either account for any one year.

Q. How can I determine whether my IRA contributions will be deductible for Federal income tax purposes?
A. Your IRA contributions will be deductible for Federal income tax purposes if:

• Neither you nor your spouse is an active participant in an employer-maintained retirement plan, or

http://www.vanguard.com/educ/lib/retire/faqira.html

Tax laws are always changing, but on the pages of The Vanguard Group's IRA FAQ you'll find up-to-date answers to any questions you might have about IRA contributions, deductions, withdrawals and tax implications.

As it stands right now (2:57 a.m., 11/27/96) the maximum that anyone can contribute into an IRA is $2,000 per year. But not everyone can contribute the full amount. There are special rules for nonworking spouses, income levels, and age requirements to consider as well.

http://www.vanguard.com/educ/lib/retire/faqira.html#deduct

FAQs on IRA Deductions

All taxpayers who are NOT active participants in an employer-maintained retirement plan can continue to take the full deduction for IRA contributions. Those who participate or who are married to an active participant must earn an adjusted gross income of no more than $25,000 (single) or $40,000 (married filing jointly) to take the full deduction. The deduction is phased out in increments of $200 per $1,000 of adjusted gross income for incomes between $25,000 and $35,000 (single) and $40,000 and $50,000 (married, filing jointly), as shown above. Note that for simplicity this chart shows the phase-out in $1,000 increments; the actual phase-out is calculated in $10 increments.

Q. My spouse and I both work, and we will have an adjusted gross income of $44,000 for the year, before we take any IRA deductions. We plan to file a joint return. If one of us is covered by an employer-maintained retirement plan, how much of our IRA contributions will be deductible?
A. In this case, your excess adjusted gross income ("excess AGI") over the $40,000 limit is $4,000. The following formula is used to calculate your IRA deduction amount:

($10,000 - excess AGI/$10,000 X Maximum IRA Contribution = IRA Deduction

Applying this formula, the IRA deduction limit for both you and your spouse would be $1,200 (assuming you each earned at least $2,000), calculated as follows:

($10,000 - $4,000)/$10,000 X $2,000 = $1,200

In addition, both you and your spouse would be eligible to make nondeductible IRA contributions of $800 each, resulting in total IRA contributions per spouse of $2,000 and a combined total of $4,000.

Q. To what extent can I make nondeductible IRA contributions?
A. You are permitted to make designated nondeductible contributions to your IRA to the extent you are not eligible to make

FAQs on Withdrawals

Q. When can I start to make withdrawals from my IRA?
A. Generally, you may start withdrawals from your IRA as early as age 59-1/2. Withdrawals must begin by April 1 following the year you attain age 70-1/2.

Q. How will my IRA withdrawals be taxed?
A. Withdrawals from your IRA will be taxed as ordinary income, with the exception that if you make any nondeductible contributions to your IRA, your IRA withdrawals will be treated partly as a non-taxable return of your nondeductible IRA contributions, and partly as a taxable distribution of your IRA earnings and any deductible IRA contributions. For these purposes, every IRA you maintain, whether you contribute to it or not, is required to be aggregated.

Q. What if I withdraw before age 59-1/2?
A. Because an IRA is intended to provide for your retirement, the law imposes an additional tax of 10% if you withdraw prior to age 59-1/2 for reasons other than your disability. This 10% tax is applied, in addition to ordinary income tax, to the taxable amount of your withdrawal. The 10% additional tax will not apply to distributions made to your beneficiary upon your death. In addition, the 10% tax will not apply to certain installment or annuity payments made for your life or life expectancy, or for the joint lives or life expectancies of you and your beneficiary, regardless of when these payments begin.

Q. When is the latest date at which I may begin withdrawals from my IRA?
A. The law requires that you begin to receive distributions from your IRA no later than April 1 following the calendar year in which you reach age 70-1/2. If you elect to make withdrawals at that time in installments, certain minimum distributions (based on your life expectancy or the joint life expectancies of you and your beneficiary) must begin. A 50% penalty tax will be imposed if the amount actually distributed to you after age 70-1/2 is less than the amount required by law.

IRAs were set up by the federal government to help people help themselves save for retirement. To assist in that end the IRS defers taxes on earnings and, if you qualify, on contributions until the money is withdrawn. The flip side of the IRS's generosity is that they get miffed if they feel their benevolence has been taken advantage of. Take your money out before age 59 1/2 and the withdrawal will be subject to a penalty. Ditto on waiting too long; you must begin withdrawals before age 70 1/2 or face the wrath of a vengeful IRS.

http://www.vanguard.com/educ/lib/retire/faqira.html#withdraw

Remember, like other retirement specific plans, an IRA is a tax-sheltering framework for investments not an investment in and of itself. Many IRA brokers can handle the investment end of things for you or you can choose to make and manage all the investments decisions yourself. You can invest in anything from futures to savings accounts, the choice is yours, just as long as the investment vehicle is IRS approved. For some odd reason the IRS doesn't consider a mint condition #1 Action Comics an approved vehicle.

http://www.vanguard.com/educ/lib/retire/faqira.html#death

FAQs on IRAs and Taxes

Q. How will an IRA lower my taxes?
A. In two ways:

1. Your IRA earnings will not be subject to Federal income tax until withdrawal
2. Your IRA contributions may be deductible for Federal income tax purposes, as explained above.

Q. Will I need to file any special forms with the IRS?
A. If you are eligible to make deductible contributions to your IRA, you may claim the deduction on your Federal income tax return (Form 1040 or Form 1040A) even if you do not itemize deductions. Each tax year, Vanguard will provide you with a Form 5498 showing your IRA contributions from the previous year. If you make any designated nondeductible contributions to your IRA, or if you receive any distributions from your IRA, and you have at any time made nondeductible contributions to any of your IRAs, you must attach Form 8606 to your Federal income tax return (Form 1040 or Form 1040A).

When you receive a distribution from your IRA, Vanguard will send you the IRS forms you may need to file your income tax return.

You may owe additional IRA taxes because of:

1. An excess contribution
2. A premature distribution before age 59-1/2, or
3. An under-distribution after age 70-1/2

You may be required to file Form 5329, which you may obtain from the IRS.

You can use the Smith Barney IRA Calculator to see how the value of your IRA can grow over time.

Fill in all of the blanks and use their guides to determine the hypothetical rate of return that you might expect to see on any taxable investments you make. Use the Tax-Exempt space for securities such as federal savings bonds which have a historically lower rate of return than other investments but are guaranteed and incur no income tax. When you're through click on the "Calculate" button for the results.

http://www.smithbarney.com/cgi-bin/ira/ira1.cgi

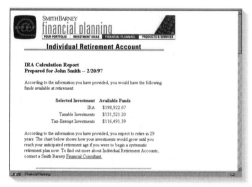

The calculation report that you will get based on the information that you provided shows how much assets you can expect to have available to you for retirement. It compares what you would have available to you in a tax-deferred IRA account, a taxable account and a tax-exempt account and shows you a year-by-year breakdown of the three accounts.

You may want to note that tax-free bonds are a poor investment for an IRA since their earnings would be treated like all other IRA earnings and taxed accordingly when withdrawn.

http://www.smithbarney.com/cgi-bin/ira/ira1.cgi

RRSPs

The Canadian equivalent of an IRA is the RRSP or Registered Retirement Savings Plan. While RRSPs work very much like their American counterparts there are lots of little differences. The Art of Investment Web site is here to explain them all.

The Art of Investment has put together a good collection of RRSP related articles on their site. You can explore to your heart's content or click on "Search" for a quick list. If you think you know your stuff you can click on Quizzes and take the RRSP challenge.

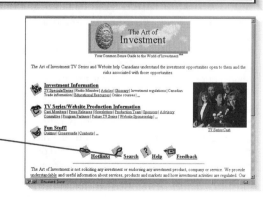

http://www.aofi.com/

From their search utility you can type in "RRSP" in the space provided, select "Articles" from the drop down list and click on "Search" for a long list of articles to check out.

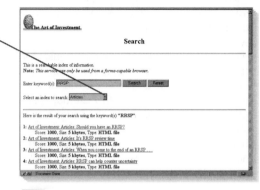

Click on any title to read that article. You can always click your browser's back button to come back to the search results page and continue on from there. Once you feel like you're up to the challenge be sure to return to the Art of Investment Home Page and take the RRSP Quiz.

http://www.aofi.com/search/index.html

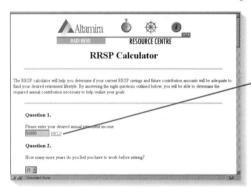

Once you've finished doing your homework and you're done taking the quiz it's time to calculate the results with Altamira Investment Services RRSP calculator. Each of the eight fields has a help link you can click on for guidance—just in case you don't happen to know the historical rate of inflation in Canada. Click on the "Calculate" button for one of the more "user friendly" results screens of any of the on-line calculators on the Net. And if you don't like the answer you get you can always click on "Try Different Scenarios" and try it again.

http://www.altamira.com/altamira/rrsp_calc.html

 ## Annuities

Tax Deferred Annuities aren't so much a retirement plan as a useful tool when doing your retirement planning. Basically, tax-deferred annuities are life insurance plans that pay up while your still around to enjoy the benefits. You can buy an annuity in one lump sum payment or pay into them monthly and have them provide for a steady income upon retiring. Sound simple? Think again. There are umpteen different annuity plans available and picking the right one is important. Bank of America has more to say on the subject.

http://www.bankamerica.com/p-finance/baistax.html

Deferred annuities are similar to qualified retirement plans in that the interest and/or earnings grow tax-free until you begin to receive payments and there's a penalty to be paid for early and/or late withdrawals (60 1/2 and/or 70 1/2, respectively). But unlike a qualified retirement plan annuity contributions are paid for with after-tax income. So while an annuity won't lower your current taxable income, there is no set limit on the amount that you can contribute.

http://www.bankamerica.com/p-finance/baistax.html

There are two basic types of deferred annuities, fixed and variable. With a fixed annuity you get a set interest rate on your investment and the piece of mind that comes with it. With a variable annuity you get to choose from various stock and bond portfolios which offer the potential for higher returns but carry the risk that those investments could turn sour. Many variable annuities guarantee at least the principle to your heirs if you happen to die before the annuity matures—which won't help you much but your heirs might appreciate it.

http://www.bankamerica.com/p-finance/baistax.html

The "deferred" part of deferred annuity refers to when you begin receiving the payments, not when you begin paying the taxes. As soon as a deferred annuity commences payments it becomes an Immediate Annuity. If you are in line for a lump sum payment upon retirement an Immediate Annuity might be a good way to supply yourself with a steady income for a specified period of time, like life. But be sure to take a look at <u>Richard F. Bregstein's Guide to Immediate Annuities</u> before committing yourself to something so *final*.

http://www.chesco.com/~rbreg/immedann.html

Put to good use, an annuity can supply you with a lifelong guaranteed income, decrease your taxes, and even help provide for your survivors. But like any other investment there are things to watch out for and things to avoid. Use trusted insurers and avoid annuities with high fees. Avoid annuities with surrender charges that don't disappear after seven years and check out what Retirement Planning Associates has to say about "Bonus" Annuities. If you plan on sticking around for a while they may be no bonus at all.

http://www.datadepot.com/~rpa/bonus.htm

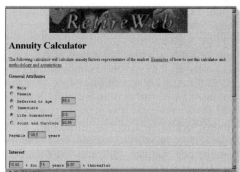

Finally, Hutchison Avenue Software Corporation's Retire Web has an on-line annuity calculator for you to play with. You can use this calculator to compare one annuity to the next or test out different scenarios and see, in dollars and cents, which one is right for you. See what happens if you defer payments for an extra 5 years or add another 10 on to your life expectancy. Put in your own numbers and click on "Calculate" to see the results and look at additional examples that you can use to interpret your own numbers.

http://www.retireweb.com/annuitycalc.html

 Professional Advice

Even after you've read this entire chapter and visited all the sites talked about, you may still have questions about retirement planning. Understandable. The subject is as vast as it is confusing. That's why financial planners spend a long time in school learning what no introductory book can teach in a few short hours, what no Web site can impart with a few quick clicks. But fear not, the Web holds one last trick up it's sleeve, the Financial Services Directory by Financial Profiles, Inc. Click on any state or on the International link.

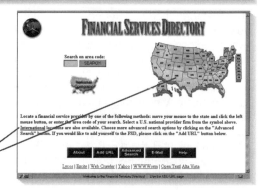

http://www.profiles.com/directory/

You get a long list of financial service professionals, both individuals and companies, that you can contact with your questions. I haven't personally called and asked each and every one of them, but my guess is that they's be more than happy to lend their assistance.

Under the name is a phone number and address. Often you will also be able to click on their e-mail address and/or Web address for easy access.

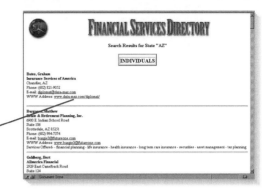

http://directory.profiles.com/cgi-bin/search?state=AZ

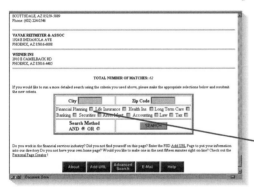

This is not a complete listing of every single financial service company in existence, but it is the most complete one available on the Web today and new links are added regularly.

You can narrow your search down to a specific city, zip code, or area of expertise or confine your search to only those with expertise in more than one area, such as both Accounting *and* Law. Just fill in the blanks and tick off whatever it is that you're looking for to see what the Web can come up with for you.

http://directory.profiles.com/cgi-bin/search?state=AZ

Remember What It's All About

When you're going through all the trouble of planning and saving, remember to keep your eye on the prize. Because in the end this is what it's all about. No, not golf necessarily. But you, your retirement, and doing what you've got to do now so that when the time comes you have what it takes to follow your dreams, whatever they are.

And if you dreams happens to include bright baggy pants and little white balls you can always stop by GolfWeb to remind yourself what it's all about.

http://www.golfweb.com/

Planning for College

The Cost of a College Education
- The Going Rate
- What You Can Expect to Pay in the Future

Aid, Loans and Scholarships
- The Ambitious Student's Guide to Financial Aid
- Where to Turn for a Loan
- Finding a Scholarship

Paying for School
- The Future Value of Your Current Savings
- What You Need to Set Aside
- Financing a College Education
- The Most Common Savings Instruments and Investments
- Pre-Paid Student Loans

Choosing a School
- Schools That Meet Your Exact Criteria
- Education Pays

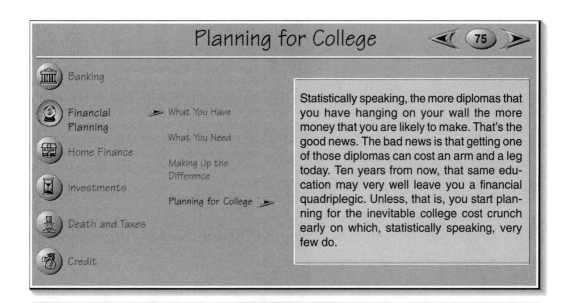

Banking

Financial
Planning

Home Finance

Investments

Death and Taxes

Credit

What You Have

What You Need

Making Up the
Difference

Planning for College ➤

Statistically speaking, the more diplomas that you have hanging on your wall the more money that you are likely to make. That's the good news. The bad news is that getting one of those diplomas can cost an arm and a leg today. Ten years from now, that same education may very well leave you a financial quadriplegic. Unless, that is, you start planning for the inevitable college cost crunch early on which, statistically speaking, very few do.

The Cost of a College Education

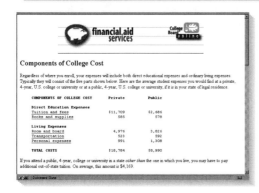

College is expensive. But "expensive" is such an ambiguous word. $3 for a 12-ounce bottle of water is expensive, $5 for a comic book is expensive, $200 for a pair of sneakers ... Exactly how much money is "expensive?" And more to the point, how much is an expensive education going to set you back? At an average of $18,784 a year for a private education, the answer may be unwelcome but at least it's no longer ambiguous. Visit the College Board and you will be given a complete breakdown.

http://www.collegeboard.org/expan/html/cost001.html

When I said "breakdown" a moment ago I meant it in the quantitative analysis sense. But with college costs rising at almost twice the rate of inflation, what's it going to cost you when your child goes to school 10 or 12 years from now? The financial aid web site has a calculator to figure that out. Fill in the blanks, click the "Calculate Projection" button and brace yourself for an entirely different type of breakdown; the type that leaves *you* in need of some analysis.

http://www.finaid.com/finaid/calculators/cost-projector.html

When your toddler starts applying to schools in about 17 years you could be looking at a cost of over a quarter of a million dollars (that's a two and a five followed by a whole whack of zero's). Ouch. And that's just for an *average* private school. Speaking of average, if you're one of the lucky ones with 2.3 children you could be looking at over $600,000.00 before your youngest ever dons a cap and gown. "My son, the high school dropout" never sounded so good.

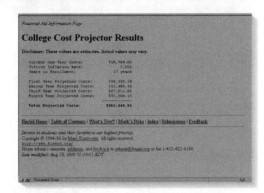

http://www.finaid.com/finaid/calculators/cost-projector.html

Aid, Loans, and Scholarships

It's time that you started thinking about where that money will come from. If it's any consolation, chances are that you won't have to come up with all of it yourself. Financial aid in the form of low interest, deferred payment loans will help.

We looked at a program from the College Board in the *Loan Lessons* chapter that will estimate how much financial aid you will be entitled to. Now read up on the subject with The Ambitious Student's Guide to Financial Aid from the Web pages of Signet Bank.

http://www.signet.com/collegemoney/toc1.html

The Financial Aid web site might also be of some assistance with their links to lenders that issue educational loans. There are a whole lot of lenders on this list that will be glad to help you out in a pinch. The problem is that sooner or later, they're all going to want their money back. Plus interest. Can you picture yourself still paying for you child's education when he or she is thirty-something? Probably not. Small wonder than that it's the kids that are usually saddled with the loan payments.

Lenders that Issue Educational Loans

This page presents information about banks, credit unions, savings & loan associations, and other financial institutions that provide funds to students and parents for educational loans under the Federal Family Education Loan Program (FFELP) or alternative loan programs. (Schools that participate in the Federal Direct Student Loan Program (FDSLP) do not use a private lender for the Stafford and PLUS loans, since loan funds are provided by the US Government.)

In addition to the lenders listed here, Secondary Markets, Guarantee Agencies, and Servicers may also issue educational loans (See, for example, the listings for the Connecticut Student Loan Foundation (CSLF), Sallie Mae, Southwest Student Services Corporation, and the USA Group.)

Additional details about private educational loan programs offered by these lenders appears on the Alternative Loans page.

Directories of Lenders

National Financial Services Network (NFSN), Student Loan Marketplace
NFSN provides a directory of lenders that provide various consumer services, including educational loans, organized by state. Entries in the directory consist of the lender's telephone number and links to the lender's web page. Access is free to consumers. At present, educational lenders are not charged for their listings. Lenders who wish to be included in the directory should send mail to register@nfsn.com. For more information, call 1-619-793-8334, write to National Financial Services Network, 3525 Del Mar Heights, Suite 190, San Diego, CA 92130, or send email to feedback@nfsn.com.

Lenders

Access Group
Access Group is a nonprofit organization offering federal and private loans for graduate and professional education.

http://www.finaid.org/finaid/loans/lenders.html

Scholarships can also help defray part of the price of admission. There are thousands of unheard of scholarship programs available but finding them isn't always easy. Some have turned to commercial search services that charge a fee to help match students to grants. FastWEB offers a free alternative for both American and Canadian students. Click on begin the fastWEB scholarship search and make a note of the "check your fastWEB mailbox" link, you're going to come back to it again later on.

http://www.fastweb.com/

You'll need to fill out the forms requesting information about yourself. Some might consider the questions nosy. You will be asked about your race, for example, and your religion. Don't be offended, if the Latino Hare Krishna league is handing out money and you're entitled, who are you to argue. FastWEB notes that most of scholarships are granted on the basis of organizations and activities. If you were on the pom-pom squad tick off the box, if you wear contact lenses, x marks the spot.

http://www.fastweb.com/

After answering five or six pages of personal information you can submit the information and play around on the Net while fastWEB matches your answers against the thousands of scholarships in its database. Fifteen minutes later you can check your fastWEB mailbox to see what they've come up with. FastWEB is even thoughtful enough to include form letter replies for you to print out and send in with your applications. Remember to check your mailbox often, over 1,200 new scholarships are added daily.

http://www.fastweb.com/

Financial aid and pom-pom scholarships will only take you so far. Let's say that between the two they'll cover half of your expenses, how much are you going to have to set aside to make up the difference?

Sallie Mae offers a two-in-one calculator that can either estimate the future value of your current savings or go the other way around and figure out how much you should be setting aside to meet your future financial needs. Just fill in the blanks and click the appropriate button.

http://www.salliemae.com:80/calculators/savings/

First, see how far off you are, given your current savings. Then go back and try the second calculator to see how much you need to be saving from now on.

Be careful about raising the interest rate from the 5 percent default. Projecting a 43 percent annual return on your investment might make you feel better, but the results won't necessarily be realistic. Likewise, increasing the number of years that you have left to work with will make for a more palatable answer, but don't expect your children to play along.

http://www.salliemae.com:80/calculators/savings/

The U.S. Department of Education has published a resource book for parents entitled Preparing Your Child For College and has made it available on their Web site.

I would suggest that you don't worry about preparing the kids for college right now, let them figure out how to tie a toga and chugalug brewskies on their own. Your job is to click on the Financing a College Education chapter title so that you can figure out how you're going to pay for all that higher learning.

http://www.ed.gov/pubs/Prepare/

So far in this chapter we've looked at college costs, both now and projected in the future. We've seen that you'll need to set money aside and we've calculated how much. We've looked at ways to supplement your educational savings through financial aid and scholarships. This Web page ties it all together and puts it into perspective.

Just above the Financial Aid section is a link that reads Chart 8 -- Examples of Savings Instruments and Investments—follow it.

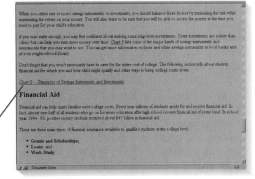

http://www.ed.gov/pubs/Prepare/pt4.html

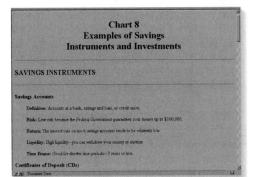

Saving and investing for college is no different than savings and investing for any other reason. You have to look at your options and weigh the pros and cons. Are you willing to take your chances on the stock market in the hopes of making a killing or would you rather have the security of a savings bond at a potentially lower return?

The Dept. of Ed. lists some of the most common savings instruments and investments, defines them, and describes the risks and returns involved with each.

http://www.ed.gov/pubs/Prepare/chart8.html

Some states now offer a tax-deferred alternative to traditional savings and investments designed specifically with college expenses in mind.

Crestar discusses these tuition account programs (TAP) and their tax implications. Some states have taken the concept a step further and have begun offering prepaid tuition at current prices. Sadly, not all states have one of these programs in place and of the few that do there are some serious issues that need to be worked out with the IRS.

http://www.student-loans.com/TaxTips.html

Canada has long offered a tax deferred <u>Reg-istered Education Savings Plan</u> (RESP) as outlined here in <u>CNNet's Money Sense</u>. Currently, RESP contributions are limited to no more than $1,500 per year up to a maximum of $31,500 per student. When the time comes to tap into the RESP, the profits are taxable at the student's (presumably lower) tax rate. On the downside, if your child decides to pass on college and chooses instead to try his or her hand as an *artiste*, all of the accrued interest is forfeited.

http://cnnet.com/syoung/young14.htm

Choosing a School

OK, your kid got the pom-pom squad leaders, Latino Hare Krishna scholarship, took out a low-interest student loan, and, somehow, you managed to raise the rest of the money yourself. The question remains; where is your little darling going to go to school?

<u>CollegeNET</u> offers a database of colleges that can help narrow down the search to a select few. Choose your country and pick from four year or community, technical and junior colleges to get started.

http://www.collegenet.com/search.html

Tick off whichever states that you are interest in or see schools from across the country that meet your criteria. You can set preferences for tuition (free would be nice), number of students, majors offered, sports programs, religious affiliation, and choose between public and private institutions.

To search for a specific school, enter in part of the name in the box supplied. Once all of your preferences are set, click on the "Search" button at the bottom of the screen.

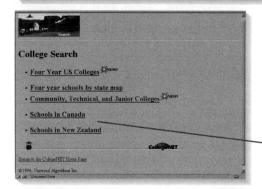

http://www.collegenet.com/cgi-bin/
Webdriver?MIval=cn_search_*_input

Long before the Internet took center stage it was primarily a way for students to share their work. It should come as no surprise then that most colleges have their own Web sites. You can click on the name of any underlined school on the list to jump to that school and learn a little more about what they have to offer.

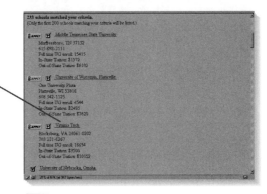

After seeing what there is to see on one college's site you can click your Web browsers's back button repeatedly to return to this screen and go on to the next school.

http://www.collegenet.com/cgi-bin/
Webdriver?MIval=cn_search_*_input

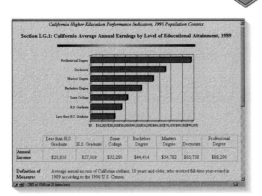

Once the kids are packed off to college the house will seem empty. So will your savings account. But all is not for naught. After the toga is back in the linen closet and the diploma is hanging on a wall your child will have much to thank you for—not that the ingrates ever do, mind you. This graph from the California Postsecondary Education Commission clearly shows what we knew all along: Education pays. Good thing too, now that your money is all gone someone's going to have to support you in your old age.

http://www.cpec.ca.gov/ab1808/final95/section1/inclevel.htm

Mortgage News

Information for an Educated Decision

⊣ Interest Rate Trends

⊣ Analysis

⊣ Current Financial Columns

⊣ Searching by Subject

On-Line Newspapers

⊣ Local News Around The World

Insider Information

⊣ Top Mortgage Tips

⊣ Mortgage Rates by City

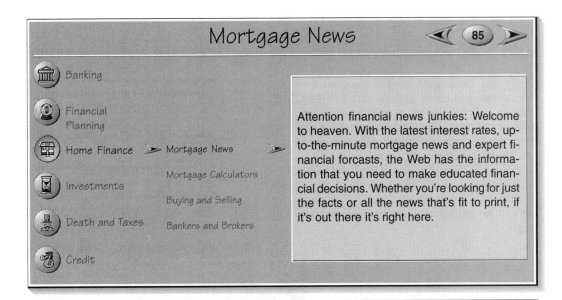

Banking

Financial Planning

Home Finance ➤ Mortgage News ➤

Mortgage Calculators

Investments

Buying and Selling

Death and Taxes   Bankers and Brokers

Credit

Attention financial news junkies: Welcome to heaven. With the latest interest rates, up-to-the-minute mortgage news and expert financial forcasts, the Web has the information that you need to make educated financial decisions. Whether you're looking for just the facts or all the news that's fit to print, if it's out there it's right here.

 # Information for an Educated Decision

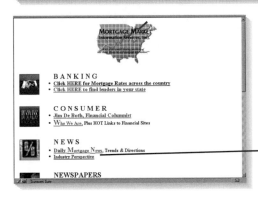

Go straight to the same source that over 300 newspapers rely on each week for their mortgage, real estate, and financial news coverage. At the Mortgage Market Information Services (MMIS) Web site you'll find the insightful, independent information that you need to make educated decisions about your home finances.

Click here for the Daily Mortgage News Report.

http://www.interest.com/

This chart gives you a historical sense of where interest rates were yesterday and where they stand today. Continue on down the page to read the Daily Mortgage News Report and find out where the experts think rates will be going tomorrow, and why.

You'll find the latest breaking news on the home front and some analysis on what it all means. Let's face it, unless you're some kind of financial freak, what the Federal Reserve Bank has to say on the subject of interest rates makes for some mighty unexciting reading. Unfortunately, it's exactly this kind of boring stuff that will help you to make an informed decision. It might even save you a lot of money, and saving money is most definitely not boring.

> **Friday March 29, 1996**
>
> Some weak economic news and end-of-quarter trading activity in the bond markets helped interest rates to edge a bit lower on Friday, giving some lenders an opportunity to ease their mortgage rates slightly this weekend.
>
> Factories continue to operate at less than desired levels, at least according to the Chicago Association of Purchasing Managers. The trade group released the results of its survey of business conditions for the Chicago area. The overall index edged higher to 47.3, but remained below 50, indicating a slowing of factory activity.
>
> Winter weather kept home sales down in the Midwest, dragging national sales levels lower in February. The Commerce Department reported that sales of new homes fell 1.3% to a seasonally adjusted annual rate of 700,000 units.
>
> Consumer confidence was also not as strong as previously thought. The University of Michigan's index of consumer sentiment came in at 93.7 in its final March reading, up from the 88.5 reading in February, but down from a preliminary 95.7 March reading reported a couple of weeks ago.
>
> These reports were encouraging to the emotionally battered bond markets, which have been reeling from Fed Chairman Alan Greenspan's forecasts of an improving economy. Bond prices moved sharply higher, putting downward pressure on long-term interest rates. The price on the benchmark 30 year Treasury Bond was higher by 25/32, pushing its yield down to 6.66%. The bond market rally was also believed to be aided by

http://www.interest.com/news.htm

BANKING
- Click **HERE** for Mortgage Rates across the country
- Click **HERE** to find lenders in your state

CONSUMER
- Jim De Both, Financial Columnist
- Who We Are, Plus HOT Links to Financial Sites

NEWS
- Daily Mortgage News, Trends & Directions
- Industry Perspective

NEWSPAPERS

Click the back button on your Web browser to return to the home page. From here you can click on the link that says Jim De Both, Financial Columnist for a list of, you guessed it, Financial Columns by Jim De Both.

http://www.interest.com/

Many sites on the Internet publish financial related articles and opinion pieces. The quality and depth of the articles available varies considerably from site to site. This site, in particular, has an especially good library of worthwhile articles. The latest of these are listed on this page for easy access. For a wider selection, you can click on Search the MMIS Archives and find articles written in the not-so-distant past that are still appropriate to your current mortgage quest.

Featured Mortgage Related Articles

James R. De Both
President, Mortgage Market Information Services, Inc.

🔍 SEARCH the MMIS Archives

● Determine how much house you can afford before you begin shopping (Jan. 1996)

http://www.interest.com/column.html

The ability to search through many articles for a specific subject is handy. You can type in any word or phrase in the space provided (like equity for example, or balloon payments) and click the "search" button for a list of all of the articles in the archives that deal with that subject.

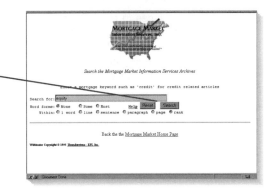

http://www.interest.com/search.html

Article titles are listed followed by the first couple of lines from each. Click any title to read the article. The search engine has some special features as well; to see the context in which the searched for word or phrase is used in the article click on the magnifying glass icon. To see more articles that cover similar subject matter click on the ≅ icon.

http://www.interest.com/search.html

After reading an article you can click your Web browsers back button to return to the previous screen and go on to read any other articles that look interesting.

http://www.interest.com/sa951101.htm

One of the best places to read about events that can affect your new home purchase is your local newspaper. With more local dailies publishing on the Web everyday, home delivery through the Net means never having to fish a soggy paper out of the begonias.

Take a look at the World News Index page and click on the map to find your area's local e-rag.

http://www.stack.nl/~haroldkl/index.html

This extensive list of on-line newspapers is organized by region. Clicking on a link will bring up the Web site for that paper.

Thinking about moving to Eden? Click on Maui News and discover what property taxes are like in paradise.

http://www.stack.nl/~haroldkl/usa.html

Each on-line newspaper site is different from the next. Some offer extensive search capabilities, for example, so you can search all recent articles for key words like "mortgages" or phrases like "toxic waste dump." Convenient if that open lot behind your new dream house is being eyeballed by the E.P.A.

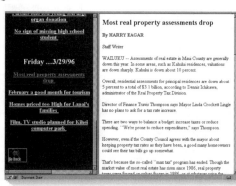

http://www.maui.net/~mauinews/news.html

The banking industry pays big bucks for the insights offered by the financial experts at Bank Rate Monitor, but you can access their comprehensive Web site for free. The information is well informed, plentiful, and, did I mention, free.

From this page you can click on the Home Equity or Mortgages buttons for current news and bank rates.

http://www.bankrate.com

Click on any article for a detailed, expert analysis on rates and rate directions or click on the Mortgage rates by city link for the latest bank rates in your neck of the woods.

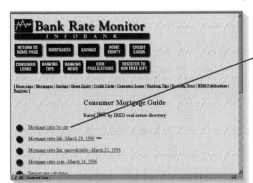

http://www.bankrate.com/bankrate/MORTHOME.HTM

Interest rates vary from lender to lender, so it's important for you to look around for the best rates before leaping into a 30-year financial relationship.

Here you can compare the rates of numerous lenders in your area without having to make a gazillion phone calls or visit a single branch. Just click on the name of the city that's nearest you.

http://www.bankrate.com/bankrate/mrtgcity.htm

The city listing includes the largest banking institutions in the area and their rates on 15 and 30-year fixed-rate loans and 1-year adjustable-rate mortgages.

If the bank's name is highlighted you can click on it to automagically visit that bank's Web site for more info. If it's not highlighted, and the bank doesn't yet have a Web site, you can always call the bank up and politely tell them to wake up and smell the 90's.

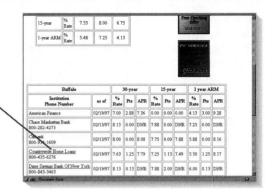

http://www.bankrate.com/bankrate/rates/brm34m.htm

Mortgage Calculators

How Much House Can You Afford?
⊢ How Much Will They Lend You?
⊣ Calculating Your Monthly Payments

Refinancing
⊣ Are You Better Off Refinancing?

Paying Points
⊣ Should You Pay Discount Points To Get a Lower Rate?

Comparing Mortgages
⊢ Fixed vs. Adjustable
⊣ Comparing Term Lengths

Closing Costs
⊣ Good Faith Closing Cost Estimate

Buying vs. Renting
⊣ Calculating for Cash Flow, Income Tax, and Net Worth

More Programs to Play With
⊢ Web Based Calculators
⊣ Home Finance Software

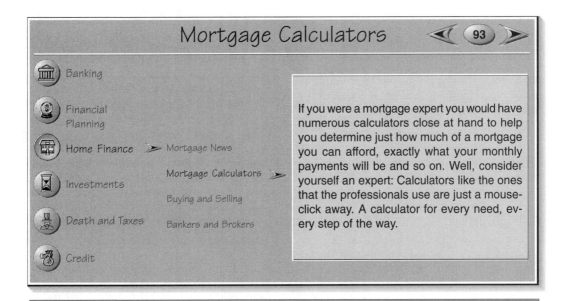

Banking

Financial Planning

Home Finance — Mortgage News

Mortgage Calculators

Buying and Selling

Investments

Death and Taxes — Bankers and Brokers

Credit

If you were a mortgage expert you would have numerous calculators close at hand to help you determine just how much of a mortgage you can afford, exactly what your monthly payments will be and so on. Well, consider yourself an expert: Calculators like the ones that the professionals use are just a mouse-click away. A calculator for every need, every step of the way.

How Much House Can You Afford?

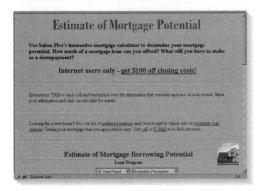

Unless you just hit the Lotto jackpot you probably don't have enough cash stashed away under your mattress to buy a house without resorting to a loan. You will need at least 10 percent for a down payment plus enough cash in reserve to cover closing costs. The rest you will have to borrow from a mortgage lender.

Pay a visit to the Salem Five Web site and discover how much lenders are likely to let you borrow.

http://www.salemfive.com/potential

During the initial stages of a house hunt you may not have the answers you'll need to fill in all the blanks. Not a problem. Do your best to supply estimates and come back to this site as often as you wish to plug in your updated numbers and recalculate your results. Because you may visit this site numerous times, you may want to add the address to the bookmark that comes with your Web browser.

http://www.salemfive.com/potential

Once you've plugged in your numbers you can scroll down the page and press the "Calculate" button to see what you get.

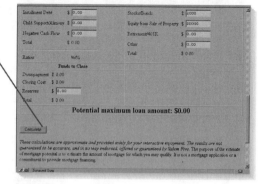

Here under the "Proposed Monthly Mortgage Payment" section you will find the total for what lenders assume that you can afford to pay for combined monthly mortgage payments, property taxes, home insurance and fees. You may think that this sum may be more or less than what you can really afford, but like it or lump it, it's what the lenders think that you can afford and therefore, it's what a lender is likely to let you borrow.

A bit further down the page, in big, bold, letters, is the calculated maximum amount that lenders are likely to let you borrow. Add your down payment to this total and you now know the maximum price range of homes that you can reasonably afford.

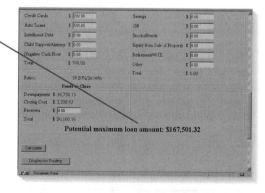

Knowing your price range is great when you are searching for a house, but debt with so many zeros behind it is a hard concept to grasp. The real question is how much are you going to have to cough up at the end of each month?

You'll find the answer by using this Monthly Mortgage Payment Calculator on Hugh Chou's Web page. Fill in all of the fields and click here to calculate your results. Canadians should put a "c" (e.g., 8.5c) after the annual interest rate.

http://www.ibc.wustl.edu/mort.html

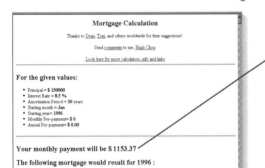

You will see a summary screen that looks something like this. And here, once again in big, bold numbers, are your monthly payments.

You may want to print these results out for future reference by clicking on your Web browser's print button.

http://www.ibc.wustl.edu/mort.html

Below the summary you will find a table detailing principle, interest, and balance remaining on your mortgage.

Be warned, this table can get rather lengthy on a 30-year mortgage, so have plenty of patience and paper if you choose to print the whole thing out.

Your monthly payment will be $ 1153.37

The following mortgage would result for 1996 :

Month	Prin	Int	Balance
Jan	90.87	1062.50	149909.13
Feb	91.51	1061.86	149817.62
Mar	92.16	1061.21	149725.45
Apr	92.81	1060.56	149632.64
May	93.47	1059.90	149539.17
Jun	94.13	1059.24	149445.03
Jul	94.80	1058.57	149350.23
Aug	95.47	1057.90	149254.76
Sep	96.15	1057.22	149158.61
Oct	96.83	1056.54	149061.78
Nov	97.52	1055.85	148964.26
Dec	98.21	1055.16	148866.06

- FOR 1996 : Int=$ 12706.50 Prin=$ 1133.94 Bal=$ 148866.06

http://www.ibc.wustl.edu/mort/mortnew.cgi

What if you don't want a mortgage on a new home? What if you want to take out a new mortgage on the home you already have? In other words, what if you want to refinance?

Take a look at the <u>Refinancing Calculator</u> at the <u>Financenter</u> Web site and see if refinancing makes sense for you.

http://www.smartcalc.com/cgi-bin/smartcalc/HOM12.cgi/FinanCenter

This calculator is fairly complete. It has to be, the decision to refinance involves more than just calculating how much lower your payment will be each month.

Add your own numbers in each of the "input" fields. In the "Other Costs to Obtain Loan" field, be sure to include any prepayment penalty fees incurred. Ask your current mortgage holder what fees, if any, would be applicable in your particular case.

http://www.smartcalc.com/cgi-bin/smartcalc/HOM12.cgi/FinanCenter

Scroll down and click on the "Calculate Again" button to see your results.

Here you will see the Total Monthly Payments as well as the Total Cost if Paid Today for both your existing mortgage and the mortgage were you to refinance.

http://www.smartcalc.com/cgi-bin/smartcalc/HOM12.cgi/FinanCenter

The refinancing calculator takes into account numerous factors such as the cumulative interest paid and yearly tax savings in order to calculate the real cost of both the old and new loans.

The cumulative interest paid on the loans is easy enough to understand; the less you have to pay out in interest charges the better. Another, less straightforward, part of the equation is explained when you click on the Tax Savings link.

http://www.smartcalc.com/cgi-bin/smartcalc/HOM12.cgi/FinanCenter

Upfront costs, potential return on invested savings, interest charges, and tax savings are all taken into consideration when determining whether or not refinancing is right for you. Put to good use, this refinancing calculator should help to cut through some of the clutter and help make an otherwise complex decision a little bit easier to make.

http://www.smartcalc.com/docs/hom/taxsave.htm

 Paying Points

By now you've probably come across the term points numerous times. The concept can be confusing. Deciding whether or not to pay points, and if so how many, is enough to make you want to tear your hair out.

Use the Financenter point calculator to test out various point scenarios on your unique situation. It's cheaper than Minoxidal and less painful than plugs.

http://www.smartcalc.com/cgi-bin/smartcalc/HOM5.cgi/FinanCenter

The point calculator has two columns so that you can test out different point scenarios for side-by-side comparison.

This calculator can also factor in Adjustable Rate Mortgages and even serves as a quick personality test. Optimist or pessimist? If you consider yourself a realist you can test both best and worst case scenarios, then assume the worst and hope for the best.

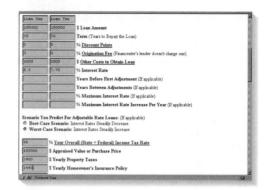

http://www.smartcalc.com/cgi-bin/smartcalc/HOM5.cgi/FinanCenter

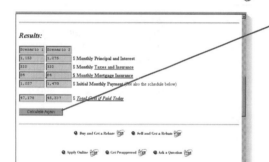

Press the "Calculate Again" button to see your results. Want to try a different point scenario? Just scroll back up the page, put in your new numbers and try it again.

http://www.smartcalc.com/cgi-bin/smartcalc/HOM5.cgi/FinanCenter

Scroll down the page for all the gory details.

Compare the bottom numbers in the Cumulative Interest Paid columns. Now add up the Yearly Tax Savings column and see if you're any further ahead after paying taxes.

Try your own numbers and see for yourself if paying points pays off, or if what the points giveth, the taxman taketh away.

Year	Monthly Payment	Remaining Amount Owed	Yearly Principal Paid	Yearly Interest Paid	Cumulative Interest Paid	Yearly Tax Savings
0	0	150,000	0	0	0	0
1	1,153	148,866	1,134	12,706	12,706	5,740
2	1,153	147,632	1,234	12,606	25,313	5,702
3	1,153	146,289	1,343	12,497	37,810	5,661
4	1,153	144,827	1,462	12,378	50,188	5,616
5	1,153	143,235	1,591	12,249	62,438	5,567
6	1,153	141,504	1,732	12,109	74,546	5,513
7	1,153	0	141,504	11,955	86,502	5,455

Loan With Points:

Year	Monthly Payment	Remaining Amount Owed	Yearly Principal Paid	Yearly Interest Paid	Cumulative Interest Paid	Yearly Tax Savings
0	0	150,000	0	0	0	0
1	1,075	148,683	1,317	11,579	11,579	7,022
2	1,075	147,261	1,422	11,473	23,052	5,272
3	1,075	145,725	1,536	11,359	34,411	5,228
4	1,075	144,065	1,660	11,236	45,646	5,181
5	1,075	142,272	1,793	11,102	56,749	5,131
6	1,075	140,334	1,937	10,958	67,707	5,076
7	1,075	0	140,334	10,803	78,510	5,017

http://www.smartcalc.com/cgi-bin/smartcalc/HOM5.cgi/FinanCenter

After weeding through just about every house on the market today and finally selecting the right one, the next most difficult decision you will make as you prepare for moving day will likely be between a fixed rate mortgage and an adjustable rate mortgage (ARM).

Use this fixed rate vs. adjustable rate calculator on the Interactive Home buying on the Web site and see which makes sense for you.

http://www.maxsol.com/cgi-bin/cgih/hweb

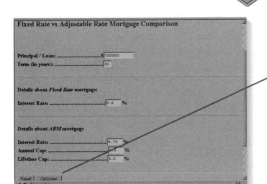

Click the "Fixed Rate vs. Adjustable Rate" button and you will see this screen. Here you can enter in your numbers and click on the "Calculate" button for your results.

http://www.maxsol.com/cgi-bin/cgih/hweb

You will see a summary screen like this one. Notice that this calculator necessarily makes some assumptions for its calculations—namely that the adjustable rate mortgage increases by the maximum amount each year and that the two loans being compared are otherwise the same in terms of fees, points, and other related costs.

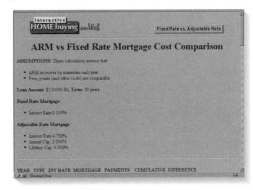

http://www.maxsol.com/cgi-bin/cgih/hweb

Below the summary screen is a more detailed analysis of your results.

Which type of mortgage you should choose to go with often depends on how long you intend to own the property before selling. Based on the numbers you've supplied, the calculator will draw some conclusions and highlight the point at which one choice is likely to save you money over the other.

http://www.maxsol.com/cgi-bin/cgih/hweb

15- and 30- year mortgages are the most common, but what's right for you? At the Open House America site you can use this calculator to see what different term lengths mean to your monthly payments and overall loan costs.

Fill in the details of your loan. For the loan length, enter a term you would like to test out. You will come back to this screen later to try another term and compare the results. Press the "Calculate" button when done.

http://www.openhouse.net/calculator.html

Here are the results of your initial calculation. The two numbers that are of most importance to you are the monthly mortgage payment and, at the bottom of the table, the cumulative amount of interest you will end up paying out before finally burning the mortgage.

Make a note of these numbers for comparison and click your Web browser's back button to return to the previous screen.

http://www.openhouse.net/calculator.html

This time around you'll change the term length and press the "Calculate" button again to compare the results.

What you find might save you a lot of money: For example, a 30-year, $150,000 loan at 8.5 percent will cost over $149,000 more in additional interest charges than the same loan paid off in 15 years. Monthly payments will go up, but if you can afford to pay it off faster you'll save a bundle in the long run.

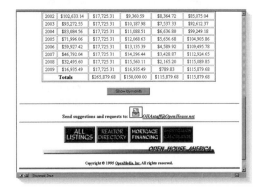

http://www.openhouse.net/calculator.html

 Closing Costs

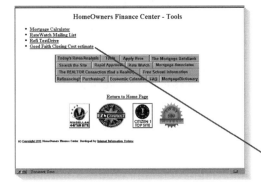

Not really a calculator so much as an estimator, the "Good Faith Closing Cost Estimator" on the HomeOwners Finance Center Web site is, at the very least, interactive: If the amount of your loan is not represented by these typical closing costs, you can always contact the good people that run the site for an estimate that more closely matches the particulars of your loan.

From this page click on Good Faith Closing Cost Estimate.

http://www.homeowners.com/toolstop.html

Here you are provided with some tables for standard closing costs. You can use these tables to better estimate the closing costs you will incur on both refinanced and first time mortgages.

http://www.homeowners.com/goodfaith.html

The list includes an estimate of just about every kind of fee those sneaky old bankers and lawyers might throw your way. Read it and weep.

(A quick, personal note to my banker and lawyer: Linda, Bill, I just want you both to know that I wasn't referring to either of you in the above sentence.)

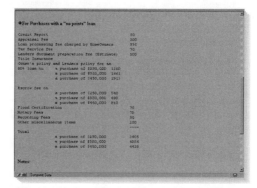

http://www.homeowners.com/goodfaith.html

 # Buying vs. Renting

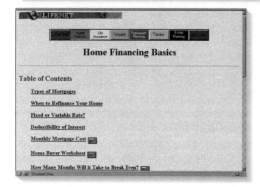

To buy, or not to buy, that is the question ... To own! Perchance to build equity;—ay, there's the rub.

Use this buying vs. renting calculator on the Lifenet Web site and answer the eternal question for yourself.

Continue to scoll down the screen and you will see the Buy or Rent calculator pictured below.

http://lifenet.com/home2.html

The calculator will analyze your data and compare the differences between buying and renting in terms of cash flow, income tax and net worth.

Fill in the blanks and click the "Calculate" button for your results.

http://lifenet.com/home2.html#buyrent

You will get a screen like this one that details all of the most common costs involved.

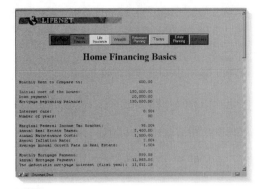

http://lifenet.com/life-cgi/buyrent

Further on down the page are some important notes about the calculations and what they all mean to you. Notice that while standard maintenance costs are factored into the calculations, costly emergency repairs are not. Midwinter furnace breakdowns aren't something you can plan for, but as a home owner, it is a financial possibility that you had better be prepared for.

http://lifenet.com/life-cgi/buyrent

These estimates assume that you will be staying put for the span of time covered by a mortgage. With mortgages of 15 and 30 years so common and people moving an average of every seven years, it is wise for you to not make that same assumption.

How long are you planning to own or rent before moving on? See where you would stand each year and base your decision on your own particular time frame.

http://lifenet.com/life-cgi/buyrent

Here is where you can weigh the financial pros and cons for yourself. You'll find the true cost of home ownership (and no, the calculator isn't broken), the amount of equity built up over the years and the total rent paid out.

Unfortunately, there's nothing yet on the Web that can sum up the precise amount of joy you will feel when given your first plumbing bill or calculate, to the decimal point, the ultimate satisfaction of ownership.

http://lifenet.com/life-cgi/buyrent

 # More Programs to Play With

The Web has an on-line calculator to work out just about any mortgage problem you can throw at it. One of the brightest spots on the Web for mortgage related information, Hugh Chou's Mortgage and Financial Calculators, Information and Links page brings together many of the finest of these on-line calculators.

http://www.ibc.wustl.edu/mort_links.html

Scroll down the page and click on "Mortgage Freeware/Shareware for your Mac or PC".

From here you can click on the name of any program and easily download dozens of great little software programs that can help you to analyze mortgages on your own computer and find the best deals.

Mortgage Freeware/Shareware for Mac/PC

http://www.ibc.wustl.edu/mort/shareware/

Buying and Selling

Finding the Information You Need

⊣ ired.com, The Real Estate Directory

 └⊣ Real Estate Books and Publications on the Web

⊣ R.E. Infonet

 ⊣ Home Sellers Information

 └⊣ The Resale Value of Renovations

└⊣ Hometime's How-To Center

Choosing an Agent

 ⊣ The Realty Referral Network

 ⊣ Links to Realtor Home Pages Around the World

House Hunting

 ⊣ Virtual Home Tour

 └⊣ Finding the Perfect House

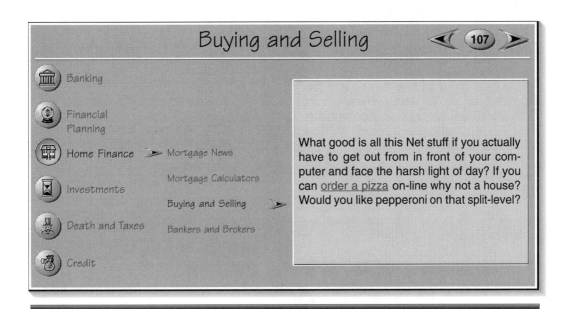

- 🏛 Banking
- 💰 Financial Planning
- 🏬 Home Finance ➤ Mortgage News
  - Mortgage Calculators
  - Buying and Selling ➤
  - Bankers and Brokers
- ⌛ Investments
- ⚖ Death and Taxes
- 💰 Credit

What good is all this Net stuff if you actually have to get out from in front of your computer and face the harsh light of day? If you can order a pizza on-line why not a house? Would you like pepperoni on that split-level?

🏠 Finding the Information You Need

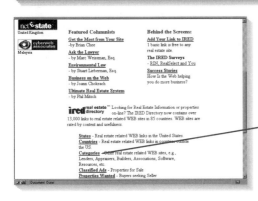

Here's a spot to bookmark if you're serious about buying, selling, or owning a home. With over 6,000 real estate links from around the world and more than 3,000 pages of information on hand, ired.com is a site worth visiting again and again.

Rummage around and click on Categories when ready.

http://www.ired.com

The sheer quantity of links found here can be almost overwhelming, but ired.com helps to make order out of the chaos. Finding what you're looking for is made simpler by having the links rated for content and quality and then neatly divided into categories.

Browse through Books/Publications for a list of on-line real estate documents available for your fiscal edification.

http://www.ired.com/cgi-bin/ssi.cgi/dir/index.html

This eclectic library borrows heavily from the best of the Net. You'll find articles ranging from "The Complete Guide to Immigration and Successful Living in the United States" to "Real Estate Nightmares."

Click on R.E. Infonet for one of the better general information real estate sites on the list.

Service affords real estate agents an edge
Discount Real Estate Book Store ☆
The Ultimate Collection of News Links ✹☆
"The Complete Guide To Immigration And Successful Living In The United States"
Quantum Books ✓
Real Estate Nightmares ☆
Is this the Net's version of "Pacific Heights?"
Creative Real Estate Online
An infomercial online, but better than we expected.
Real Estate Library ☆
Today's Realtor® NAR Magazine ☆
National Historic Preservation Act of 1966 ✓
Gregory A. Laycock - Grubb & Ellis, Seattle Newsletter ▤☆
Real Estate Industry News ✓
R.E. InfoNet ▤▤ ☆
Some of the best RE articles on the WWW for buyers and sellers.
Real Estate Journal Interactive ▤▤ ☆
Relocation Journal & Real Estate News
RE/MAX Times ▤▤
Wine Country Weekly Real Estate Reader ▤▤
Review Net Listing of Real Estate Newsletters and Resources
How To Find Your Ideal Country Home ☆
Home Financing Primer -- December 93
Land Sales Scams -- November 92
Timeshare Resales -- November 92
Timeshare Tips -- October 92
Guide to Single Family Home Mortgage Insurance

http://www.ired.com/cgi-bin/ssi.cgi/dir/relibr.htm

R.E. Infonet has information and suggestions for buyers and sellers alike. The site might be short on visual flash but with article titles like "Nice House - But Where is the Furniture?" and "Owning a Hammer Does Not Make You a Contractor," it doesn't lack its own distinctive style.

Take a look at the Home Sellers Information area for tactics and financial strategies that will help you to sell your home sooner and maximize its sales price.

http://www.reinfonet.com/

Live in a home for long enough, and the natural urge to improve it will inevitably take precedence over any financial instinct that you might posses.

Before you call in that contractor, you might first want to consult the How Much is That Home Improvement Worth chart and see how much of that investment you can expect to recoup when the time comes to move on.

Home Sellers Information

Tactics and financial strategies to help home sellers maximize the sales price of their home regardless of market conditions in their area

- How Much is That Improvement Worth
- Prepare Your Home For Sale
- Sale Preparation Checklist
- Caveat Emptor but Seller Disclose
- Going it Alone - FSBO Considerations
- Determining the Gain or Loss in Your Sale

http://www.reinfonet.com/homesellers.html

This chart shows the average amount of money that you will recover on a major renovation at the time of sale. These numbers are national averages, so you will want to consider the area that you live in to better estimate how much that home improvement is really worth to you.

The addition of a swimming pool, for example, will generally show a better return on investment in Phoenix than in Anchorage—vice versa for that fireplace.

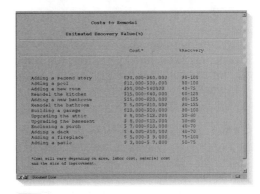

http://www.reinfonet.com/improvement.html

Installing a marble-tiled hot tub in your bathroom may help to sell your home faster, but don't count on ever getting all of that money back. Bang-for-the-buck wise, you're usually better off just fixing that leaky faucet.

When the problem is too small to call in a professional contractor and too large to ignore, get advice from Hometime's How-To Center.

http://www.hometime.com/

You know all of those little do-it-yourself projects that you've been putting off ever since you bought the house? Yeah, well, now that you're trying to sell the place it's time to dust off the toolbox, click a button and get to them.

http://www.hometime.com/projects/plmbelec.htm

I think my wife would agree with me if I said that I am not the handiest guy in the world. Heck, I'm not even the handiest guy in the house: My five-year-old son repaired some shaky lawn furniture today. I'm sure I would have gotten to it eventually, no doubt when it came time to sell the house.

I'll have to get my son to go through the Plumbing section on Hometime. He can start with Plumbing Basics and work his way down to Fixing Leaky Faucets.

http://www.hometime.com/projects/plmbelec.htm#plumbing

Kind of makes you want to go out and buy a 200-piece ratchet set or something, doesn't it?

Join us next week when my 18 month old daughter will demonstrate proper drywalling technique.

http://www.hometime.com/projects/howto/plumbing/pc2plm8.htm

Choosing an Agent

Finding a real estate agent is rarely a problem. Finding a *good* agent, however, one that knows the area, understands the market, and is willing spend the time it takes to get to know your needs, that requires some effort.

The Web offers a couple of shortcuts you can use to help review the qualifications of agents in your area before selecting the right one.

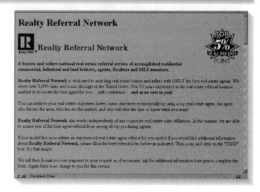

http://mmink.com/mmink/dossiers/rrn/rrn.html

The <u>Realty Referral Network</u> offers a free service that can help to match you up with the right real estate agent in over 5,000 cities and towns throughout the United States. The service operates independently of any real estate companies in a notable attempt to provide more objective recommendations.

Fill out the form as completely as possible and click the "Send Request" button when done. Realty Referral Network will then e-mail you a list of agents for review.

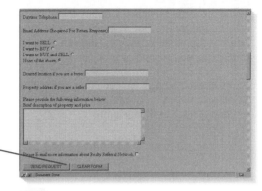

http://mmink.com/mmink/dossiers/rrn/rrn.html

Many real estate agents and agencies now have their own Web pages that you can use to learn more about them before engaging their services. Unfortunately, finding those Web pages without knowing in advance where they are can be something of a hit-and-miss affair.

Use <u>RealtyGuide</u> to give yourself a head start in your search. From the home page you can <u>click here</u> to find the sites of real estate agents in your geographical area.

http://www.xmission.com:80/~realtor1/

At the rate that real estate agents are putting up their own Home pages there should soon be a real estate Web page for every man, women, and child in North America. All right, that might be a slight exaggeration, but while we may never reach true Realor® Home page to population parity, you *will* find links to thousands of agents from the <u>United States</u>, <u>Canada</u>, <u>Mexico</u>, and <u>around the world</u>.

Welcome to RealtyGuide

Info | RealtyGuide | Finance | 411 | Library | Software | Tour | Main

RealtyGuide is presently text-based. It's not that we can't afford pictures or fancy graphics. We believe that you're here looking for lots of raw information and quick connections. Since our data is dynamic (it changes often), be sure to use your browser's *RELOAD* function at each visit. This is the Main Index and there's a similar "menu bar" at the bottom of every page (click here for menu definitions). Also, don't forget how to return to RealtyGuide because lots of the links are one-way (hint: the "back arrow" works great!). See What's New on the "INFO" page for system news and more information.

Here are the *Menu Definitions:*

* Info - RealtyGuide's system information. What's new? How do I use it?

RealtyGuide - World wide real estate resources, geographically indexed.

Finance - Global financial resources and lenders, alphabetically sorted.

411 - Resources galore! RealtyGuide's Real Estate Business Directory.

RealtyGuide to the World

RealtyGuide uses a step-down menu system. Select an area to view and you will be presented with choices arranged alphabetically by continent, country, state/province and city or region. Just highlight one and click on it to be transported! More detailed instructions on using RealtyGuide is found on the Info page.

There is a menu bar, an e-mail form and an Add-Link command at the bottom of each page. Send us your URLs we'll include them in the next update, without charge. We encourage user support and really appreciate your comments!

George Dodge, Realtor * **RealtyGuide** * Salt Lake City, Utah * 801-569-9618

Select one

* United States (1,380)

* Canada

http://www.xmission.com/~realtor1/relinks1.html

The nationwide services (Century 21's corporate headquarters, for example) are posted near the top of the list with the individual Realtors® grouped by state or province below.

Scroll down the page until you find something of interest or click on a state or province name to jump quickly to that section.

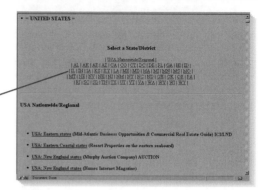

http://www.xmission.com/~realtor1/relinks1.html#USA

Click on any link to begin your review of agents. If you plan on using this site frequently to aid in your search for the perfect agent, you may want to bookmark this page. Otherwise you can click the back button when you're done with one agency site to return here and go on to the next site.

http://www.xmission.com/~realtor1/relinks1.html#IL

House Hunting

Why is it that the coolest things in life are always just around the corner? While most of the virtual home tours were "under construction" when we visited, this one from Anderson Homes, and a hundred others just like it, should be up and running in the not-so-distant future. Access the on-line home of tomorrow's real estate agent and take a virtual tour of homes for sale around the world. All from the comfort of your own ergonomically-designed, pneumatically-adjusted chair. Say "gee whiz" and click on the front door to begin your tour.

http://www.anderson-homes.com/virtualtour/index.html

Navigate through the house by clicking on any door or entryway or choose the floorplan link at the bottom of the page and jump to any room in the house. Click on a closet and search for skeletons from the relative safety of your computer.

I would like to take a second here to thank the gracious homeowners of their fine home in picturesque Sunnyslope Village for allowing all 30,000 of us to take a quick peek through their house. We'll just shut the door behind us on the way out.

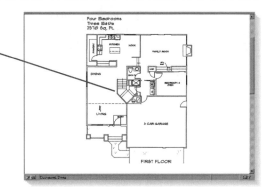

http://www.anderson-homes.com/ss_floorplan.html

The two biggest Web browser developers are currently in the process of introducing their next generation of Internet software with built-in real-time 3-dimensional capabilities. The mind staggers at the home hunting possibilities.

And, of course, it's just around the corner.

http://www.anderson-homes.com/virtualtour/stair_case.html

The National Association of Realtors® has a mighty slick Web site. Best of all, it's available today. From here you can search through a database of hundreds of thousands of homes for sale from all across the country. With more properties being added every day, you should soon be able to select from over 1,000,000 homes—a major undertaking and a taste of things to come.

Select a state from the map or the list below it to begin your search.

http://www.realtorads.com/

From the State map you begin to narrow the scope of your search further by clicking on the city or town that you are interested in.

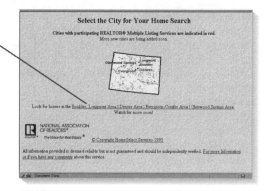

http://www.realtorads.com/selco.htm

From the community level you can select neighborhoods from the list to the right of the map. If you would like to search across multiple neighborhoods you can click on the names of several neighborhood in the list while holding down the Control (a.k.a. Ctrl) key on your keyboard.

Once you've selected the communities you would like to search for homes in, click the "Continue" button.

http://www.realtorads.com/boulder/region.htm

Before you can complete your search you will need to fill out a form detailing exactly what features you are looking for in your new home. Get as specific as you want, but at a minimum, you will need to supply the type of home, approximate price range, and minimum number of bedrooms.

When you're satisfied with your search criteria click on the "Start Search For Homes" button and see what you get.

http://www.realtorads.com/boulder/region.htm

Paydirt. Starting from a map of the entire United States you have now zoomed down to a list of homes that meet your exact specifications in precisely the neighborhoods of your choice. This list comes complete with descriptions and, if available, pictures of the property.

Remember to <u>print</u> this list out for future reference if you find something you like.

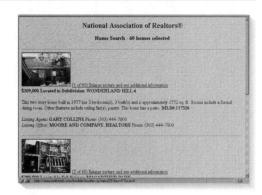

http://www.realtorads.com/boulder/region.htm

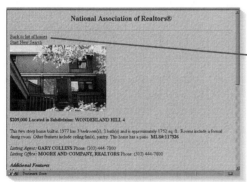

You can click on any picture to bring it up in greater detail and see additional information about the property. The homes are listed in groups of three. Click here to display the next three homes or start a new search.

If you find something that you like, jot down the MLS number for an agent to use as a reference. Not to worry if you don't know what an "MLS number" is, your agent will. Happy Hunting.

http://www.realtorads.com/boulder/region.htm

Bankers and Brokers

Banks on the Web
- The BankWeb Directory
- The Sort of Things You Can Expect

Mortgage Options
- Types of Mortgages
- On-Line Applications
- Which Mortgage is Right for You?
- The Mortgage Lending Resource Center

Mortgage Brokers
- Finding a Mortgage Professional
- Seeing What Each Has to Offer
- Doing the Paperwork

Getting the Best Deal
- CLN MortgageNet

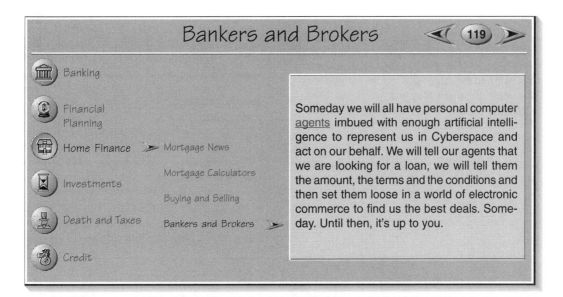

Banking

Financial Planning

Home Finance ➤ Mortgage News

Mortgage Calculators

Investments

Buying and Selling

Death and Taxes Bankers and Brokers ➤

Credit

Someday we will all have personal computer agents imbued with enough artificial intelligence to represent us in Cyberspace and act on our behalf. We will tell our agents that we are looking for a loan, we will tell them the amount, the terms and the conditions and then set them loose in a world of electronic commerce to find us the best deals. Someday. Until then, it's up to you.

Banks on the Web

Every day more banks clamber aboard the Internet bandwagon to head out and stake their claim in cyberspace. Hot on the heels of the first few fiscal pioneers is a stampede of banks from all over the world just itching to join the electronic gold rush.

Click on BankWeb's exhaustive list of banks and pay a visit to your bank's virtual homestead. If the bank you're looking for isn't amongst the many on this list with a World Wide Web site, wait a minute.

http://www.bankweb.com/

U.S. banks are organized by state. Click on the name of any state to bring up the list of banks from that state with Web sites, or click on the link that says International Banks for a list of on-line banks from around the world.

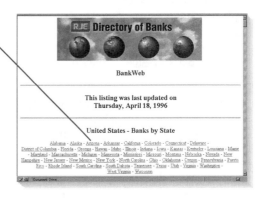

http://www.bankweb.com/bankweb.html

You will find the larger U.S. banks listed under the state in which they are headquartered; CitiBank, for example, would be listed under New York and Bank Of America can be found under California.

Click on any bank name to make personal banking a bit more personal and bring home finance home.

http://www.bankweb.com/bankweb.html#ca

Electronic banking is still in its virtual infancy. Only recently have the staid institutions of finance begun to open their eyes and focus on the World Wide Web. But time on the Net passes by so quickly, and electronic commerce seems to grow even as we all look on in wonder. Already, many banks have taken their first, tentative steps towards offering a full range of on-line consumer services, and as these services continue to mature, electronic banking begins to come of age.

http://www.bankamerica.com/

The best of the on-line bank offerings deliver more than just repackaged advertising and offer home finance services that you can really use. Bank of America has created one such site.

Most bank sites offer a way to contact a bank rep and will forward any questions you might have to a specialist. Just be careful. Unless the e-mail facility is secure, err on the side of caution and don't send confidential or personal account information.

http://www.bankamerica.com/contact/email_expert.html

Banks offer many different types of loans and options—"products" in banking lingo. These products range from the traditional (no point ARMs) to the incidental (how about the "Good Neighbor" mortgage). Some banks even have mortgage "specials" for Internet users, a marketing gimmick that can save you some dough.

Examine the products a bank has to offer and compare them with what the other banks are flogging on the Net.

http://www.bankamerica.com/p-finance/athome/athome_loanbuy.html

The ancient Greek philosopher Heraclitus once noted that you can never step in the same river twice. He could have said the same of the World Wide Web, except, of course, for the fact that no one would have known what the heck he was talking about for another 2,500 years.

The only thing that even approaches the Web for rate of change is the change in rates. Interest rates are posted on the sites of most banks and are updated daily.

http://www.bankamerica.com/p-finance/athome_rerates.html

Most, but not all, banks offer the ability to fill out a loan application on-line. Most, but again, not all, also charge an up-front, nonrefundable application fee for the privilege. So if the bank requires you to furnish your credit card number as part of the application process, you had better be sure that this bank is the one you want to have your mortgage with. Just like real life. Clicking "undo" on your Web browser won't bring the money back.

http://www.bankamerica.com/cgi-bin/hloan_app.cgi

Another staple service to be found on the Web sites of most banks is the reference library. They tend to offer useful information about different types of loans, how loans work, and so on.

The depth and quality of these articles vary from bank site to bank site, so even if you want to deal with one particular bank, it's worth paying a visit to several others, if for no other reason than to check out their reference libraries.

http://www.bankamerica.com/p-finance/athome/athome_refbuy.html

The Bank of America Web site has been used in this section to illustrate the sort of things that you can expect on the sites of most other banks. However, there is one great feature found only on the Bank of America site. The Interactive Which Loan is Right for Me? figureouter is definitely worth the visit, regardless of whether or not you actually want to bank here. Check off your priorities, concerns, expectations, and income level and the figureouter figures out which type of loan is best for you. Cool.

http://www.bankamerica.com/tools/athome_whichloan.html

The Mortgage Mart Web site is a one-stop resource center for mortgage shoppers.

Sample something like thirtyonederful mortgage flavors by clicking on the Mortgage Market link, then be sure to click on Mortgage Library and check out some publications to take with you on your trip to the bank.

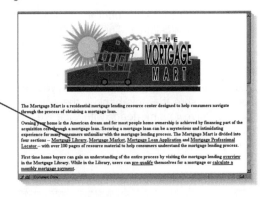

http://www.mortgagemart.com/index.html

Before taking that final plunge into the prover-bial Sea of Red Ink, see what you're getting yourself into with the Overview of the Ins & Outs of Getting That Loan, check your rights with The Overview of Consumer Protection Laws, make any last minute adjustments to your calculations and get your feet wet with some warm-up articles. When you're ready to swim with the loan sharks, er, professionals, take one last, deep breath, click the Locator button and jump right on in.

http://www.mortgagemart.com/library.html

 Mortgage Brokers

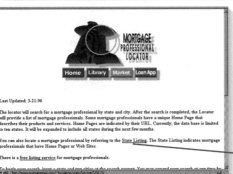

Mortgage professionals, a.k.a. mortgage bro-kers, work as middlemen between you, their client, and several lending institutions. The idea is that because they are not tied to any one particular lender they are free to shop around on your behalf for the best deals. An added bonus of using a broker is that brokers can sometimes find lenders for you when more traditional means of financing prove fruitless.

Click on State Listing to begin your search.

http://www.mortgagemart.com/locator.html

Money knows no borders and the World Wide Web transcends physical boundaries. Many of the brokers to be found here can make loans on properties outside of the state in which their office is geographically based. With that in mind, click on a state name to find links to the Web sites of brokers that reside in that state or look elsewhere on this growing list and ex-pand the horizons of your search.

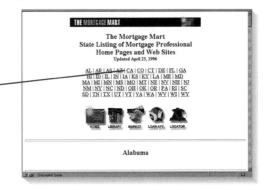

http://www.mortgagemart.com/state.html

Use this list to shop and compare between different brokers. Not all brokers or mortgage companies are the same. A good broker can save you a lot of money but a poor one will just waste your time.

A few cautionary words of advice: Don't get sidetracked by the slickest looking Home pages, the substance is in the savings and the service. Also, watch for bait and switch tactics; if a deal looks to good too be true, it probably is. When in doubt, get it in writing.

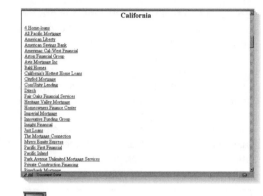

http://www.mortgagemart.com/state.html#cal

The HomeOwners Finance Center is a fine example of the sort of thing you can expect from the better mortgage broker Web sites.

You will find the latest rates and analysis, information about the company and its services, pointers on how to get the best loan for your needs, and even the ability to apply for a loan on-line.

http://www.homeowners.com/

Explore to your heart's content and click on the Forms link to begin filling out the forms required to begin your loan application.

http://www.homeowners.com/

Every mortgage broker's site that you visit will be different. Previously stated advice aside, this site has some especially slick little features that are worth getting sidetracked on.

Click on the Rate Watch Mailing List to request free rate and trend updates via e-mail. You are under no obligation and no salesman will visit. Clicking on Complete Loan Application brings up form 1003, the Uniform Loan Application.

http://www.homeowners.com/forms.html

This is the form that you will have to fill out at some point in the loan process whether you are applying for a mortgage on a new piece of property or refinancing property that you already hold a mortgage on. The advantages of filling out this form on-line are that your loan application will be expedited and since you are doing most of the "paper" work, the broker will often offer a discount. In this case, the brokerage firm will deduct $250 off closing costs for essentially doing the work for them.

http://www.homeowners.com/onlineapp.html

It's a shame that the world isn't a more trusting place. It would be nice if lenders could just take you on your word that you both need and deserve a loan and simply cut you a check. In a perfect world they would just electronically transfer the funds and have the cash pop out of your floppy drive. But just in case you hadn't noticed, this ain't a perfect world. You will have to fill out this lengthy form, submit it, and wait for the broker to mail it back to you via snail mail for you to sign. Good luck.

https://w3.internet-is.com/homeowners/app1.html

You've seen how to access the Web pages of banks and brokers to shop around for the best deal on your mortgage. Now take a look at the Computer Loan Network and see how the best mortgage deals can find you.

Click on Add a Loan Profile.

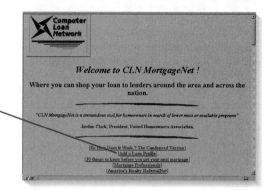

http://www.clnet.com/

Hundreds of lenders will look here and see your loan requirements in the hope that they can give you the best terms and secure your note. It's a great way for you to leverage the extraordinary scope of the Internet to ensure that you get the best possible terms on your loan. If you can use this system to shave just one point off of your loan, you will have saved yourself thousands of dollars. Ralph Nader would be so proud.

http://www.clnet.com/CLNform1.htm

When filling out the loan profile, you may not wish to fill in certain sections (such as your credit rating). For those instances, select "X—Not Stated" from the drop down list. Click the "Submit" button when you are done.

The information that you enter contains no sensitive data such as credit card numbers or personal information, so lenders see only what they need to see. Any lender who can beat the stated terms of your loan will contact you for additional information.

http://www.clnet.com/CLNform1.htm

Introduction to Investing

First Things First

⊣ Glossary of Financial and Investment Terms

⊣ Understanding and Controlling Your Finances

⊣ Working With Your Cash Flow

⊣ Emergency Money

Defining Your Goals

⊣ How Long Until You Meet Your Goals?

⊣ Why Are You Investing?

Balancing Risk and Reward

⊣ Considering Your Investment Horizon

⊣ The Historical Rate of Return

⊣ Risk Tolerance Quiz

⊣ The Efficient Frontier

⊣ Your Personal Investment Profile

⊣ The Power of Diversification and Optimization

Learning by Example

⊣ Avoiding the Major Investment Mistakes

⊣ The American Association of Individual Investors

⊣ A Little Levity: Doubtful Accounts

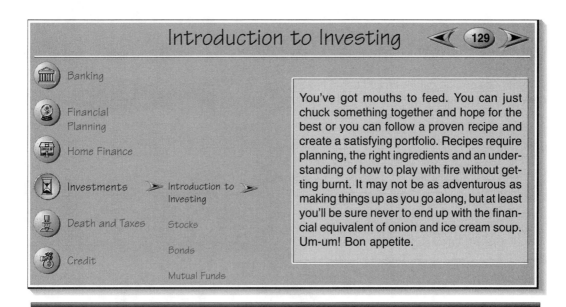

 Banking

Financial Planning

Home Finance

Investments ➤ Introduction to ➤ Investing

Death and Taxes   Stocks

Bonds

Credit

Mutual Funds

You've got mouths to feed. You can just chuck something together and hope for the best or you can follow a proven recipe and create a satisfying portfolio. Recipes require planning, the right ingredients and an understanding of how to play with fire without getting burnt. It may not be as adventurous as making things up as you go along, but at least you'll be sure never to end up with the financial equivalent of onion and ice cream soup. Um-um! Bon appetite.

First Things First

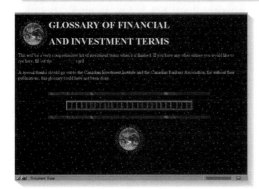

Maybe the best way to introduce an intro to investing chapter is with a glossary of financial terms. So here goes: Reader meet glossary. Glossary, reader. There, now that those niceties are out of the way ...

This particular glossary is brought to us by Daniel Feuer's Web Site of Investments. It's fairly complete, alphabetically indexed and cross-referenced. So if you look under "S" for "Strike Price" and the definition refers in turn to a "Put Option" you can click on that term and define the definition.

http://www.myna.com/~invest/glossary.htm

When we say "investments" we're really covering a lot of ground. We're talking about anything from savings accounts to aggressive growth funds.

Interface Technologies offers a quick way to get a handle on Understanding and Controlling Your Finances without talking down to you or talking over your head. It's worth the read even if you have a basic idea of what stock is, for example, but you're not exactly sure how the whole thing works.

http://www.iftech.com/centers/finance/finance8.htm

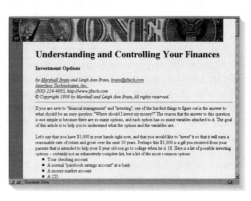

Before you go and get all excited about how you're going to invest your money, you might want to spare a second and use the First Tennessee Bank Cash Flow Calculator to figure out how much money it is that you have to invest. If some long lost granduncle just died and left you sole beneficiary in his will, great— well, not great, I certainly don't wish your family harm, but at least then you'd know what you're working with. If, on the other hand, you plan to invest from your income, you'd better make sure you've taken your outgo in account.

http://ftb.com/personal_dreams/cashflow.html

Speaking of cash flow ... Someone asked Women's Wire financial columnist Cash Flo (I suspect that's not her real name) about setting money aside for emergencies. Most financial planners use three months worth of living expenses as a rule-of-thumb, but given the uncertainty of today's job market, Ms. Flo wisely suggested boosting that number to six.

That's not to say that you shouldn't invest until you've set aside an emergency nest egg. Just the opposite in fact, a nest egg is *precisely* the place to start investing.

http://women.com/wwire/archives/html/qacash/960110.qa.cas.html

⧖ Defining Your Goals

Psst, want to see how long until you become a millionaire? Use the Investing For Kids Java Goals Calculator to see how long it will take you to reach any financial goal. Type in the financial goal, the capital that you'll be starting with, how much you'll be investing each month and the return on investment that you expect to make. Click on "Calc" and see what you get.

$1,000,000 is a nice round number, but you can use this calculator to see how long it will take to reach any financial goal.

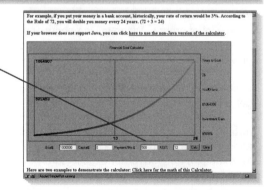

http://tqd.advanced.org/3096/3goal.htm

Investments don't exist in isolation, they should be part of an overall strategy that takes into account your situation and your goals. If you were to sit down with a professional financial advisor like Jim Hetherman of Financial Network Investment Corporation he would start by Defining Your Financial Goals. To do this he would want to know when you need the money, for what reason(s) are you investing, whether your goals are realistic, and how much tolerance for risk do you have.

FINANCIAL NETWORK INVESTMENT CORPORATION
Member NASD and SIPC

DEFINING YOUR FINANCIAL GOALS

We all want to achieve certain financial goals in our lives, but where do you begin? An important first step is to define your investment objectives. Everyone's financial needs are different, so you need to ask a few important questions:

What is my investment time horizon? When do you need the money? In 5, 10, or 20 years?.

What do I want from my investment? If you are young, you may be trying to achieve goals such as funding a child's education and purchasing a home. In these cases, your goal may be liquid short term income and capital growth. If you are older, you may also be planning for retirement. Thus you may need both growth and income from your investment.

Are my goals realistic? Your strategy to help work towards your goals should consider your age, income, taxes, immediate cash risk and risk tolerances.

What is my tolerance for investment risk? When considering investments, you should remember one thing: *in most cases, the greater the potential reward, the greater the risk.*

Am I comfortable risking some of my principal for a potentially greater reward? You may want to accept a lower return in exchange for greater safety of principal.

How many years do I have to invest? Age is one factor that will influence the risk you're willing to take. Generally, the longer your investment horizon, the greater risk you can tolerate. For example, if you are young,

http://www.hetherman.com/fnic/ideana14.html

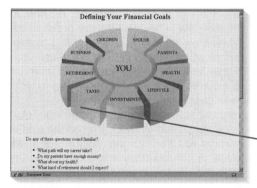

Defining Your Financial Goals

YOU — CHILDREN, SPOUSE, PARENTS, HEALTH, LIFESTYLE, INVESTMENTS, TAXES, RETIREMENT, BUSINESS

Do any of these questions sound familiar?

- What path will my career take?
- Do my parents have enough money?
- What about my health?
- What kind of retirement should I expect?

There is no right strategy, there is only a right strategy for you. And even that will change with age, income, and goals.

Prudential Bache Securities does not promise to supply you with easy answers, but they do aim to help you better define your goals with links to information on some of the most common concerns: children, parents, spouse, health, business, taxes, retirement, and lifestyle. You can click on the ones that are relevant to you and see what advice they have to offer.

http://www.prusec.com/goals.htm

 ## Balancing Risk and Reward

As Vanguard so aptly points out, Considering Your Investment Horizon means looking at how long you have to invest and finding the investments that best fits the time frame that you have to work with.

Obviously, age plays a major factor when looking at investment horizons, but you have to look at all of your goals in order to come up with a plan appropriate to your particular situation. Planning for retirement would dictate one time horizon, planning for a child's college education would dictate another.

http://www.vanguard.com/educ/module2/m2_3_2.html

Considering Your Investment Horizon

The amount of time you have to reach your destination often helps to determine the most effective mode of transportation. Likewise, the number of years you will be investing is one of the most critical factors in creating your investment mix.

Your investment objective is closely related to your investment horizon, or the time frame in which you will be investing. As noted above, a short time frame suggests a more conservative approach, while a longer time frame allows for a more aggressive approach because you have more time to weather the markets' periodic swings.

Determining your time horizon is relatively easy. Suppose, for example, you are 30 years old and are investing for retirement. You should anticipate an investment time frame of 50 to 60 years. Why not 35 years - which would bring you to the traditional retirement age of 65? Quite simply, your time horizon is tied to your life expectancy, which is likely to be 80 years or more. And if you plan to leave a portion of your retirement savings to heirs, your investment horizon will extend well beyond your life span. For college planning, establishing your investment horizon is somewhat easier since you have a pretty good idea of when your child will be attending school and how long he or she will be enrolled.

Lesson 3: The Asset Allocation Decision
1. Balancing Your Investments
2. Determining Your Investment Goal
3. Considering Your Investment Horizon
4. Assessing Your Risk Tolerance
5. Weighing Your Financial Resources

Go to Lesson 4: The Right Investment Mix

The reason why time horizons affects the investments you should make can be summed up in one word: Risk. As a general rule, the riskier an investment is, the more money you stand to make, or lose, on it. Compare the higher returns of the volatile stock market to bonds in this graph from Ibbotson Associates. Over the long term stocks outperformed bonds, but in any given year many of the stocks went down in value. If time is on your side you can afford to be more aggressive, if it's not you had better take a more conservative approach.

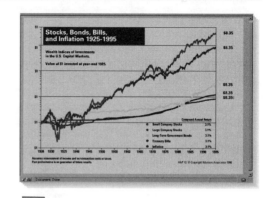

http://www.ibbotson.inter.net

Which brings us to risk tolerance. You see, all investments bring some degree of risk to the table. How much risk you're willing to take before you start losing sleep over your investments depends on your personality as much as your time horizon. You have to gear your investment decisions accordingly. Mass Mutual has put together a Risk Tolerance Quiz. Start off by clicking on the type of investor you *think* you are (aggressive, moderate, or conservative) and go on to see the type of investor you *really* are.

http://www.massmutual.com/pension/retire/riskquiz.html

You are going to have to base your investment decisions on the answers you came up with for your time horizon and risk tolerance. Use this chart from Legg Mason to help you match your needs to the right investments. The chart is based on the Efficient Frontier, a Nobel Prize winning theory based on the concept of balancing risk and return.

Find the type of investor you are and see the types of investments that fall under that risk category.

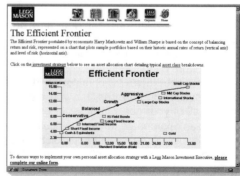

http://www.leggmason.com/Invest/AssetAlloc/effront.html

Now it's time to start putting all of this information together into a more focused financial plan. The Bank of America has a small questionnaire that incorporate your goals, objectives, time frame, experience, personal feelings and tolerance for risk. Check off the answers to the 12 questions and click on submit. Just remember that while this Personal Investment Profile serves as a good indication of which direction you should head in with your investments, it's no replacement for good judgment or in-depth planning.

http://www.bankamerica.com/tools/sri_assetall.html

The results go beyond merely saying that you should consider a conservative or aggressive approach, by now you already know that. The "What Your Answers Say About You" screen goes on to suggest which investments would best suit your needs and why. It offers some sample portfolios and gives the breakdowns of the sorts of investments that would go into them.

At the bottom of the screen is a button marked "Worksheet." You can click on it and compare the sample portfolios with your actual one.

http://www.bankamerica.com/tools/sri_assetall.html

Fill out the form and "Submit" it. Bank of America will show you a comparison of your current investments and the model profile that you generated earlier. You can then see how closely they match and where you might want to consider making adjustments.

It's worth noting that the "model portfolios" are just that, models. Exactly 34% in this type of investment, 26% in that, 34% in the other ... It would be nice if we could all measure up to those very precise standards, but let's face it, we can't all be Money Magazine centerfolds.

	Market Value	% of Total	Model Portfolio
Your Current Investments			
Stock Investments:			
Individual Shares	500.00		
Mutual Funds	0.00		
Variable Annuities	0.00		
Total Stocks	$ 500.00	5%	%
Fixed Income Investments:			
Individual Bonds	7000.00		
Mutual Funds	1000.00		
Fixed Annuities	0.00		
Total Fixed Income Investments	$ 8000.00	84%	45-60%
Short-Term Investments:			
Money Market Mutual Funds	0.00		
FDIC-insured CDs/Other Bank Deposits	1000.00		
Total Short-Term Investments	$ 1000.00	10%	10%
Other Investments:			
Real Estate, Precious Metals, etc.	0.00	0%	
TOTAL For All Categories	9500.00	100%	100%

Let us help

To discuss this personal investment profile, your financial objectives and how you may want to adjust your current portfolio to match your profile, please call your BA Investment Services Investment Specialist or call Invest by Phone(sm) at 1-800-427-9633.

http://www.bankamerica.com/tools/sri_assetall.html

Minimizing risk and maximizing profits are not mutually exclusive concepts. Balancing the two is the idea behind portfolio diversification. Primenet offers a good primer on The Power of Diversification and Optimization.

At its most basic, the wisdom behind diversification can be summed up in the old phrase "don't put all your eggs in one basket." Optimization takes the idea one step further and looks at how each investment in the portfolio responds to every other one.

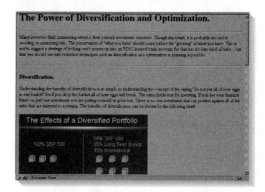

http://www.primenet.com/tutor/2_table_contents/d_invest_plan/powerof.html

 Learning By Example

As you invest you are bound to make some mistakes, nobody's perfect and even if they were, the market certainly isn't. The trick is to learn from the mistakes of others and avoid the expense of having to learn them firsthand. In that vein the Stock Signals Group presents 25 ways of Avoiding The Major Investment Mistakes. No doubt, these tips were culled from personal experience. Nameless martyred investors laid down their cash and lost their savings to bring you this offering. Please, don't let their sacrifice be for naught.

http://www.crl.com/www/users/up/uptime/literatures/dontdo.html

As you approach the end of this introduction you may still find yourself with a host of unanswered questions. To which, as the author of this chapter, it is my solemn duty to reply "tough boogies." If you want any more answers you're going to have to find them on your own.

Still, I suppose that I can at least get you started, so here goes: Seek out the Web site of the American Association of Individual Investors. Click and all questions will be answered.

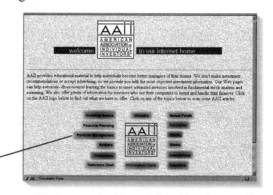

http://www.aaii.org/home.html

Efficient Frontiers, risk tolerance, investment horizons ... Who could blame you if your eyes have long since glazed over. Only a warped mind can see humor in this stuff. But then warped minds are something that the Internet has in abundance.

Meet Doug Pike, creator the Stock Market cartoon series <u>Doubtful Accounts</u> and local yokel of the investment world's far side. Stop by for a quick chuckle or do someone else a good turn and favor your favorite investor with a comic of the week gift subscription.

http://www.doubtfulaccounts.com/

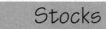 

Stocks

Why Bother?

⊣ What's the Worst That Can Happen? (Scripophily)

⊣ Why Do People Buy Stocks?

⊣ Investment FAQ: The Basics

⊣ Investment FAQ: Dividends

The Riches of the Net

⊣ Invest-O-Rama!

⊣ Directory of Investing Resources

Research It!

⊣CNNfn

⊣ The Reference Desk

⊣ Hoover's Online

⊣ Research: InvestorNet

⊣ PointCast

⊣ The Stock Club

⊣ Investor Newsgroups

Stock Selection Strategies

⊣ Investing for Kids

⊣ The Warren Buffet Way

⊣ The Warren Buffet Way Spreadsheet

⊣ Stock Selection Tutorial

⊣ Dogs of the Dow

⊣ Strategies for Daytraders

⊣ The Conductor: Computerized Forecasting

Choosing a Broker

⊣ Full Service vs. Discount

⊣ The Wall St. Directory

⊣ On-Line Trading

⊣ Commissions Pricer

⊣ DRIPs and DPPs

Quotes and More

⊣ The Big Kahuna: Quote.com

Profits and Portfolios

⊣ Stock Profit Calculator

⊣ Tracking Your Portfolio On-Line: Microsoft Investor

Freebies and Fun Stuff

⊣ Free Portfolio Review

⊣ The NVestor Stock Game

⊣ A Trip to the Floor

⊣ The CNNfn List of Exchanges

⊣ The New York Stock Exchange Visitor's Center

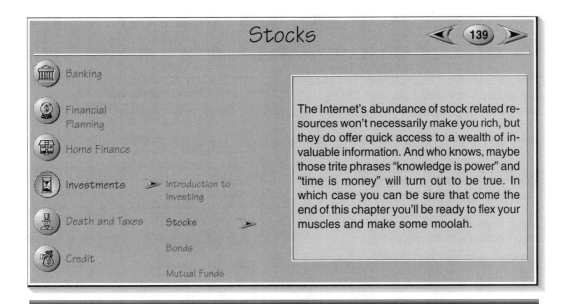

- 🏛 Banking
- 💰 Financial Planning
- 🏠 Home Finance
- ⌛ Investments ➤ Introduction to Investing
- ⚖ Death and Taxes   Stocks ➤
- 💰 Credit   Bonds
    Mutual Funds

The Internet's abundance of stock related resources won't necessarily make you rich, but they do offer quick access to a wealth of invaluable information. And who knows, maybe those trite phrases "knowledge is power" and "time is money" will turn out to be true. In which case you can be sure that come the end of this chapter you'll be ready to flex your muscles and make some moolah.

⌛ Why Bother?

Buy low, sell high. At least that's the idea. You buy pieces of a company, shares, hope the company does well and that your shares become more valuable. And more often than not, that's exactly the way things work out. If things don't work out, you end up with a pretty, but worthless, stock certificate suitable for framing. The pessimists amongst us can forgo the anxiety and visit the Dietz Associates catalog of scripophily. Any certificate that you buy here will never be worth much but at least your walls will look like a million.

http://www.robinsoft.com

Markets crash. Companies go belly-up and people lose their shirts. Those are just the cold, hard facts of life. So why do so many people continue to pour so much money into something so unsure? Come on. Do you really need a book or a Web page to answer that for you?

As Legg Mason tells it people participate in the stock market in one of three (clickable) ways; by Investing, Speculating, or Trading. But no matter how you participate you do so for one reason and one reason alone—Money.

http://www.leggmason.com/Learning/stocklrn.html

The Stock Market is a complicated beast. Seeing hordes of frenzied traders on the nightly news screaming "buysellsellbuybuy," swigging back Pepto Bismol and waving bits of paper around in the air for no apparent reason only makes it seem more so. Not to worry, The Investment FAQ Introduction to Stocks section won't replace an MBA from Wharton, but it's a good place to get your feet wet.

Read to your heart's content and click on the next article link to continue.

http://www.cs.umd.edu/users/cml/invest-faq/articles/stock-a-basics.html

In addition to the value of the stock itself, one of the appeals of owning stock is that many (but not all) companies offer dividends to their shareholders.

Dividends are a board of directors way of saying "thanks" in the best way that they know how—cash. By themselves dividends aren't likely to make you wealthy but you'll apreciate them even when the stock itself isn't appreciating. And really, what can any investor say to a cash "thank you" except "you're welcome."

http://www.cs.umd.edu/users/cml/invest-faq/articles/stock-dividends.html

The Riches of the Net

Once you've got the basics down pat it's time to start exploring the riches of the Web. There are so many good investment-related sites on the Net that you can begin just about anywhere and lose yourself in a seemingly endless parade of links. That's OK, getting lost on the Web is half the fun. Bookmark invest-o-rama! and make it home base for your explorations. Click on the directory. With 2,513 links (but who's counting) arranged into 48 categories you will always have someplace to return to when you hit the end of a trail.

http://www.investorama.com/

You're probably acquainted with Web directories like <u>Yahoo!</u> Same idea here except that invest-o-rama! deals only with sites of interest to individual investors. All of the links are organized, grouped into categories, and summarized so that you have an idea what you're getting into before you actually get into it.

From the <u>American Stock Exchange</u> to <u>Zack's Investment Research</u>, invest-o-rama! lists them all.

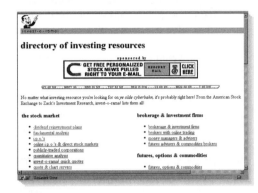

http://www.investorama.com/director.html

Since you can go virtually anywhere from here but the question is, where should you go?
Try putting yourself in the shiny shoes of a successful Wall St. tycoon. You've just stepped into the office. The starting bell has yet to ring but everyone around you is already buzzing. You pour yourself a cup of coffee, quickly check you pulse, and scan the latest headlines. The bell rings and you're off ...
Down near the bottom of the directory is the news & commentary area. Click on <u>financial & investing news</u> and it's on to <u>CNNfn</u>.

http://www.investorama.com/director.html

Research It!

While there is always risk involved when playing the stock market it should not be confused with gambling. There are two fundamental differences between buying stock and playing poker. First, the law of averages; In Las Vegas individuals can win but it's the house that always comes out ahead. On Wall St., individuals can lose, but the market keeps going forward, taking all those left in the game with it. Second, in Las Vegas they'll boot you for sneaking a peek at the dealers hand. On the Street however, <u>research</u> is required.

http://cnnfn.com/

It should come as no real shock to you that the CNNfn Web site is one of the best places on the Internet to find the latest breaking business news. What may not be as readily apparent is that CNNfn is also a great place to begin more in-depth research into any company that you are considering buying into.

It all starts here in the "Research It" section. Click on <u>Reference Desk</u> for links to references, resources, company Web sites and perhaps most importantly, a way to search <u>Hoover's MasterList corporate directory</u>.

http://cnnfn.com/researchit/

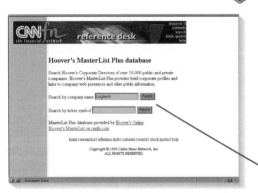

When you bought your computer you probably did your homework. You compared megs, mips, cache, gigs, bauds, megahertz, refresh rates, and all the rest of it. When you buy stock you are actually buying a piece of a company. At the very least, you should spend as much time shopping for the right company as you spent shopping for the right PC.

Hoovers Directory is where you will begin. Type in a company name or ticker symbol and click on "Find It".

http://cnnfn.com/researchit/referencedesk/hoover/

Hoovers lists over 10,000 public and private companies in their database. They charge a fee to access their in-depth company profiles but make a wealth of company related information available for free. You get a company snapshot (sales, number of employees, etc.), and links to the company's Home page, latest quarterly financials, SEC fillings, stock quotes and charts, related new stories, press releases and even a map to each company's headquarters. Try clicking on the company's "latest quarterly financials."

http://www.hoovers.com

The current financials page gives you all the vital statistics. It lists the sales, net income, earnings per share, and number of shares outstanding for the last quarter, last six months, and last full fiscal year. You can see where the company is at compared to the same time period the year before.

Up at the top of the page is the company's stock ticker symbol (the call letters by which the company is known on the exchange). Click on it for more detailed information.

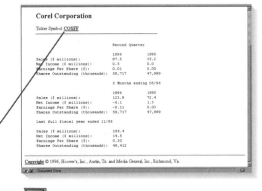

http://www.hoovers.com

This is where things start to get down and dirty. These are the keys by which you will be able to make an informed decision. It's all here, even if it doesn't make much sense to you. Debt-to-equity ratio, book value, price-to-earnings ratio, the whole enchilada. You can click on any of the underlined terms for a quick definition of what it means or print the page out and bring it to your broker. If you already know a bit about the market then you understand how invaluable this kind of information is. If you don't, rest assured, you will.

http://www.hoovers.com

Just about the only things missing from Hoovers were free in-depth reports. Fair enough, everyone has to make a living. Be that as it may, you still want to get your hands on a report, and if you can do it without having to pay for it all the better. Enter Research:. A lot of time goes into preparing a company profile, so it's no wonder that the people that prepare them want to be paid for their efforts. Research: is paid, but for many of the reports available they're paid by the companies being profiled, not you. Click on InvestorNet.

http://www.researchmag.com/

Before you access InvestorNet you will need to register yourself. It's straightforward enough, just click on the "Free Registration" button and follow the instructions. Research: promises not to sell your personal information or give out your e-mail address, so no worries there.

Once you've registered you can pop in a ticker symbol if you happen to know it or find a symbol by clicking on Ticker/Company Name Search directly above.

http://www.researchmag.com/investor.htm

Besides the ubiquitous stock charts you can access an investment report in Adobe Acrobat format and a one-page Wall St. analysis written in plain English. The more detailed eight page S&P report (S&P stands for Standard & Poor's, a giant in the industry) is available as part a subscription plan but if you're serious about investments the subscription could easily pay for itself.

What's so amazing about it all is that this sort of stuff used to be available only to professionals.

http://www.researchmag.com/cgi-bin/newcorp.exe?name=msft

The companies that you'll find reports on are followed by Wall St. professionals and are updated daily. Research: makes a point of covering themselves by pointing out that the reports are for information purposes only. In other words don't sue if they're wrong. Caveats and warning aside, the pros that follow these things make their recommendations—buy or sell, tell you how they came up with their recommendations, and even go so far as to let you know how confident they are about their predictions.

http://www.researchmag.com/cgi-bin/newcorp.exe?name=msft

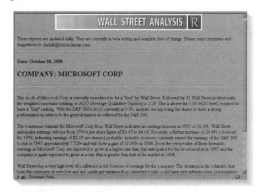

PointCast is another very, very cool way to keep on top of things as they happen. It's like having a customizable news station on your computer. It hunts down the information you're after, updates itself without intervention and plays it back whenever you're not busy.

If you haven't seen PointCast yet you've got to see it, and if you haven't downloaded it yet now's your chance.

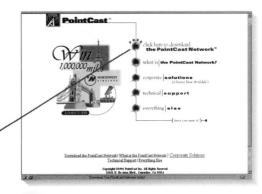

http://www.pointcast.com/

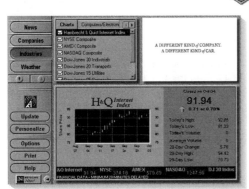

PointCast is more than just business, it'll fetch the latest sports news, weather reports, and People magazine for you if you tell it to. But for investors there's no beating it. You can define and track up to 25 companies and 10 industries, and it keeps you up to date with the latest business news, a scrolling ticker, market charts and graphs, a daily edition of Money Magazine, and new "channels" are being added all the time. You do have to put up with the animated commercials, but it's certainly no worse than TV.

http://www.pointcast.com/

Sometimes just chatting with other would-be tycoons can be entertaining, if not enlightening. The Stock Club offers numerous party-line-like forums where you can "speak" with other investors in real time. Enter the Free-For-All or pick a specific forum and track a particularly hot prospect you've got your eye on. A word to the wise though; just because someone says something on the Net doesn't necessarily make it so. In the anonymity of the forum you're never really sure who you're taking advice from, or why they're giving it.

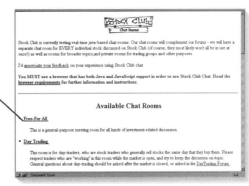

http://stockclub.com/chat/index.html

Like chat forums, investor usenet newsgroups are another way to listen and be heard. The trouble comes from trying to weed out the good advice from the noise. But as long as you don't mind putting in some effort you're likely to find some savvy investors willing to share their knowledge with you.

Yahoo! lists the most popular investment newsgroups, each with it's own focus; investments in general, news, and analysis. Find one you like and you can subscribe to it and be notified as new messages are added.

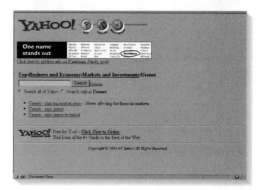

http://www.yahoo.com/Business_and_Economy/
Markets_and_Investments/Usenet/

Stock Selection Strategies

Please, don't be offended by the choice of this next site. Because despite its name, this site is an outstanding resource for anyone interested in knowing more about how the pros do it. Neither the fact that the site is called Investing For Kids nor the fact that it was designed, written, and maintained by a high school student and his not-quite-in-high-school-yet buddy should deter you from exploring it to the hilt and learning everything you can from these two *wunderkinds*.

http://tqd.advanced.org/3096/41pick.htm

Even if you have no interest in taking investment advice from a couple of teenagers you might be interest to learn how Warren Buffett goes about Picking Stocks for himself. And Warren's not alone. There are different approaches that investors take to improve their chances of picking a winner. Here are three fundamental approaches, none of which are quite as original as picking stocks by the stars but they do have their proponents. And more importantly they are time-tested and broker approved.

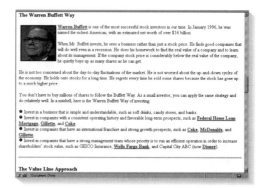

http://tqd.advanced.org/3096/41pick.htm#The Warren Buffett Way

Bill Gates and Warren Buffett are the two wealthiest people in America. Both of whom have made most of their fortunes in stock. If you hope to follow in their footsteps you should do what they do. In Mr. Gates's case that means buying lots of <u>MSFT</u> and hoping that Bill and Co. continue to take over the world. In Mr. Buffett's case it means getting out your pencil and calculating a company's earnings, margins, return on equity, and capitalization. That or grab a copy of <u>InvestorWEB</u>'s <u>The Warren Buffett Way spreadsheet files</u>.

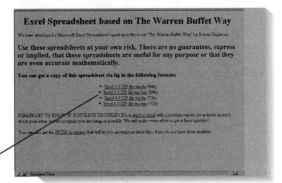

http://www.investorweb.com/TWBW.HTM

Stock Selection Guide Tutorial

By Douglas Gerlach

The Stock Selection Guide is a paper form developed by the not-for-profit National Association of Investors Corporation (NAIC) in the 1950's to aid individual investors in the fundamental analysis and selection of stocks. The relatively-simple two-sided form enables an investor to identify the characteristics of a growth stock, and plot potential future growth from the historical trends. The SSG (as it is known) also helps an investor determine a reasonable value for the stock, suggesting purchase when the stock is temporarily on the cheap side of a value assessment.

The SSG is **not**, however, a "black box" analysis tool, one that uses mathematical formulas to prognosticate the future. It requires an investor to apply his or her own judgement to many factors in the analytical process. The SSG can be an important aid to the individual investor in discovering those stocks which are most likely to increase in value over the next five years.

The following tutorial attempts to de-mystify the Stock Selection Guide, to explain its components step-by-step, and to point out areas where an investor's judgement should be carefully applied.

The NAIC Web Site has more information about NAIC and the Stock Selection Guide, as well as details about a number of software implementations of the SSG. Blank SSG forms can be ordered from the Web Site, or via e-mail from NAIC Customer Service (a pack of 20 forms is $4).

Did any of that stuff about equity and capitalization make any sense to you? If not, you may want to take a peek at <u>The Stock Selection Guide</u> developed by <u>National Association of Investors Corporation</u> (NAIC) and made available on <u>invest-o-rama!</u> before tackling Warren Buffett style spreadsheets.

While there is no such thing as a substitute for good judgment, the tutorial helps clear up some of the mystery surrounding the stock selection process with step-by-step guidelines.

http://www.investorama.com/features/ssg_00.html

If you read and follow the advice laid out in the NAIC Stock Selection Guide you'll end up with a good understanding of the fundamentals of stock analysis. You'll also have your work cut out for. There are no easy answers with stock selection—or are there? <u>Dogs of the Dow</u> suggests otherwise. Pay the Dogs a visit. Read about a simple technique that has outperformed the Dow Jones Industrial Average overall return for a time period of some 23 years. Not bad for an easy answer. Click on <u>Dog Steps</u> for all the details.

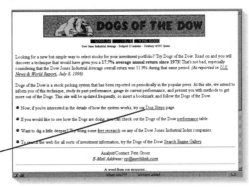

http://www.dogsofthedow.com

All of the trading strategies that you've looked at so far make the assumption that you're in the market for the long haul. As far as strategies go the long-term approach has a lot going for it. But the St. is rife with tales of overnight millionaires. To be sure, there's a quick buck to be made on the market and you won't make it quick by playing it safe. If the very real prospects of ulcers doesn't frighten you take a look at the Daytraders Web site and read up on the trading strategies that the pros use.

http://www.daytraders.com/trade.html

Without actually getting into the specific advice to be found here, the following snippets should give you an idea of what you can expect: "... the market is made up of emotional sheep ... you must be the cold, cunning and calculating wolf looking over the herd for your kill ... Buy when there is blood in the streets!" It's safe to say that daytrading is not for everyone, it is not for the weak and it is not for the mild. Daytrading is not an investment plan nor is it a hobby. It is all out fiscal warfare, potentially profitable, pitiless, and proud of it.

http://www.daytraders.com/trade.html

If you're looking for a forecasting method that can give you an edge on the market, take a guided tour of The Conductor and see what quantitative analysis tools have to offer.
Thought by many to be the next big thing a few years back, neural networks, fuzzy logic, genetic algorithms, and knowledge-based systems fell out of favor because of their generally poor track records. Now, with more powerful computers and better programming at their disposal, quantitative analysis like this one are ready to take another crack at it.

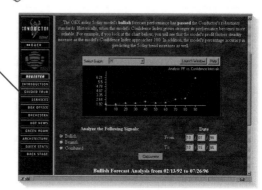

http://www.HHConductor.com/pub/

You're up to date on the latest news, you've settled on a strategy, done your research and picked out some winning companies. No doubt you're just itching to get out there and buy, buy, buy. But first you'd better stop by <u>The Motley Fool</u>, a Web site of infinite jest, of most excellent fancy and follow their suggestions on choosing a broker. For as the fool's might say, "there's the rub."

How many goodly choices are there here!
How beauteous the market is!
O trading floor, that has such brokers in't!

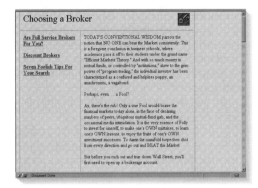

http://www.fool.com/school/sch_06.htm

The service that you receive from a broker ranges from holding your hand, doing the research and making all the investment decisions on the one extreme to just pushing through the paperwork that you specifically tell them to on the other. A discount broker can save you money on commissions while a full-service broker can make you money on trades you wouldn't have come up with yourself. Which you prefer, a full-service relationship or a deep-discount quickie, depends on both your priorities and your personal tastes.

http://www.fool.com/school/sch_06.htm#2

In the end, no matter which type of broker you choose, you'll be sure to find many brokerage firms that would more than happy to fill your needs, or at least your order. And here's where you're going to find them; <u>The Wall Street Directory</u> maintains an extensive database of brokerage firms that you can search through and select from.

Choose either "Brokerage Services" or "Brokers—Discount" and click the "Category Search" button for a long list of brokers around the world and around the Web.

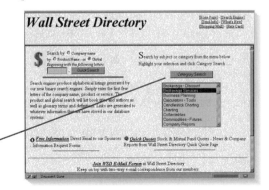

http://www.wsdinc.com/search.shtml

For $1,250,000 you can buy a "seat" on the New York Stock Exchange and stand amongst a screaming mob of frenzied traders. Or, for substantially less, you can pull up a chair and trade stock from the quiet and comfort of your own computer. Tough call, I know, but if you opt for the later you can choose from any number of on-line brokers.

E*Trade is one of a new breed of Web based brokerage firms. Click on Trading Demo and see what it's like to buy and sell stock over the Net.

http://www.etrade.com/

In the future you will probably see the full-service brokers enter the fray with on-line trading services of their own, but for the moment, the Net is the exclusive trading domain of the low-ball discount broker. You won't find any bells and whistles here, no recommendations, no custom tailored in-depth portfolio analysis, and no red carpet treatment. But if you pick your own stocks or options and prefer to do your own trading, you will find rock bottom commissions.

http://www.etrade.com/visitor/demo

In the demo area you can afford to play around. Place an order to buy or sell stock with a couple of clicks of your mouse. You can't lose any money here but you will get an idea how the system works.

Just be careful, once you're out of the demo area and start buying real stock for real money it's no longer a game. In terms of commissions, ease of use, and accessibility, Web based trading can't be beat. But if you need financial advice, this isn't the place. If you're looking for a quick rush try The Casino.

http://www.etrade.com/visitor/demo

Full-service or discount, on-line or not, which-ever broker you end up going with you'll have to pay a commission each time you buy or sell. You can use the Java-based Calculator written by Dr. Robert Lum of Intrepid Technology to estimate how much of a commission you can expect to pay.

Select either stock or option, put in the price per share and the number of shares being traded. The calculator automatically computes the results.

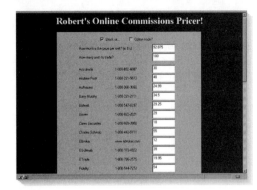

http://www.intrepid.com/~robertl/commissions-pricer3.html

Dividend Reinvestment Plans (DRIPs) and Direct Purchase Plans (DPPs) are two ways to buy stock while reducing commissions or avoiding them altogether. With a DRIP you must first own stock in a company that offers the plan before you can apply dividends to-wards additional shares. You can learn more about DRIPs and DPPs from Investor Guide and follow the links at the bottom of the page. In particular, try clicking on All About DRIPs for a good overview or on DirectInvestor for lists of companies that offer the program.

http://www.investorguide.com/DRIPs.htm

Compared to the total number of companies that you can purchase stock in, relatively few offer DRIPs and DPPs. NetStock Direct makes the process of finding the companies that do offer the plans much easier. Click on "DirectINVESTOR" for a complete index of Direct Purchase Plans or on "The Clearinghouse" and have company prospectus and enrollment forms e-mailed to you. Or click on "Search" and narrow your selection down to a manage-able number of companies that meet your ex-act criteria.

http://www.netstockdirect.com/

Whether following along in this chapter or just poking around on the Net by yourself, you've no doubt come across quite a few sites that offer time-delayed stock quotes. No surprise there, something like a googol (that's a 1 followed by 100 zeroes) offer the service. Well, here's the Big Kahuna of quote services— Quote.com.

As far as quote services go this one is as complete as they get, but to start out all you have to do is type in a ticker symbol and click the "quote" button.

http://fast.quote.com/fq/quotecom/quote

You get a lot more than just the latest quote. You get the open, high, low, last, change, and the volume on the day. Under "Fundamentals" you'll find the earnings per share, price-to-earnings ratio, dividends per share and the 52 week price range. Plus you have access to two intraday charts and three historical charts—and that's just for a "quick quote."

Like all of the free quote services on the net this one is time delayed. If every second counts you may want to subscribe to Quote.Com's real-time quote service.

http://fast.quote.com/fq/quotecom/quote?symbols=nscp

Use the intraday charts for tracking the minute-by-minute progress of the stock throughout the day. The historical charts are better suited for getting a sense of the bigger picture.

In any of the charts the vertical lines represent the high and low range that the stock traded at during that day, week, or month. The small horizontal lines between are what the stock closed at on the day. You can see the volume, or number of shares the stock traded at the bottom of the chart and compare the whole shebang to the rest of the market.

http://fast.quote.com/fq/quotecom/quote?symbols=nscp

Assuming that the company you bought stock in doesn't go under, no matter how high or low the stock price goes, you don't actually make or lose any money until you sell it. It's only then that you can count you money and see how you did. When that time comes take a look at Webpoint's stock calculator.

Put in the initial purchase and final selling prices, the total number of shares traded and click the "calculate" button for your results.

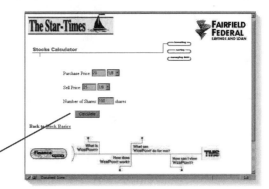

http://www.webpoint.com/calcstox.htm

And there you have it, expressed as both a dollar amount and a percentage.

What the calculator doesn't show is your *real* bottom line. That's not quite as simple. You have to look at inflation rates; how much is the dollar you made worth compared to when you put it into stocks? You have to subtract any commissions that you paid to buy and sell the stock, and, finally, you have to take taxes in account. Forget the IRS if you want, but you can be sure that the IRS won't be forgetting you come tax time.

http://www.webpoint.com/calcstox.htm

Seeing where your stock prices sits at any particular moment and getting quotes on individual trades is all well and good, but it doesn't give you an indication of where you're really at. For that you need to look at your overall portfolio.

There are any number of places that will let you enter all of your investments and track them but the slickest one has got to be on MSn, the Microsoft Network. Start by clicking on "Portfolio Manager."

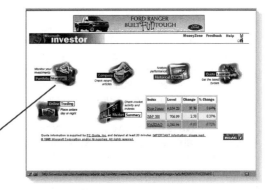

http://investor.msn.com/Contents.Asp

It may interest you to know that the information that you put into your portfolio is stored locally on your hard drive so no one but you can access your private data. Not that you shouldn't trust Microsoft, but ...

Type in a name for your portfolio. Call it anything you want, you can rename it later. Check off the "Watch Portfolio?" box if you don't actually own the investments but would like to track their progress. When you're done, click on "Create Portfolio."

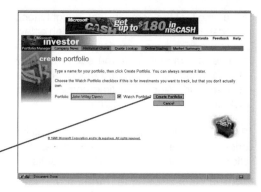

http://investor.msn.com/portmgr/pmedit.asp

Start setting up all of the stocks that you would like to track here and click on "Submit."

This is the only time that you will ever see this screen. Once you've created your first portfolio Microsoft Investor is smart enough to bypass the initial setup stage and instead automatically takes you to your account. As an aside, MS Investor will optionally take advantage of <u>Active X code</u>, so depending on which browser you use you may see a slightly different screen than the one shown here.

http://investor.msn.com/portmgr/pmedit.asp

This (or something very close to it) is the screen that you will see from now on. It lists all of the investments that you have set up in your portfolio. You can set up more than one portfolio and use the drop down boxes at the top of the screen to select which one you would like to view and how you would like to view it.

You really have to hand it to good ol' Microsoft. With the notable exception of access speed, MS Investor feels less like a Web page than a program running locally on your computer.

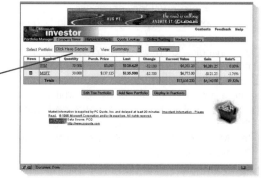

http://investor.msn.com/portmgr/pmedit.asp

On this next site is one of the all-time great freebies of the Internet. The Wall St. brokerage firm Legg Mason was offering a limited time only free portfolio review on their Home page. When the firm learned that we would be visiting them in this book they agreed to extend the offer to our readers indefinitely.

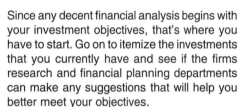

Do yourself a favor and take advantage of their generosity. You can choose between a free customized equity portfolio review and a free asset allocation analysis.

http://www.leggmason.com/

Since any decent financial analysis begins with your investment objectives, that's where you have to start. Go on to itemize the investments that you currently have and see if the firms research and financial planning departments can make any suggestions that will help you better meet your objectives.

Obviously, Legg Mason hopes to use this service to show you how they can improve upon and manage your portfolio for you. And, as long as they're willing to do the work for free, more power to them.

http://www.leggmason.com/Portfolio/index.html

The saddest part of learning the stock market ropes is that wisdom comes through experience and experience rides shotgun with loss. Usually. Now The League of American Investors has come up with a way for you to learn the ropes without risking the loss.

nVESTOR, the stock market simulation, is a very serious "game" where you trade real stock from real companies with not so real nVESTOR $. Sound like fun? First you have to register yourself and let nVESTOR know that you're a player.

http://www.investorsleague.com/index.html

Fill out the form and choose a password for yourself, you're going to need it every time you want to review your portfolio or trade some stock (wouldn't want some white collar criminal messing with your game).

If you've ever played Monopoly™ you know how serious people can get when they get a whiff of hard, cold pseudo-cash. If anything, nVESTOR players are more serious. After all, it may not be real money on the line, but the winner gets the bragging rights, and that's something that money can't buy in this game.

http://www.investorsleague.com/Register.html

You start with $100,000 and use your prowess to parlay that pittance into some major money. You'll be trading in real companies so you can use the resources found elsewhere in this chapter to research them as you would any other public offering. There's even a link to Hoovers to help you in your analysis.

Play like it was for real and see how well you do. But if you find yourself getting a little *too* caught up in the simulation try to remember, it's only a game.

http://www.investorsleague.com/Register.html

What would a trip through the World Wide Web's financial resources be without paying a call on the exchange floors where all the action actually takes place?

CNNfn has links to virtually every virtual exchange out there. Not just the ones you hear about in the news either, the list starts at the African Stock Exchange and doesn't stop until it gets to the Zagreb Exchange. Somewhere in the middle of the pack is the mother of all exchanges, the New York Stock Exchange.

http://www.cnnfn.com/researchit/webconnection/exchanges/

In the time it takes you to read this sentence, the equivalent of roughly 4.3 million dollars worth of shares will trade hands at 18 Broad Street, home of the NYSE. It would have been more if I hadn't used the Exchange's acronym. Not bad for a loose conglomeration of traders founded under a tree back when the "Wall" in Wall Street was a wooden stockade and the "Street" had yet to be surveyed. More fun factoids and the on-line home of one of New York's 10 biggest tourist attractions await you in the Visitors Center.

http://www.nyse.com/

Bonds

Bonds for Beginners

    ⊣ Glossary of Bond Terms

    ⊣ A Definition

    ⊣ Bonds and Market Risk

Savings Bonds

    ⊣ The Bureau of the Public Debt: All About Bonds

    ⊣ Savings Bonds Calculator

    ⊣ The Do-It Yourself Investment

Types of Bonds

    ⊣ Corporate Bonds

    ⊣ U.S. Government Securities

        ⊣ Treasury Bills

        ⊣ Treasury Notes

        ⊣ Treasury Bonds

    ⊣ Municipal Bonds

        ⊣ General Obligation Bonds

        ⊣ Revenue Bonds

    ⊣ Mortgage-Backed Securities

        ⊣ Fannie Mae

Building a Bond Ladder

    ⊣ Merrill Lynch: Bond Strategies

Interest Rates

    ⊣ CNNfn: Today's Rates

    ⊣ Canadian Bond Yields

    ⊣ An Inverse Relationship

    ⊣ Charting the Past

Bond Ratings

    ⊣ The Alphabet Soup Explained

    ⊣ Junk Bonds

Callable, Convertible, and Zero Coupon Bonds

    ⊣ Callable Bonds

    ⊣ Zero Coupon Bonds

    ⊣ Convertible Bonds

        ⊣ Convertible Bond Calculator

Price and Yields

    ⊣ Bond Quotes

    ⊣ Calculating Bond Prices

    ⊣ Calculating Yield to Maturity

    ⊣ Tax Exempt vs. Non-Tax Exempt

Finding and Buying Bonds

    ⊣ Upcoming Bond Issues

    ⊣ Treasury Direct

    ⊣ Ask the Bond Professor

    ⊣ Portfolio Recommendations

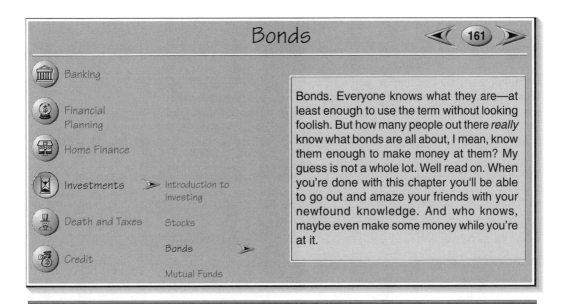

Banking

Financial Planning

Home Finance

Investments ➤ Introduction to Investing

Stocks

Death and Taxes

Bonds ➤

Credit

Mutual Funds

Bonds. Everyone knows what they are—at least enough to use the term without looking foolish. But how many people out there *really* know what bonds are all about, I mean, know them enough to make money at them? My guess is not a whole lot. Well read on. When you're done with this chapter you'll be able to go out and amaze your friends with your newfound knowledge. And who knows, maybe even make some money while you're at it.

Bonds for Beginners

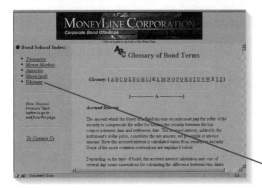

In the *Intro to Investments* section we visited a site that had a glossary of investment terms. As far as investment glossaries go, it was pretty good, but bonds have a language all their own and as such, deserve a glossary all their own. MoneyLine has the best bond-specific glossary on the Web, bar none. It's one of those sites though that uses frames. So if you want to bookmark this page for reference later on you'll have start off at the "Bond School" and click on "Glossary" to get where you're going.

http://www.moneyline.com/mlc_bond.html

Tucker Anthony offers a more detailed definition of what a bond is but to make a long story short, a bond is a loan.

Unlike an equity investment such as stock where you own a piece of the company you've invested in, bonds are closer to an IOU; You lend the issuer a set amount of money and as gratitude they agree to pay you a set amount of interest for a set amount of time. When the bond matures, the loan agreement ends and the original loan amount is returned to you none the worse for wear and tear.

http://www.tucker-anthony.com/bonddef.htm

With set interest rates and an agreed upon return of the original loan amount comes a certain degree of safety. But bonds are not entirely without their risks. The most obvious being that the bond issuer won't be able to pay up. Less obvious, but more common, is that although you are making money on the bond, you're not making as much as you could have elsewhere. Vanguard shows how holding a bond at a lower interest rate translates to lowered earnings and how the longer you hold that bond the more you stand to lose.

http://www.vanguard.com/educ/module2/m2_2_5.html

Savings Bonds

If you ever overhear some big shot investors talking about how they're going long in the bond market, chances are that they're not talking about U.S. Savings bonds. That said, savings bonds do make a great gift and The Bureau of the Public Debt's all encompassing *All About* series of Savings Bonds articles has all the information on the subject you could ever hope for.

If you've ever had a question about savings bonds now's your chance.

http://www.publicdebt.treas.gov/sav/sav.htm

When Aunt Selma pinched your cheeks and gave you your first savings bond all those many years ago, she probably told you how someday it would be worth a lot of money. You promptly stuck it in a drawer and haven't thought of it since. Go dig it out now and use the Federal Reserve Bank of New York Savings Bonds Calculator to see how much it's worth. Your bond will have the denomination, series (S, E or EE) and issue date printed on it. Put in the values and click on "Compute Values" and see if Aunt Selma was right.

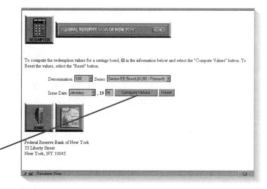

http://www.ny.frb.org/pihome/svg_bnds/sb_val.html

Savings bonds are purchased at a fraction of their face value and earn interest every six months until maturity. If you redeem a savings bond before the specified maturity date the bond will be worth that much less. If, however, you hold on to the bond after it reaches maturity it will continue to accrue interest—for a while. Humberto Cruz of the Salt Lake Tribune writes that with bond owners holding almost $2 billion in bonds that have stopped earning interest, savings bonds are The Do-It-Yourself Investment that many do wrong.

SAVINGS BONDS: DO-IT-YOURSELF INVESTMENTS

By Humberto Cruz

Nobody can question the popularity of U.S. savings bonds: about 55 million Americans own them, slightly more than invest in the stock market. Given those numbers, you'd think savings bonds were a simple investment, easy to understand.

And you'd be wrong. The rules that govern savings bonds are so wretchedly complicated even the government can't get them right.

"Buy U.S. Savings Bonds in any of the eight denominations for just half their face value," says an ad from the Department of the Treasury running in financial magazines. (So far so good). Now comes the error: "If you keep them five years or more, you'll earn competitive, market-based rates or a guaranteed minimum rate, whichever is higher."

That's not true anymore, the part about the guaranteed rate, for any Series EE bonds you bought on or after May 1, 1995, or in the future (unless they change the rules again, of course).

And that's part of the problem. Each bond is governed by a unique set of rules and earns a particular rate of interest, depending on when you bought it. Another problem is that the government never sends you a statement showing how much your bonds are worth at any one time, how much interest they are making, when they mature, or whether they have reached "final maturity" and are not earning any interest at all.

"It's a do-it-yourself investment," said Daniel J. Pederson, author of the book U.S. Savings Bonds: A Comprehensive Guide for Bond Owners and Financial Professionals.

And unfortunately, many do-it-yourselfers do it wrong.

http://www.sltrib.com/96/APR/21/tbz/20510942.htm

Types of Bonds

CORPORATE BONDS

- Typically provide interest income semiannually.
- Return principal on the maturity date.*
- Backed by the good faith of the corporation.

Corporate bonds have many of the same characteristics as other bonds except that creditworthiness becomes an added factor. Such instruments range from AAA rated companies with very solid creditworthiness to "junk bonds" with less than certain futures (see Major Rating Agencies section). Obviously, applying the risk versus reward theory, the high-quality bonds will offer lower yields than lesser rated securities, because investors who purchase the lower quality bonds demand compensation for their added risk in the form of a higher interest rate.

There, now that savings bonds are out of the way we can pop over to OLDE Discount and look at the big three, treasury, municipal, and our first contender, corporate.

Corporate bonds are backed by "the good faith of the corporation." That is, the corporation puts their good reputation up as collateral. Corporate bonds tend to pay higher interest rates then other types of bonds and, following the risk to reward scale, the less faith the rating agencies have in the corporations reputation, the more interest they pay.

http://www.oldediscount.com/fixed/hii5net.htm

Nobody can run up a tab like the U.S. Government, and they can get away with it because they always pay their bills, usually by borrowing more. All things being equal, the U.S. Treasury generally pays a lower rate of return when it borrows because its debts are backed by the "full faith and credit" of the U.S. Government—in terms of creditworthiness it doesn't get much better than that. Government issues are split up into Treasury Bills, Treasury Notes, and Treasury Bonds. Let's first take a look at T-Bills by clicking on Treasury Bills.

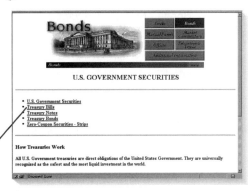

U.S. GOVERNMENT SECURITIES

- U.S. Government Securities
- Treasury Bills
- Treasury Notes
- Treasury Bonds
- Zero-Coupon Securities - Strips

How Treasuries Work

All U.S. Government treasuries are direct obligations of the United States Government. They are universally recognized as the safest and the most liquid investment in the world.

http://www.oldediscount.com/fixed/treasury.htm

T-Bills, T-Bonds, T-Notes ... It's really not so confusing when you look at it. The big difference between the three is that they are all aimed at different time frames. T-Bills tie your money up for the shortest span, either 90 days, 180 days, or one year.

T-Bills are somewhat different than the other two Treasury securities in that, like savings bonds, they are sold at a discount below their face value (or "par value" in investorspeak). You get to keep the difference between par and purchase price.

http://www.oldediscount.com/fixed/hii10net.htm

TREASURY BILLS

Treasury bills are sold at a discount ($10,000 face minimum) and are redeemed at par, whereas treasury notes and bonds have a fixed interest rate and maturity date. For example, a T-note may have a coupon of 8.5% and a maturity date of June 15, 1998. An investment of $10,000 will pay $850 interest (8.5% x $10,000) each year; $425 every December 15 and June 15, up to and including June 15, 1998. At maturity, the principal of $10,000 will also be returned to the investor. If sold prior to maturity the principal value may fluctuate depending on current market conditions.

[Treasuries Menu] [Bonds] [Home Page]

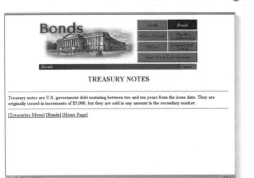

TREASURY NOTES

Treasury notes are U.S. government debt maturing between two and ten years from the issue date. They are originally issued in increments of $5,000, but they are sold in any amount in the secondary market.

[Treasuries Menu] [Bonds] [Home Page]

Treasury Notes are aimed at investors taking a slightly longer view of things. They're available with maturity dates of two, three, four, five or seven years. They are purchased at face value and earn interest every six months until they mature. Two- and three-year T-Notes are originally issued in increments of $5,000, four years plus are issued in increments of $1,000.

All U.S. securities are exempt from state and local taxes making them particularly attractive for investors living in areas with high tax rates.

http://www.oldediscount.com/fixed/hii11net.htm

Treasury Bonds are available with maturity dates of 10 and 30 years.

As long as you continue to hold on to a bond you will always have the security of knowing exactly what interest rate you will be getting. If you ever want to resell it however, how much you will get for that bond depends on the rates that bond buyers are able to get elsewhere at that time. The longer the spread between issue date and maturity the more chance those rates have to fluctuate, making resale values of long-term T-Bonds more volatile.

http://www.oldediscount.com/fixed/hii13net.htm

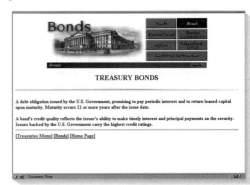

TREASURY BONDS

A debt obligation issued by the U.S. Government, promising to pay periodic interest and to return loaned capital upon maturity. Maturity occurs 11 or more years after the issue date.

A bond's credit quality reflects the issuer's ability to make timely interest and principal payments on the security. Issues backed by the U.S. Government carry the highest credit ratings.

[Treasuries Menu] [Bonds] [Home Page]

Of course the U.S. Government isn't the only government in town that has to feed a voracious debt. States, cities, counties, school districts and just about any other municipal agency you can think of also have to raise money by selling bonds. Collectively, these are knows as Municipal Bonds or, by their cute name, "Munis." Sound like a kids cartoon: The Smurfs, The Care Bears, The Munis—but I digress. Just as the municipalities can't charge tax on federal bonds, the Federal Government can't charge tax on municipal bonds.

http://www.oldediscount.com/fixed/taxfbnet.htm

THE TAX-FREE ADVANTAGE - MUNICIPAL BONDS

If you're in a high tax bracket and your financial goal is to obtain interest income, tax-free bonds may be right for you.

Municipal bonds are issued by states, cities, counties, school districts, housing authorities, hospitals and other municipal agencies. Proceeds from these securities are used to fund local governments, build roads, bridges, sewer systems, schools and other projects.

Many investors in the higher income-tax brackets find municipal securities attractive because they generate tax-free interest.* The following formula, will allow you to compare the yield on a tax-free municipal bond with a comparable taxable bond:

Equivalent Taxable Yield = Tax-exempt Yield/(1-Marginal Tax Rate)

General Obligation Bonds

Summary

General obligation bonds (GO bonds) are legally backed by the full faith and credit of the issuing government. In other words, the government is obligated to use its taxing power, if necessary, to repay the debt.

In Texas, state GO bonds are secured by the first moneys coming into the Treasury that are not constitutionally dedicated for other purposes. Because the Texas Constitution prohibits debt, issuing general obligation debt requires a constitutional amendment.

Advantages

- GO bonds usually sell at the lowest rates of interest because they are considered very low risk.
- General obligation bond issues often are not as complex as revenue bonds so there may be reduced administrative costs in preparing the issue.
- The passage of a bond referendum by the voters confirms popular support for the project or program that is being financed.

Disadvantages

- Voter referendums may delay financing of projects.
- If voters do not approve bonds, officials must devise alternative methods of financing the project, or cancel the projects outright.
- The ability to issue general obligation bonds may be constrained by legal debt limits.

The type of bond that a municipality issues depends on what purpose the money raised is intended to serve. The two most common are the General Obligation (GO) and Revenue bonds as explained here on the Texas Web site Window on State Government.

A government is legally bound to repay its General Obligation debts , using its authority to raise taxes if necessary to do so. In terms of safety and liquidity, GO bonds come in second only to Treasury Securities. At the bottom of the screen click on Revenue Bonds.

http://www.cpa.state.tx.us/localinf/debtguide/ch3.1.html

Revenue bonds are secured by a specified revenue source. For example, a bond issued to pay for the building of a new road might be subsidized through tolls collected for its use. If the road should happen to collapse into a sinkhole, the municipality is not legally obligated to make good on the bonds. It may repay it anyway or else face a tough time raising money the next time around, but the point is that it doesn't *have* to. Rating agencies measure the risks involved with each individual bond issue and rate them accordingly.

http://www.cpa.state.tx.us/localinf/debtguide/ch3.2.html

Revenue Bonds

Summary

Revenue bonds, also referred to as limited obligation bonds, are legally secured only by a specified revenue source. If that specified revenue source is insufficient to make debt service payments, the state is not legally obligated to appropriate other revenues for debt repayment. In Texas, the issuance of revenue bonds require legislative approval but does not require voter approval.

Advantages

- Revenue bonds are not subject to the constitutional prohibition against debt and therefore do not require a constitutional amendment to be approved by voters.
- Beneficiaries of the projects are often the ones paying for the debt service on the bonds if the bonds are repaid with a revenue source associated with the program or project that is being financed.

Disadvantages

- Revenue bonds generally carry higher interest rates than general obligation bonds because the risk of default is greater.
- Revenue bonds are typically more complex than general obligation bonds, thus resulting in higher administrative costs.

Revenue Bonds

Agencies, including securities issued by both federal entities and federally sponsored private enterprises, round out the list of major bond issuers. Ginnie Mae, sister Fannie Mae, and cousin Freddie Mac are the biggest bond issuers in the agency family. I'll leave it up to Prudential Securities to tell you where those fanciful names come from.

Once again, security is not a big issue, Big Brother stands firmly behind Ginnie Mae and looks on sportively as Fannie and Freddie go about their daily business.

http://www.prusec.com/mbs.htm

Besides their ridiculous names, what Fannie, Ginnie, and Freddie have in common is that they're mortgage-backed securities. What you are actually buying in to is a pool of outstanding mortgages (at least they're "outstanding" in the sense that they're still being paid for). If interest rates happen to fall and homeowners pay off their mortgages early the bond that you hold on those mortgages will mature early as well. Mortgage-backed securities may not have precise maturity dates, but as Fannie Mae tells it, they're big business.

http://www.fanniemae.com/FinancialInfo/Investor/MBS/index.html

 ## Building a Bond Ladder

If we have any bonafide psychics in the audience, please, call me. Until I get that call, I've got to assume the same thing that the rest of the financial world does. Namely, that no one knows for sure where interest rates are heading. And if you don't know where the rates are heading you can't be sure what the best bond strategy would be. In light of that uncertainty, many financial pundits, Merril Lynch being a prime example, suggest Building a Bond Ladder. What's a bond ladder you ask? If you don't visit their Web page you may never know.

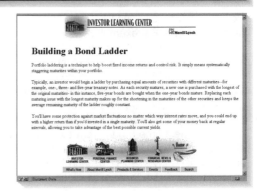

http://www.ml.com/investor/bondladder.html

I've been alluding to the fact that interest rates affect the bond market, now I'm going to clarify what I mean by that with the assistance of this nice Interest Rates table from CNNfn as a backdrop. When a company, municipality, agency, or the U.S. Treasury itself issues a bond they have to pay the going rates. Those rates are determined by the latest unemployment figures, the trade deficit, and whether or not a butterfly flapped its wings over China on that particular day. The wings flap, the market responds, and CNNfn posts the results.

http://www.cnnfn.com/markets/rates.html

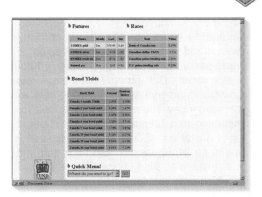

At $5+ trillion and counting, the U.S. is the biggest fish in the Sea of Debt. It follows that the U.S. is also the world's largest bond issuer. Compared to that, Canada, with a national deficit of a measly $600 billion is more of a guppy. Per capita debt however, is roughly equal across the two countries, giving Canadians something to be proud of and the Bank of Canada a good reason to constantly revise the interest rates that Canadian-issued bonds are ultimately based on. You can find the latest Canadian bond yields on The Fund Library.

http://www.fundlib.com/~wsapi/cfusion?action=Query&template=/SQLTFL/markets.dbm

So you buy a new bond issue at the going rate only to discover that your kid needs braces and that a herd of monarchs have taken up residence in Chengchow. Interest rates have skyrocketed. No one's going to pay you what you paid for yesterday's bond when they can buy a new one at the better rate. In short, the price of your bond has gone down. ICMA-RC Services illustrates this inverse relationship well. You see the people climbing up the mountain? Those are interest rates. The people walking down, those are bond prices.

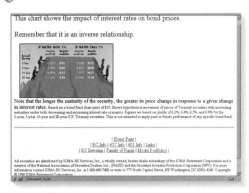

http://www.icmarc.org/Invest/article/bonds/rates.html

The Stock Room offers a way to chart Bond Yields and Treasury Note Interest Rates. The people that run the Stock Room try to keep their information straight but make a point of noting that the data is not guaranteed and that they accept no responsibility for any losses incurred because of it. It would seem that investors can be a litigious bunch.

T-Bills, T-Notes, T-Bonds, Fed Funds, Prime Rates, and the various Dow Jones's are all listed. Pick one and click on "Submit Request." And please, don't sue.

http://www.stockroom.org/stockroom/bond.html

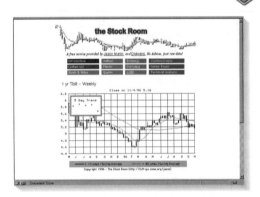

And there you have it.

As many a purveyor of bonds information is wont to add at the bottom of their Web pages, "past performance is no guarantee of future performance." Duly noted. Past interest rates however can serve as an indication of where rates are today. You wouldn't want to lock your money in on a 30-year commitment if interest rates are at an all-time low. Unless, that is, you're an ultra-pessimist and think that rates will continue to slide unabated forever more. In which case, buy!buy!buy!

http://www.stockroom.org/stockroom/bond.html

Bond Ratings

Almost all bonds are rated in terms of the issuers ability to make good on interest payments and repay the principle. There are several widely quoted rating agencies including S&P and Moody's. Each one uses a slightly different scale to rate bonds but they all look more or less like this one from Fitch Investor Service. At the top of the list are the crème de la crème, the select few that warrant a AAA rating (or Aaa, depending on who you're quoting). At the bottom of the list are the lepers of the bond industry, the dreaded Ds.

http://www.fitchinv.com/ratdefs.htm

Bonds with a rating at or below BB (or Ba, depending again on who you're quoting) are considered junk bonds. A far scarier moniker than say "Fannie Mae" but one which some feel is highly underrated, so to speak. Eager Street Asset Management for one prefers the term "High Yield." They point out that investors require an interest premium for assuming the credit risk of these lower rated securities. So as long as the bond isn't amongst the 2 percent to default each year you can expect a higher return by buying junk.

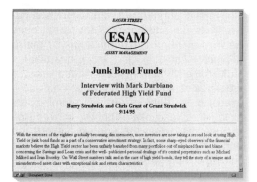

http://lifenet.com/esam/durb914.html

A callable bond is a bond that can be redeemed (bought back) by the issuer before the bond matures. For example, let's say IBM has issued $10 million in bonds to the public to finance a new manufacturing plant. These bonds sell for $1,000 each and have a 12% coupon rate. Suppose, however, that IBM will not have to pay back the principal on these bonds—that is, the $1,000 for each bond it issued—until 20 years and that these bonds are callable in five years. In other words, IBM can buy back these bonds within five years—usually at a premium, such as $1,080 or $1,050 per bond

Now, after six years, interest rates have fallen to 7%. Since IBM is currently paying 12% on its bonds, this company will probably want to pay the lower 7% rate. IBM can do this if it calls the 12% bonds and then issues new bonds at the lower 7% rate. This is called refinancing corporate debt, which helps corporations lower their interest costs.

Unfortunately, investors are at a disadvantage, because they have to sell their high yielding bonds back to the issuer and will probably only be able to reinvest their money back into equivalent bonds that have lower coupon rates. This is known as reinvestment risk.

Interest yields and alphabet soup ratings are the biggest indicators of a bonds value, but whether or not a bond is callable also plays a part in the equation. Web IPO explains that a callable bond can be bought back before it's full maturity date and, presumably, reissued back onto the market at a new, lower rate. It's good for the issuer because they're not stuck paying high yields long after the going rate has dropped, but it's not so good for investors who now find themselves shopping around for a new place to park their money.

http://www.webipo.com/gi/bo/gi-ub2.html

Zero Coupon bonds are something of a newcomer on the bond scene but in many ways they work just like the first bonds that a lot of us had experience with, savings bonds. The word "coupon" in investorspeak refers to the interest paid on a bond. It follows then that a zero coupon bond pays no interest. Instead, zeros are sold below face value. The difference between what you pay for the bond and its value on maturity is the implied interest. Web IPO details the intricacies of zeros, including their rather unusual tax implications.

http://www.webipo.com/gi/bo/gi-ub6.html

A zero-coupon bond is a bond that does not pay interest (that is, has a zero coupon payment) but is sold at a deep discount to its face value. Then, usually within five to 25 years, the bond will mature and you will receive the face value. The difference between the purchase price and the face value is the implied interest you have earned over the years. For example, let's say you buy a 10-year zero-coupon bond for $558 that has a face value of $1,000. If you hold onto this bond for ten years, you will receive $1,000. The difference between the $1,000 and $558 is the interest you earn, which is 6 percent. Unfortunately, even though you do not receive any cash interest payments during the ten years, the IRS still requires you to pay taxes on this implied interest every year. This is known as "phantom interest." Because of this tax situation, many investors put their zero-coupon bonds in tax-sheltered retirement accounts, such as IRAs and 401(k)s. Or investors might put zero-coupon bonds in a custodial account for their children, who are usually in lower tax brackets.

The zero-coupon bond is a recent innovation. In 1983, Merrill Lynch began selling the first zero-coupon bonds, which were called TIGRs (Treasury Investment Growth Certificates). Since this time, there has been an incredible amount of new types of zero-coupon bonds

Convertible bonds are a strange hybrid between stocks and bonds. They're not quite debt, they're not exactly equity, they're debtquity. And <u>Friedland Associates</u> takes a look at the attractiveness of these unusual creatures from the perspective of the issuer.

In addition to paying interest and returning principle like other types of bonds, convertibles provide the owner the right to convert the bonds into a specific number of shares in the issuing company, usually at a specified price at a predetermined time in the future.

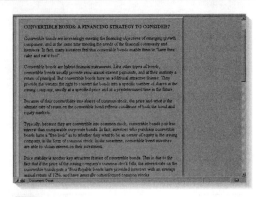

http://www.friedland-fin.com/corp/fcr9555.htm

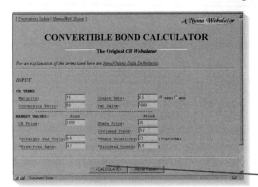

<u>Numa Financial Systems</u> has a <u>Convertible Bond Calculator</u> to help you decide when it's in your best interest to take advantage of your option to convert a bond to stock shares.

In order to properly assess the offer the calculator requires a fair bit of information. If you don't understand what it is that the calculator is asking you for, you can click on any term for an explanation. If that still doesn't help, you may need to call a good broker. Once you've got all the numbers in place you can click on "Calculate" and scroll down for the results.

http://www.numa.com/derivs/ref/calculat/cb/calc-cba.htm

Price and Yields

Unlike stocks where quoting services abound on the Net, finding a bond tends to be more difficult and the services that quote them more scarce. <u>Bondtrac</u> is one of the few free services on the Net that lets you do just that. They list the bond inventories of hundreds of broker/dealers and give you the ability to search those inventories for one bond in particular or any and all that meet your conditions.

You can choose to search the database for <u>Municipals</u>, <u>Agencies</u>, <u>Treasuries</u>, or <u>Corporate</u> issues.

http://www.bondtrac.com/

The more you know about the bond you're looking for the more you can pinpoint your search. CUSIP numbers are something like the bond equivalent of a stock symbol. They can often be found on bond statements or by calling a broker. Ditto for the Issue Description and Dealer Abbreviation. If you happen to know any of the above you can put them in, otherwise type in a range for the Maturity Year, Block Size, and Coupon Rate you're interested in and click on "Search" to find all the bonds in the database that meet that description.

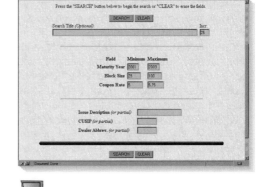

http://www.bondtrac.com/FreeCorp.html

You'll get a list of bonds, one screen full at a time. If more bonds were found then will fit on a single screen you will see a button at the bottom of the page that you can click for the next screen full.

Each bond has a Rating, Description, Coupon Rate, and Maturity Date. Unfortunately, the dealer contact and pricing information are not shown on the free service, you'll have to $ubscribe if you want that. Buy hey, the price is right and it should give you a good idea of what's out there.

http://www.bondtrac.com/FreeCorp.html

Fidelity Investments has a two-in-one bond calculator that will help you estimate a bonds price and its yield to maturity. The yield to maturity value is the total return on your investment expressed as a percentage. The bond price is the going rate for a bond on the secondary market, not its face value. You need to know one value to solve for the other. Pick which one you want to calculate and choose which type of bond you'll be calculating, either Corporate/Municipal issues or Treasury Notes/Bonds. Click "Continue" when done.

http://personal.fidelity.com/fidbin/bonds?10

I've said it before and I'll say it again; you have to know one set of numbers to solve for the other. If you're trying to find a bond price you first need to know the yield-to-maturity, coupon rate, etc. If you don't know this stuff you don't need a calculator, you need a broker. Settlement dates can be confusing. It's the date the transaction is executed, usually a few days after the terms have been agreed upon. If you're finding a price beforehand you'll want to estimate this date. Once you've got all the numbers straight click on "Results."

http://personal.fidelity.com/fidbin/bonds?10

Bond prices are kind of wacky. With stock prices you know that if the stock is listed at $135.67 you will have to pay $135.67 per share. Simple. Bond prices though are expressed in terms of number of dollars per $100 of the face amount. And nobody sells bonds by the $100. Ugh! What the numbers that you see mean are that for every $100 of the original par value on the bond you will have to pay X. So if the bond price is 99.071 on a $5,000 issue you would pay 99.071 multiplied by 50, or $4,953.55. Got that?

http://personal.fidelity.com/fidbin/bonds?10

You may think at first that calculating the yield-to-maturity is pointless. After all, if you buy a $1,000 par value bond for $1,000 and it pays a 5.5 percent coupon rate, what's there to calculate? And, as long as you paid par value for that bond, you would be right. If, on the other hand, you purchased the bond at either a discount or a premium, the coupon rate will be different from the real return that you will end up seeing on your investment. And that's the point. As with the other calculator, fill in the numbers and let 'er rip.

http://personal.fidelity.com/fidbin/bonds?10

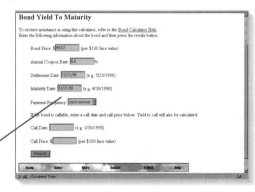

On behalf on the entire Internet I would like to apologize. Determining Whether You're Better Off With a Tax Exempt Bond or a Non-Tax Exempt Bond is a prime example of how the Internet could make your life easier. You could throw away your calculator and your pencil and use an interactive Web-based calculator thingamajig to do the work for you. But no such luck. The best the Net has been able to come up with so far is this page of instructions from Equity Analytics on how you can do it by hand. Java programmers, get on it.

Determining Whether You're Better Off With a Tax Exempt Bond

Or a Non - Tax Exempt Bond

One of the things people want to know the most about bonds is whether they are better off buying a tax exempt bond or one which is subject to taxes. Assume that an individual is in the 28% tax bracket. Further assume that this individual is considering whether to purchase a corporate bond paying 10% in interest (nominal yield or coupon yield, the amount on the face of the bond), or a municipal bond paying a nominal yield of 7%. Either one can be purchased for $1,000. The corporate bond will pay the bond holder $100 annually (two $50 semi-annual payments) and the municipal bond will pay the bond holder $70 (two $35 semi-annual payments). After taxes are paid, the corporate bond holder will wind up with $72 ($100 X [1-.28]) Not paying any taxes on the municipal bond, the bond holder will wind up with $70.

Another way to look at tax free bonds and non tax free bonds is to compute the taxable equivalent. The taxable equivalent is the amount of interest a non tax free bond would have to pay to equal the return on a tax free bond. Anything greater than this amount would indicate that the non tax free bond is a better deal. Anything less than this amount indicates that the tax free bond is a better deal. Any bond with a nominal or coupon yield at this amount and it doesn't matter which one you choose. The formula to determine the taxable equivalent is:

Tax Free Yield (divided by) 100 - the tax bracket

For example, assume that the investor is considering that same 7% municipal bond and that the investor is in the 28% tax bracket. The calculation is:

http://www.e-analytics.com/fp28.htm

Finding and Buying Bonds

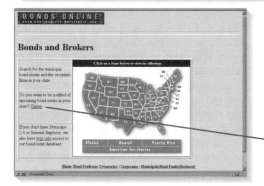

Bonds and Brokers

In terms of cool bond stuff on the Net, probably the best all-around site is Bonds Online. Starting from this map you can click on any state for a list of all the municipal bonds that Bonds Online is aware of. There are a few sites on the Web with similar capabilities but this one isn't limited to only those bond issues being managed by the security firm running the Web site.

If you like, you can Signup to be notified of upcoming bond issues in your state as they become available.

http://www.bondsonline.com/map.html

The information is a little on the scant side right now but Bonds Online seems to be adding as they update. At the very least you will find the total size of the bond issue, a description, the date it's to become available and a link to that state's treasury Web site. If you're lucky you'll also be able to link to further information about the bond. You might for example find ratings, callable dates, maturity schedules, and so on. If you find something of interest you can try the states treasury site or pass the information on to your broker.

Texas

State Treasury Site

The following bonds are to be made available in the state of Texas.

Click on the name of the offering firm for more information.

October 24

$17,000,000 Longview GO & Water & Sewer Revenue Bonds

Competitive Bid
October 23

$21,240,000 Amarillo School District General Obligation Bonds

Competitive Bid

Return to Map

http://www.bonds-online.com/issues.htm#TX

Under the Treasuries section of the site you'll find an article on the Treasury Direct Program. If you're interested in purchasing U.S. Treasury securities it's worth looking into. It details how you can participate in the Federal Reserve's regularly scheduled auctions without paying brokerage fees or transaction charges.

It's not for everyone, but if you think it might be for you you can try the links and phone numbers found at the bottom of the screen to contact the Federal Reserve Branch nearest you.

http://www.bondsonline.com/articles/treasur.htm

At the bottom of nearly every Web found on the site is a link to the "Bond Professor." Click it and you'll see something like this. From here you can access a list of frequently asked bond questions (and their answers) and the bond question of the week. If after reading the above you still haven't found an answer to your bond question you can click on Ask The Bond Professor and e-mail your stumper. The Bond Professor will e-mail you a reply and if it's a good one, may even make it the next question of the week.

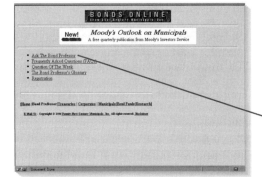

http://www.bondsonline.com/bondprof.html

BondLink is another good example of the Internet at its most interactive. This site's claim to fame is its portfolio recommendation service. You set the criteria that you're looking for in a bond and BondLink will return a table of bonds which meet your criteria, along with their most recently reported prices and yields.

You can get fairly specific in setting the criteria too, even going so far as to ask for recommendations that fit into your overall investment strategy. Just fill it out, send it off and see what they can come up with.

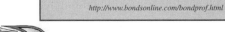

http://www.bondlink.com/criterion.html

Mutual Funds

An Overview

⊣ Getting Started

⊣ Fund Selection Tips

⊣ The Advantage of No-Load Funds

⊣ Fund Objectives

⊣ Tax-Free Mutual Fund Calculator

Digging Deeper

⊣ NETWorth

    ⊣ Fund Search by Criteria

    ⊣ Top Performers

⊣ Canada's Mutual Fund Resource Center

Fund Performance

⊣ Money Manager Profiles

⊣ Finding a Fund's Price and Charting It's Progress

Further Insights

⊣ The Prime Times Investor Newsletter

⊣ The CNNfn Mutual Funds Page

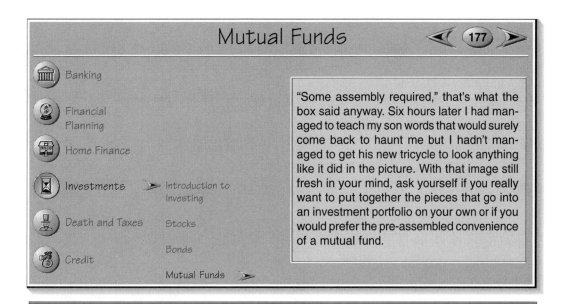

Banking

Financial
Planning

Home Finance

Investments ➤ Introduction to
Investing

Death and Taxes Stocks

Bonds

Credit

Mutual Funds ➤

"Some assembly required," that's what the box said anyway. Six hours later I had managed to teach my son words that would surely come back to haunt me but I hadn't managed to get his new tricycle to look anything like it did in the picture. With that image still fresh in your mind, ask yourself if you really want to put together the pieces that go into an investment portfolio on your own or if you would prefer the pre-assembled convenience of a mutual fund.

An Overview

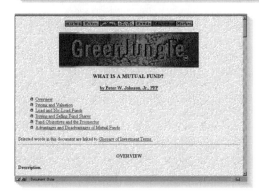

Judging by their rising popularity, there's something about mutual funds that appeal to a lot of people. Maybe it's the convenience of buying into a diversified portfolio without having to take the time or trouble to build it from scratch. Or it could be the fact that each fund is managed by an expert in the field and backed up by a team whose sole job is to see that you, and everyone else who's bought into their fund, sees a good return on their investment. Whatever the individual reasons are, mutual funds are worth some looking into.

http://www.greenjungle.com/pub/education/edartmutualfund.html

Peter W. Johnson, Jr. has put together a good overview of mutual funds on the Green Jungle Web site that can help you get started. If funds are new to you it should give you an idea of what all the fuss is all about.

The information here is equally relevant for mutual fund experts and newcomers alike. If there's one particular area that interests you you can focus on it. If it's all new to you, you can read the article from beginning to end. If you get confused by any of the terminology used, just click on the underlined word.

http://www.greenjungle.com/pub/education/edartmutualfund.html#OV

Ask half a dozen experts for advice on choosing a mutual fund and you'll get half a dozen answers. To help get things started Richard Calkins of Rich's MONEYFLO has listed six of his favorite Fund Selection Tips. Amongst other things, Rich suggests looking into no-load funds, opening an account at a firm that allows for options, avoiding the temptation to "over-diversify" and taking a hard look at each funds recent performance. Read Rich's tips, but don't forget that in the end, only your own good judgement can make you, well, rich.

http://www.harborside.com/home/m/moneyflo/fundpick.htm

There's a lot of debate about load vs. no-load funds. With load funds you pay a sales commission, which helps subsidize any research or advice you receive. Low-load funds are purchased directly through a fund company, bypassing the middleman and lowering costs. With no-load funds, the sales charges are incorporated into the funds price. The Mutual Fund Investors Center is "designed for investors who want to direct their own mutual fund investments." You can guess which side of the load/no-load debate they come down on.

http://www.mfea.com/mfframe.html

When you look into funds you will find that they usually fall into one of four basic risk categories, as described here under the "Map Out a Plan" section of the site. They are: aggressive growth funds, growth funds, growth and income funds, and, lastly, income funds. These vague descriptions are only a starting point however. They give you a general idea about the funds objectives but not much information about the makeup of its portfolio or its recent historical returns. For that you're going to want to look at each fund individually.

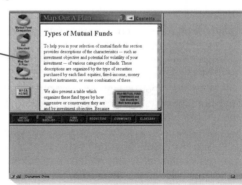

http://www.mfea.com/mfframe.html

Just as you can invest in tax-free bonds, you can also buy into a tax-free bond fund. As a general rule, you will see a lower yield with tax-free investments, but the bottom line isn't how much you make, but how much you keep. Depending on the returns of the investments you're looking at and the tax bracket that you fall into, a tax-free bond fund is definitely something to consider. SAFECO offers a simple calculator that can help point you in the right direction. Just type in your gross annual income and click on the calculator.

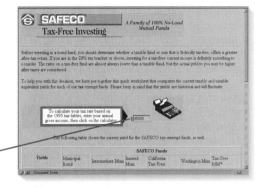

http://networth.galt.com/www/home/mutual/safeco/taxfree/
taxpage.html

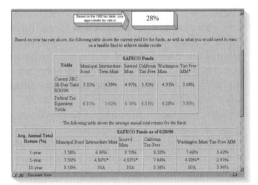

The program comes up with an approximate tax rate and below it, a table of several SAFECO funds and their current yields. The red numbers are the equivalent yields you would need to make on a taxable investment to end up with the same amount of money in your pocket after giving unto Uncle Sam what is Uncle Sam's. Obviously, the higher the tax bracket that you're in, the more money you would save by not paying taxes. Even if you're looking at someone else's funds, you can use the SAFECO numbers as a general guide.

http://networth.galt.com/www/home/mutual/safeco/taxfree/
taxpage.html

Digging Deeper

NETworth, part of the Quicken Financial Network, is one of the all-around best resources for detailed mutual fund information on the Net. You can access a sizable directory of mutual funds, delve into fund prices, check out the industry standard Morningstar Profiles, look up the best performing funds or search for funds according to your own criteria. But before you do any of the above you'll have to register. Be sure to write down the user name and ID you select, then click on Fund Search to get things started.

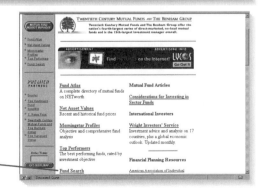

http://networth.galt.com/www/home/mutual/

There are umpteen different ways to begin narrowing down your fund search. If you have a particular fund in mind and know its name or the description it goes by you can type that in. Otherwise, you can search for only those funds that meet a stated investment objective (growth, income, etc.) or meet your criteria in terms of assets, yield, Morningstar rating, required purchase, and/or historical return. Any of the above or a combination of the lot, it's up to you. Select what it is that you're looking for and see what NETworth can come up with.

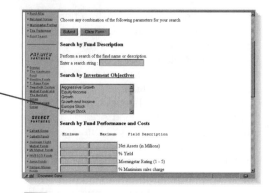

http://networth.galt.com/cgi-bin/getdb

Under the "Top Performers" section of the site you can see for yourself which funds have outperformed all others. You can choose to search for the best performers in any given class or select "All Categories" to search for the 25 funds that have fared best regardless whatever category it happens to fall under. You can choose how far back in time you want to go, anywhere from the last three months to the last ten years. Pick one and click the "Submit" button. You can always use your browser's Back Button to try another time frame.

http://networth.galt.com/www/home/mutual/top25.html

Next to the description of each fund is its symbol, the return it showed over the specified time period and links you can use to find more information about the fund.

"NAV" stands for Net Asset Value, a fancy way of describing a funds share price. Clicking on a fund's NAV brings up a graph of that fund's performance over the last 52 weeks as well as the funds closing NAVs for the last five trading days. The "Profile" link brings up the fund's Morningstar profile. Try clicking on that now.

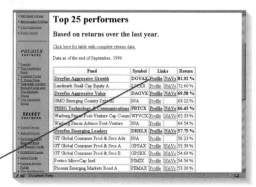

http://networth.galt.com/www/home/mutual/top25.html

Morningstar Inc. isn't the only company out there to profile and rate mutual funds, but it's the one that more investors rely on. These are the guys and gals whose job it is to look at a fund's objectives and assign it the appropriate label. They rate each fund on a one to five-star scale to indicate how well it's doing and briefly describe what the fund is all about. No profile can replace a full prospectus, but in this one little snapshot glimpse you have most of the essential information that any fund investor could want.

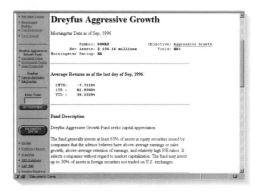

http://networth.galt.com/www/home/mutual/top25.html

Investors north of the border sometimes have to make do with less flashy Web sites then the ones their southern siblings get to surf around on. In recognizing that fact, Fundlib has managed to put together an on-line mutual fund resource that isn't just Canadian, it's Radically Canadian.

There's a bunch of good stuff here with Online Discussion Forums, Games, Newsletters, NAVs, Canadian Fund Company Profiles, and a whole lot more. None too shabby, eh?

http://www.fundlib.com/~wsapi/cfusion?action=Query&template=/sqltfl/home.dbm

Fund Performance

A mutual fund is only as good as the team that directs it. And at the head of that team is the manager, on whose broad shoulders lies the awesome responsibility of a funds performance. Mutual Funds Interactive℠ presents profiles of some of the broadest shouldered Money Managers in the business. Before entrusting your money to their care, it's worth the effort to learn where the manager is coming from and where he or she thinks the fund is going. All the more so when that effort amounts to no more than a click of the mouse.

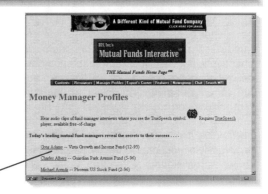

http://www.brill.com/profiles.html

Assuming that you've purchased a share in a mutual fund or have found some funds that you are interested in, you're going to want to track its progress. There are a lot of quoting services on the Net that let you track stock prices but fewer that offer the same service for funds. Stockmaster is the best of the ones that do. Start by typing in the funds symbol and clicking the "Submit" button. If you don't know the symbol, you can alternatively enter the name. And if you don't know the name, you can even get away with *part* of the name.

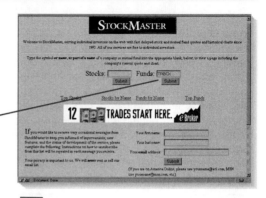

http://www.stockmaster.com/

If you got here by typing in part of the name, you may want to take a second at this point to jot down the symbol for easier reference the next time around.

At the top of the screen is the latest closing prices for the fund as well as the NAVs for the previous 10 trading days. Below that is a long range graph charting the funds progress over the last 2 1/2 years. It's a good way to get a sense of where the fund is now in relation to where it's been.

http://www.stockmaster.com/sm/mf/T/TRBCX.html

Further Insights

The Prime Times Investor offers a free in-depth newsletter each month covering a different family of funds. The newsletters includes charts, pricing, statistical information and buy/ sell recommendations. Click on "view an entire current newsletter" to download the current edition or on "mail list" to have Prime Times e-mail you educational material, instructions on reading charts, and notification when the fund family of your choice becomes available. Between newsletters, the Extra Edition will keep you on top of things.

http://www.sky.net/~primetym/

Speaking of keeping on top of things, there's no better place on the Web to find the latest mutual fund news than <u>CNNfn</u>. With an entire area of the site dedicated exclusively to its coverage, CNNfn has information for mutual fund investors who need to know what's going on and need to know it now. Breaking stories are featured on the main <u>Mutual Funds page</u> and clicking on the "continued..." link brings up a list of previously covered topics. From within each story you can jump to any related article or Web site. Nice job.

http://www.cnnfn.com/yourmoney/mutualfunds/

Death

Planning For Estate Planning

⊢ Where Should You Begin?

　⊢ Your Objectives

　⊢ Choosing an Advisor

　⊢ What Your Attorney Should Know

⊢ Choosing an Executor

⊢ An Executors Life

Wills

⊢ Glossary

⊢ Wills FAQ

⊢ Types of Wills

⊢ Wills on the Web

Probate

⊢ What it is

⊢ Who's Afraid of Probate?

⊢ Who Needs a Living Trust?

⊢ Joint Tenancy

　⊢ Rights of Survivorship

　⊢ Forms of Ownership

Estate Taxes

⊢ The Final Tax Return

⊢ Planning for Taxes

　⊢ The $600,000 Unified Credit

　⊢ The Marital Deduction

　⊢ Marital Trusts

⊢ Estimating Your Estate Taxes

Keeping It In the Family

⊢ Family Philosophies

⊢ The Family Business

Trusts and Taxes

⊢ Irrevocable Trusts

⊢ Gift Taxes

　⊢ Using Your Annual Gift Tax Exclusion

　⊢ Should You Use Your Gift Tax Exclusion During Your Lifetime?

⊢ Charitable Remainder Trusts

⊢ GRATs

⊢ QPRTs

⊢ Family Limited Partnerships

⊢ Generation Skipping Transfer Tax

Liquidity

⊢ The Importance of Being Liquid

⊢ Using Life Insurance Trusts to Protect Your Estate

Life Insurance

⊢ The Life and Health Insurance Foundation for Education

⊢ Second to Die Insurance

⊢ Finding The Right Policy

⊢ Finding an Agent

⊢ Links to Life Insurance Companies

Top Ten Estate Planning Goof-Ups

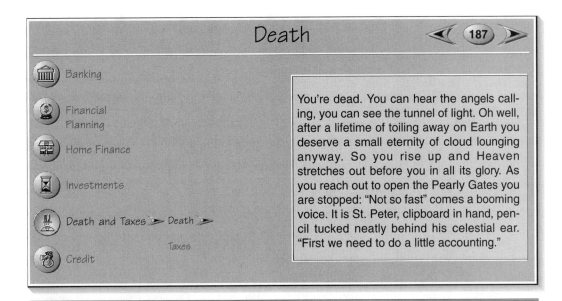

Planning for Estate Planning

Estate planning is only required reading for the mortals amongst us. If you have no intention of dying, please feel free to skip this chapter. If, on the other hand, you're reasonably certain that at some point in your life you will, in fact, die, read on. You can start with Where Should You Begin: A Guide for North Carolinians brought to you by the North Carolina Cooperative Extension Service. And forget the title, as far as I know North Carolinians aren't the only ones who can look forward to an inevitable demise.

http://www.ces.ncsu.edu//depts/fcs/docs/he2731.html

Death is kind of a big deal. Planning for it is kind of a big, depressing pain in the keister. Part of the problem is that estate planning covers a lot of ground. There's wills, wishes, insurance, taxes, the passing on of a lifetime's worth of goodies ... Just by broaching the subject you've taken the first step. Next you must consider your objectives. What are your priorities? Is it your children? Your spouse? The family business? Whatever it is you can use this checklist to get you started, and don't be afraid to check off the "Other" item.

http://www.ces.ncsu.edu//depts/fcs/docs/he2731.html

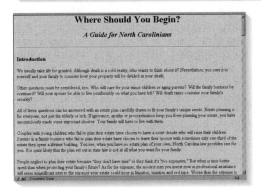

Your situation, like your priorities, is unique, but that doesn't mean that you have to go it alone. One of the wisest decisions you can make as you begin to piece together an estate plan is to seek the assistance of professional advice. A good estate plan is not a do-it-yourself project, it is a team effort. You may need the expertise of a life insurance underwriter, an accountant/tax adviser, a trust officer, a financial planner, *and* an attorney. Using all of the above may seem like overkill, but you only die once.

http://www.ces.ncsu.edu/depts/fcs/docs/he2731.html

3 Choose a professional adviser

Estate planning is extremely technical. Most people do not have time to develop the expertise needed to draw up and keep current a good estate plan. That is why you should consider a team of professionals to help you. Professionals such as a life insurance underwriter, an accountant or tax adviser, a trust officer, a financial planner and an attorney are invaluable sources of information and advice. Life insurance underwriters or agents can review your insurance coverage and help you organize information for your attorney and tax adviser. The underwriter or agent will suggest ways to help you avoid liquidity (cash flow) problems upon your death. Many companies also suggest alternatives to avoid unnecessary death taxes.

Accountants or tax advisers are also knowledgeable of death taxes. They will help you figure the tax consequences of various types of transfers. Accountants or tax advisers can advise in business or property management, valuation of assets, and business continuation or sale.

Trust officers can suggest alternatives in choosing executors or setting up trusts. They also offer management and investment services. Financial planners review your entire financial situation and identify strategies to achieve your financial goals. They work with other professionals to develop your insurance, investment, retirement and estate plan.

The attorney is a key member of the team. He or she coordinates the work and helps you evaluate the advice of the others. Final decisions about your estate plan are made with your attorney. The attorney then draws up the legal documents required.

All of the professionals will need background information before they can help you plan. Call your professional adviser, and ask what information you should bring to the appointment. You will need to review your financial situation, listing assets and liabilities. Accurate information about your net worth is particularly important for tax planning. The checklist entitled, **What My Attorney Should Know** may help you make your list.

You also need to determine how your property is owned. Do you have a life estate or do you own property outright? Whose ...

Wills

WHAT MY ATTORNEY SHOULD KNOW

Save time and money by having the necessary information in hand for that first visit to your attorney. The following checklist is a tally of information your attorney will need.

_____ PERSONAL INFORMATION (family members, names, birth dates, addresses, occupations, social security numbers)

_____ BANK ACCOUNTS (name and location, exact name on accounts, number on each account)

_____ STOCKS AND BONDS (description, years purchased, number, exact name of owner, face value, cost)

_____ LIFE INSURANCE (company, policy number, amount owned by husband, wife, joint, exact name of owner, insured, beneficiary on policy)

_____ TRUSTS (type, location, trustee, who established, exact name of beneficiary, value, owned by whom)

_____ NOTES, MORTGAGES AND ACCOUNTS RECEIVABLE (description, year acquired, value, person who owns you)

_____ REAL ESTATE (list type of property and acres, location, year acquired, cost, owned by, market value)

_____ PERSONAL PROPERTY (list livestock, motor vehicles, machinery, crop inventory, home furnishings, jewelry, art, antiques, personal items, describe cost and value and who own)

_____ LIENS AGAINST PROPERTY (property mortgage, name of creditor, date due, remaining amount due from husband, wife, jointly)

Before you go ahead and schedule an appointment with one of your advisors you should take the time to gather the information they will need. The more accurate the information that you supply the better able they will be to draw up an estate plan that you can live with (ew, yuch. No pun intended, I assure you).

Use this "What My Attorney Should Know" checklist as a starting point. Advisors can't be of much use if they don't know where you're coming from and what you want.

http://www.ces.ncsu.edu/depts/fcs/docs/he2731.html

Plan to your heart's content, but in the end someone else is still going to have to take care of the final paperwork. And there's a lot of it to be taken care of. You don't have to specify who, exactly, you trust to do it for you, but if you don't, the court will appoint someone on your behalf. Unfortunately, it won't necessarily be your first choice. Before you go ahead and choose a close family member of friend as your executor, read what the Cooperative Extension, Mississippi State University has to say on the subject.

http://www.ces.msstate.edu/pubs/pub1746.htm

Who Should Be Your Executor?

Technically speaking, a testator only names or nominates an executor in his will, the court makes the appointment.

A person can choose a friend, family member, attorney, corporate entity, or bank to serve as executor. The best choice for your situation depends on the people and circumstances involved. A Mississippi executor need not be a resident of the same county or state as the deceased; however, it is necessary that he be at least 18 years of age.

Give careful consideration to personal estate planning objectives and the consequences of each of the possible choices before making a selection of executor.

Many people choose a family member or friend thinking it is easier and cheaper for him to settle the estate, because he is familiar with it. This is not necessarily true. Most people do not share their total financial situation with friends. Even a family member may not be aware of all the intricacies of the estate. A family member or friend may take longer to settle the estate and incur unnecessary expenses, because he is unfamiliar with procedures and deadlines.

When a family member or friend serves as an executor, there is always the risk that a misunderstanding and hard feelings may arise. Certain family members may feel that the executor did not act impartially and was unfair in his actions. Sometimes they forget that even if the executor disagrees with the provisions of the will, he must carry them out anyway.

Friends and family members also may be so preoccupied with their own affairs that they may not have the necessary time and attention to devote to the problems of settling your estate. And, of course, the possibility exists that a family member or friend named as executor may die before you do. For this reason, you may want to name an alternate.

Another possibility for an executor is a bank with trust powers. Banks have the facilities, contacts, experience, and business judgment that may not be matched by an individual. In addition, banks provide continuity. A bank doesn't get sick, die, or move away. Usually, the bank selected to be the executor of an estate is the bank where the testator does business and he and his family are known.

The Royal Bank has a list of some of the responsibilities your executor will have to attend to. It's a fairly long list. Look it over and decide for yourself if these are the types of things a mourner could or even should be taking care of. Use it also to make the executor's job as painless as possible, within reason of course. There's no need to cancel your magazine subscriptions in order to spare your executor the trouble, but by knowing what will need to be done you can take a moment and make the executor's job that much easier.

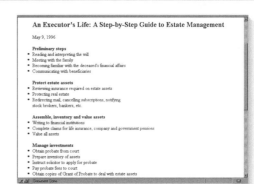

An Executor's Life: A Step-by-Step Guide to Estate Management

May 9, 1996

Preliminary steps
- Reading and interpreting the will
- Meeting with the family
- Becoming familiar with the deceased's financial affairs
- Communicating with beneficiaries

Protect estate assets
- Reviewing insurance required on estate assets
- Protecting real estate
- Redirecting mail, cancelling subscriptions, notifying stock brokers, bankers, etc.

Assemble, inventory and value assets
- Writing to financial institutions
- Complete claims for life insurance, company and government pensions
- Value all assets

Manage investments
- Obtain probate from court
- Prepare inventory of assets
- Instruct solicitor to apply for probate
- Pay probate fees to court
- Obtain copies of Grant of Probate to deal with estate assets

http://www.royalbank.com/english/wealth/04release/04a2.html

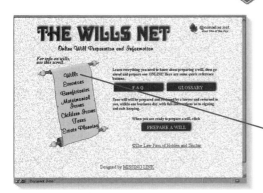

"Intestate," what an ugly word. Sounds like some sort of digestive disorder, doesn't it? What it really refers to though is someone who died without having prepared a will. Bad idea. Dying without a will means that the court gets to choose how your estate is divided and has to guess at your wishes.

On The Will's Net you can click on the word Wills on the scroll to learn how not to pass on intestate or click on Glossary and look up some more ugly will-related words like "escheat" and "testatrix."

http://www.wills-net.com/

 Probate

The FAQ doesn't get very technical, but it does cover most of the basic questions you may have. Questions like: What is a will? What is a living will? Why is it a good idea? What if you don't have a will? What does a will cover? And, lastly, when does a will take effect? Click on a topic at the top of the page or scroll down and read through them all.

From here you can also click on the Prepare a Will button and take care of things while they're still fresh in your mind. Be warned though, there is a charge for this service.

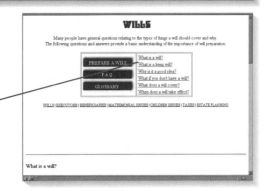

http://www.wills-net.com/wills.html

A will can be as simple as a handwritten "I leave everything I own to X." While a handwritten or "holographic" will such as this may be valid depending on where you live(d), that doesn't necessarily make it a *good* will. Wills can be amended or revised at any time, but again, you only get one last shot at it. Make a mistake and no one will know it until it's too late. For this reason do-it-yourself wills are not always recommended. What is recommended is that you visit Nolo Press and read up on the various Types of Wills available.

http://www.nolo.com/swill/2c.html

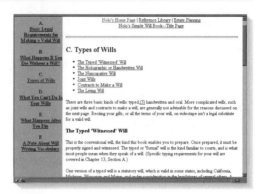

The wills of Benjamin Franklin, Elvis Presley, Jacqueline Kennedy Onasis, and a host of other celebrities past can be found on the Web site of Mark J. Welch. Depending on how you look at it, these wills can be seen as morbid memorabilia of the tabloid variety or as examples to be followed. If nothing else, they serve as a warning: Some of these people did everything they could while alive to protect their privacy. Once they died, however and their estates passed through probate court, it all became a matter of public record.

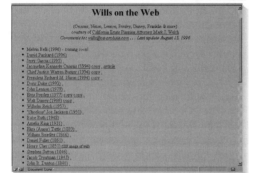

http://www.ca-probate.com/wills.htm

As Profit Financial Corporation explains it, privacy isn't the only issue at stake when an estate passes through probate. You can think of probate court as a final clearinghouse for all your earthly possessions. The court sees to it that all debts are paid off, divvies up your assets, and arranges for the care of any dependents. Unless you specify otherwise, how the assets are split and who takes care of the kids are at the sole discretion of the court. The court tries to be fair, but it may not take care of things the way you would have.

http://www.wadecook.com/probate.htm

Any property left through a will *must* go through probate piece by piece, a process which can shave off big chunks of an estate in fees and take years before finally being resolved. There are, however, ways of passing along property while minimizing the hassle of court, a hassle that some take so seriously that they'll do just about anything to avoid it. But how scared should you be of probate? Nolo Press might have an answer for you in one of their excellent articles, starting with Who's Afraid of Probate?

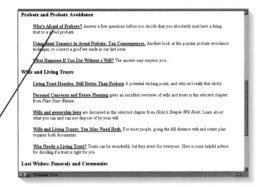

http://www.nolopress.com/estat.html

There are plenty of good reasons to minimize the time your estate spends in probate, but those reasons aren't equally valid for everybody. First off, not all assets pass through probate; jointly owned property with rights of survivorship doesn't (more on this later), neither does property with a named beneficiary, such as life insurance. If you have a simple, small estate, if creditors aren't a problem and if you don't expect a lot of infighting amongst your heirs, you may be searching for a solution to a problem you don't even have.

http://www.nolopress.com/nnprob.html

In the Who Needs a Living Trust? article Nolo Press shows how you can use a revocable living (or inter vivos) trust to avoid some of probates biggest problems. Like a will, a living trust allows you to leave property to the beneficiaries of your choice. But unlike a will, a trust passes through court as a single consolidated entity rather than a slew of individual items. The benefit is that your estate changes hands quicker, with potentially less expense and with your privacy intact. With some work, a living trust can also help reduce estate tax.

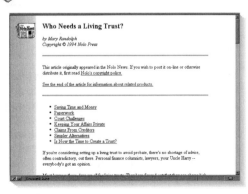

http://www.nolopress.com/nn168.html

Another way avoid the drawbacks of probate is to own property in joint tenancy with rights of survivorship. The Tennessee Bar Association explains how the process works and details some of its advantages and drawbacks but basically what it means that you own something, a house, a car, whatever, with someone else. When one of the owners dies, the surviving owners automatically gain his or her share in the property—without the need for probate. Joint tenants can be husband and wife but don't necessarily have to be.

http://www.tba.org/lawbytes/T15_2401.html

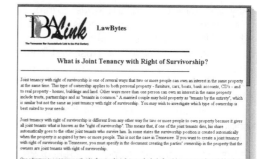

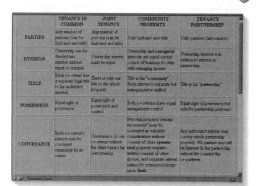

There are numerous ways to own a given piece of property. Discount Realty lists the most common in table format so that you can readily compare one against the other and decide on the one that makes the most sense for your situation. Frankly, none of them are without their disadvantages. Owning something in joint tenancy with rights of survivorship, for example, does allow the property to avoid probate, but it also has tax and other implications that you're going to want to discuss in detail with a professional.

http://discountrealty.com/own.htm

Estate Taxes

What, you didn't think actually think that a little thing like death would get you off the hook with the IRS, did you?

As Kennedy and Coe, LLC points out on their Web pages, there is a penalty for failure to file a tax return when due unless the failure results from "reasonable cause." Dying, it would seem, is no excuse. Unless you can figure out a way to file your return from beyond the grave it becomes the responsibility of your personal representative to do it on your behalf.

http://www.kcoe.com/dthtaxes.htm

One last look at your annual income doesn't mean that the IRS is ready to let you R.I.P. just yet. While yearly tax returns generally look at no more than the last 365 days, estate tax is based on everything you manage to accumulate over a lifetime. The more that federal and state governments take in taxes the less you have to leave behind.

Deloitte & Touche LLP shows how with estate planning you can lower those taxes and help see to it that your legacy finds it's way into the right hands.

http://www.dtonline.com/pfin/gtintro.htm

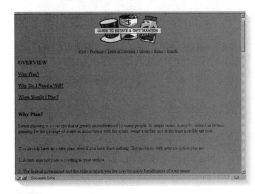

One of the problems with estate planning is that so few of us know how long we have left in which to make our plans. Estate planning therefore becomes an ongoing process. Every once in a while you should check to make sure you're still alive. If you find that you are, you may want to revise your plans to meet your current financial and familial situation. If you find that you're not, don't worry about it.

Do a quick check now; if you're still there and have a large estate, or at least hope to at some point, click on the magic number, $600,000.

http://www.dtonline.com/pfin/gtintro.htm

When you look at the value of your estate make sure to include everything, life insurance, real estate, velvet paintings of poker playing dogs- ev-ry-thing. The IRS certainly will. You are granted a $600,000 "unified credit" that can be passed on tax free. Anything beyond that is taxed, heavily. Rates start at a whopping 37% and go onwards and upwards from there. And that's not even including the inheritance tax that individual states may want to collect on top of that. With rates like these, if you weren't dead already the taxes would kill you.

http://www.dtonline.com/pfin/gttaxcmp.htm#valuation

No matter how large the estate being passed on is, if it's left to the spouse of the deceased it falls under the <u>unlimited marital deduction</u> and is not subject to estate tax. That's the good news. The bad news, as the <u>Trust Counselors' Network</u> explains it, is that this simply defers the issue of taxes until the death of the surviving spouse. If the estate is still worth more than $600,000 at that time you'll find the taxman will still be waiting for you, patient but not forgetful. You can take your time about it, but in the end you always have to pay the piper.

http://www.trustcounsel.org/articles/tcn0013/pg7.htm

THE MARITAL DEDUCTION

The Marital Deduction is a major element to be considered in tax planning for the transfers of gifts and estate assets. The Marital Deduction is available in addition to, and independent of, the Unified Credit.

Internal Revenue Code §2056 allows an unlimited Marital Deduction for property passing to a surviving spouse. This means that no matter how large and estate, the entire estate is left to the spouse, the entire amount will qualify for the Marital Deduction and there will be no estate taxes due. For example, if the gross estate is $1,500,000 and the entire estate is bequeathed to the spouse in a form which qualifies for the Marital Deduction, then the tax would be computed as follows:

- Gross Estate..............$1,500,000
- less: Marital Deduction...$1,500,000
- Taxable Estate............$0
- Tentative Tax.............$0

In the foregoing example, the Unified Credit was not used. All of the assets bequeathed to the surviving spouse will be included in the surviving spouse's estate. Thus, the Marital Deduction basically allows only a deferral of the Estate Tax until the time of the second death. The Marital Deduction does not result in a "forgiveness" of the tax.

It is advantageous to take advantage of the Marital Deduction because the value of the deferral of the tax until the time of the second death is (usually great). The assets will presumably grow and/or produce income during the lifetime of the surviving spouse, thereby providing additional assets available for ultimate distribution to the children. Also, the surviving spouse has the benefit of the full use of the funds for life.

GO ON TO NEXT PAGE
Return to This Article Index

How to **Save $240,000** Using Basic Estate Planning

Facts: Married couple with children. Husband dies first. All property in his name. Assume no appreciation in asset values between deaths of husband and wife. Also assume combined Federal and State Death Tax Rate is 40%.

Gross Estate

House Estate	$200,000
Personal Property	50,000
Investments	600,000
Retirement Plans	200,000
Life Insurance	150,000
Total	$1,200,000

Scenario 1: Simple Wills - leave everything to surviving spouse outright. (Same result if all property were held jointly with right of survivorship.)

Husband's Death	$1,200,000	Gross Taxable Estate
	-1,200,000	Marital Deduction
	-0-	Net Taxable Estate
Wife's Death	$1,200,000	Gross Taxable Estate
	- 600,000	Exemption (thru $192,800 Credit)
	$600,000	Net Taxable Estate

How big a problem you will ultimately have with estate taxes depends on how big an estate you manage to accumulate. For couples with assets of up to $1,200,000 the estate can be split up into two pieces, each falling within the limits of the $600,000 unified credit. If piece A is left to spouse B it must be done in such a way that the income is available while still being treated as a separate estate for tax purposes. Enter <u>Webb & Craven</u> with their recommendations on how a <u>marital trust</u> can save you big bucks.

http://www.sandhills.org/webb/howto.htm

Before we go any further and look at the various methods that can be used to reduce or eliminate estate taxes, now might be a good time to try out the <u>Sun Life</u> <u>Estate Tax Calculator</u> and judge for yourself how large a tax problem your heirs will ultimately have to face.

Pop in your total assets and total liabilities in the spaces provided and click on the "Calculate Taxes on Estate" button for the results. And remember, this is only an estimate, an estimate that will change as your fortunes do.

http://www.sunlife-usa.com/estate_tax.html

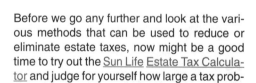

Estate Planning:
Estate Tax Calculator

A Federal Estate Tax is imposed on the transfer of the taxable estate of every deceased person who is a citizen or resident of the U.S. Each person has a Unified Credit of $192,800 that will reduce the amount of the estate tax due. This is the equivalent of having $600,000 of assets which will not be subject to the Federal Estate Tax, assuming the credit has not been used against taxable gifts during the person's life.

To determine your taxable estate, you'll need to estimate your total assets and total liabilities. When you've done so, enter them below and we'll calculate your taxable estate and your total estate tax. If your estate tax equals zero, your total estate is less than the Unified Credit of $192,800.

Please keep in mind that this is only an estimate of your estate tax. Sun Life advises you to consult your lawyer, accountant and/or tax advisor for a more accurate number.

Please enter total assets

Please enter total liabilities

Calculate Taxes on Estate

E M A I L   S U N L I F E

Paying your fair share in taxes is only fair, but paying more than you need to is just plain silly. If the government's idea of what's fair sends you into fits of nervous laughter, the onus is on you to come up with a creative solution. As it turns out, the least creative solution when the problem is too much money is to spend it. Passing a sizable inheritance on to future generations is a noble goal, but there's nothing wrong with enjoying yourself either. After all, isn't that why you worked so hard to make that money in the first place?

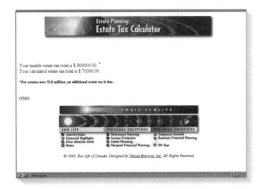

http://www.sunlife-usa.com/estate_tax.html

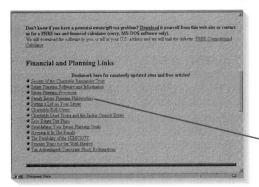

Henry & Associates has another good site with links to articles detailing some of the methods that can be used to make sure your estate makes it into the right hands.

One of the more interesting articles on the site isn't so much about tax avoidance schemes then it is about honest and timely self reflection. Before going any further with your plans click on Family Estate Planning Philosophies and pause to consider your feelings, as well as your finances.

http://web.profiles.com/Estate.html

 ## Keeping It In the Family

The technical details of who you're planning to leave what to are important, obviously, but the reasons *why* you do what you do shouldn't get lost in the shuffle. And sometimes, being clear in your own head isn't enough.

The idea of speaking with your loved ones about your wishes can be an uncomfortable proposition, but sharing your feelings about something as important as your legacy may help stave off any misunderstandings when your no longer around to explain yourself.

http://web.profiles.com/CRT-5.html

Family Philosophies

Financial planners often help clients create an investment philosophy to define the level of risk, the need for liquidity and the time frame for making their investments. Clients starting the estate planning process should create something similar. Under the typical planning arrangements of wills and trusts, those documents tell heirs what and when things are to happen, but not why you planned the way you did. A written philosophy will help clients achieve their objectives in the accumulation, management and distribution of their personal wealth. While establishing priorities, this is an opportunity to protect assets and pass down a set of values held by the client. These objectives, once stated, help your professional advisors create tools that better meet those goals. Scott Fithian has been particularly helpful in articulating these objectives in the planning process and the National Alliance of Renaissance Associates (NARA) has promoted much of it as a concept worthy of inclusion in all plans.

Wealth is a relative concept, but nobody wants to unnecessarily waste a lifetime's work. What results do you want when family assets are preserved and passed on to your heirs?
· a financial edge, giving heirs a leg-up on future successes
· improved competency through education and enhanced self-esteem
· an incentive to create and develop up to their full potential
· a sense of tradition, loyalty and family harmony
· a desire to serve others or acquire societal impact

There are conflicting concerns about passing down unearned wealth, and the different positions each have some justification. Some parents feel an obligation to pass down their wealth and leave their children better off than they were. On the other hand, a few parents have strong beliefs about having heirs make their own way. Their belief is that by overcoming adversity heirs may somehow improve their work ethic and leave their potential. Since divorce affects nearly 50 percent of marriages, a few parents may have justifiable concerns about the possible loss of family wealth. While other parents fear the dilution of family assets among many heirs will result in the complete lack of influence for those inheriting. There are no right answers, but the fact that you take

After covering some of the approaches to family philosophies, Henry & Associates go on to discuss Keeping It In The Family. With "It," in this case, being the family business.

Passing a business on from one generation to the next requires careful planning in order to ensure as smooth a transition as possible with a minimum amount erosion. "Keeping It In The Family" has some suggestions on ways to protect yourself against preventable expenses but warns against using excessively low valuations as a way to reduce taxes.

http://web.profiles.com/CRT-11.html

Keeping It In The Family

Except for bankruptcy, is it easier to get into than out of business? If so, then do some serious planning to keep that hard earned asset from being wasted. A Cornell study estimated that property in excess of $10 trillion is due to change hands during the next twenty years. With a treasure like that, could it be better protected? Since wealthy folks have a legion of tax advisors coaching them on ways to avoid problems, it turns out that middle and upper-middle class taxpayers' estates are due to take the biggest percentage of hits. Appreciated assets gathered through years of hard work, great planning or just plain luck will experience major erosion. Those losses occur because of poor planning and are generally avoidable. When the Depression era generation passes the torch to the baby-boomers, you can bet the IRS will be there for its cut, and a hefty one at is. The main goal for families affected by this generational shift in capital is to preserve value and options without paying unnecessary taxes and expenses.

Of course the IRS has a little something to say about techniques designed to reduce the tax bite. The good news is that limiting tax exposure works for everyone, but it takes action. Since liquidity is a problem for even the largest estates, a going concern needs a ready buyer to convert illiquid family businesses to cash. Good buyers could include family members, insurance trusts, key employees or competitors. Unfortunately, this solution is rarely available, since getting the best price for a business that just lost the "rainmaker" is difficult. As long as few businesses can survive without top management responsible for its profit potential, it makes sense to plan ahead. One of the best tools used to control a closely held business without a ready market is the buy-sell agreement. This arrangement is designed to avoid major shocks to management when a principal owner steps out of the picture. Triggered by retirement, death or disability, almost everyone agrees a contract provides certainty, but who really profits from a well-designed agreement?

· The family, since a fair price has already been negotiated and the funding secured for a business that has provided them with years of financial support. There

---

 ## Trusts and Taxes

TRUSTS FAQ

OUTLINE

1. What is a trust? What is the difference between a revocable and an irrevocable trust?

2. Are there limitations on the kinds of assets that can be placed in a trust?

4. What are the responsibilities of the trustee? What happens if the trustee dies?

5. Is there a difference between a trust set up during my lifetime and one set up in my will?

6. How is a trust terminated?

7. Can a beneficiary alter the terms of the trust?

8. What are the tax implications of a trust? For the beneficiary? For the person who establishes the trust?

9. How are Trustees paid? If I don't want the Trustee to get paid, what should I do?

10. Why should I create a trust?

11. Can I set up a trust that will protect assets from my child's creditors?

1. What is a trust? What is the difference between a revocable and an irrevocable trust?

A trust is a legal arrangement under which a person transfers funds to another person or an institution with directions on how to manage the property for the benefit of a third party. Trusts take a variety of forms and have many uses in estate planning. There

Once you're clear that you'd like to keep it in the family you have to start looking around at your options; A search that inevitably leads you to irrevocable trusts and the trust FAQ from Teahan & Constantino.

Unlike the revocable living trusts we looked at earlier, which can be changed or revoked as your moods dictate, you had better be real sure about your decision before setting up an irrevocable trust. Because while there are distinct tax advantages to be had through irrevocable trusts, there's no going back.

http://www1.mhv.net/~teahan/trfaq.htm

The reason why irrevocable trusts carry tax benefits as well as an air of finality is that the government taxes estates. Anything that you give away is no longer part of your estate. Simple enough, right? The catch is that you really do have to give it away. As long as you reserve the right to take it back you never really gave it away in the first place.

Reinhart, Boerner, Van Deuren, Norris & Rieselbach, s.c. looks at some of the many ways of giving it away, starting with Using Your Annual Gift Tax Exclusions.

http://www.rbvdnr.com/te/1.htm

Minimizing Estate Taxes

Using A Family Trust To Minimize Estate Taxes

How Can You Leave Your Estate To Your Spouse Estate Tax Free?

Using Your Annual Gift Tax Exclusions

Should You Use Your $600,000 Estate & Gift Tax Exclusion During Your Life?

Life Insurance Trusts

What Is A Grantor Retained Interest Trust ("GRAT")?

What Is A Qualified Personal Residence Trust ("QPRT")?

What Is A Family Limited Partnership ("FLP")?

What Is The Generation-Skipping Transfer Tax ("GST")?

Liquidity - Will Your Estate Have Enough?

Wisconsin's Marital Property Law

Marital Property Agreements

Disability Planning

If the problem is giving away too much when you die, why not just give it away while you're still alive? Each of us is allowed to give away up to $10,000 in gifts each year to as many people as we want without incurring any estate or gift taxes. Do that for enough years and the tax savings can be substantial. If you're in the position to do it, it's a good way to ease your tax burden and make your heirs happy in the bargain. And besides, think how nice it would be to see your heirs enjoy your gifts? Hey mom, dad? Wouldn't that be nice?

http://www.rbvdnr.com/te/1l.htm

Using Your Annual Gift Tax Exclusions

Every individual may give up to $10,000 to any number of recipients each year without being subject to federal gift taxes. Because a spouse may join in making such gifts, husband and wife together may give $20,000 annually to any number of recipients without incurring any federal gift taxes. Because the marginal federal estate tax brackets begin at 37% for estates subject to tax, for every $10,000 given during lifetime, at least $3,700 of death taxes can be saved. The maximum federal estate tax bracket is 55% for taxable estates of $3,000,000 or more. In addition, of course, any appreciation in the property after the date of the gift also escapes being taxed in the decedent's estate. From a tax savings standpoint, property likely to appreciate in value, often makes the most appropriate gift.

To qualify for the annual exclusion, a gift must be of a "present interest." This is intended to limit the availability of the exclusion where the gift is made to a trust. Certain kinds of trusts (such as "2503 (c)" and "Crummey" trusts), nonetheless, qualify to receive annual exclusion gifts.

Previous Article

Next Article

Previous Menu

Should You Use Your $600,000 Estate & Gift Tax Exclusion During Your Life?

A donor may wish to make a gift in excess of the annual exclusion. The $600,000 estate tax exemption can be used to offset large gifts as well as to offset federal estate taxes. Thus, a donor can give as much as $600,000 without paying any federal gift taxes. The principal advantage in making a large gift is to remove from the estate the expected appreciation in the asset after the gift is made. By making the gift, the growth in the asset occurs in the hands of the recipient, presumably the next generation. If an asset appreciated from $500,000 to $1,000,000 after the gift, the savings in giving the asset could be as much as $275,000.

It must also be noted that the level of scrutiny by the Internal Revenue Service on the valuation of gifts of property that does not have a readily ascertainable value is significantly less than the scrutiny in federal estate tax proceedings. There is significant latitude in valuing closely held stock for the purpose of making gifts.

Previous Article

Next Article

Previous Menu

Clicking on the Next Article link brings you forward, in this case to a discussion on the merits and pitfalls of large gifts.

As far as the IRS is concerned you can give away as much of your estate as you want. But bear in mind that gifts larger than what the annual gift tax exclusion allows for eats into the $600,000 that you are entitled to give away tax-free throughout your lifetime. Even then, besides putting a smile on somebody's face, you may see a tax benefit if the assets grow in the hands of the happy recipient.

http://www.rbvdnr.com/te/1m.htm

Before hitting some of the more advanced estate planning techniques, let's sidestep for a second and visit the Charitable Remainder Trusts article found elsewhere on this site.

There are various types of charitable remainder trusts but they all boil down to reducing your estate (and, not incidentally, being a nice person) by promising to give all or a portion of your assets to a worthy cause upon your death. In the meanwhile, you get to receive payments from the trust while you're still alive.

http://www.rbvdnr.com/te/7a.htm

Charitable Remainder Trusts

I. INTRODUCTORY COMMENTS.

A. A charitable remainder trust permits a taxpayer (the donor) to diversify his investments, defer the income tax consequence on the sale of capital gain property, and make a charitable gift as well. The net result is that the donor receives a distribution from the charitable remainder trust which can be diversified tax free, and, in effect, the U.S. Government shares the cost of making a gift to a charity chosen by the donor. Given the right scenario, there may be no net cost to the donor and the donor's family.

B. A charitable remainder trust is a trust to which a donor transfers property, retaining the right to receive a stream of annual payments from the trust for a term chosen by the donor. Usually, the term is for the donor's life and even for the life of the donor's spouse. After the term has run, the trust estate is paid to a public charity designated by the donor.

C. This article is designed to provide a fundamental understanding of what a charitable remainder trust is and how it operates. The comments assume a gift of low basis assets (either marketable or nonmarketable) which will likely be sold by the trust shortly after they are transferred to the trust.

II. TWO TYPES OF CHARITABLE REMAINDER TRUSTS.

A. **Charitable remainder annuity trust ("CRAT").**

1. Annual payment to donor (and/or family) is a fixed dollar amount set when trust is created; the amount does not vary if trust increases or decreases, i.e. "income" flow protection if trust estate decreases in value but no protection from inflation.

"GRITs," "GRATs," and "GRUTs" may sound like a condition you'd want to treat with a high-fiber diet but they are all ways of having your estate cake and eating it too.

In the simplest of terms, these three variants on the Grantor Retained Interest Trust theme allow you to retain some level of control over your assets during your lifetime while reducing the value of those assets from the perspective of the IRS. They are also, in a sense, a gamble: The tax saving value of the trust depends in large part on how long you live.

http://www.rbvdnr.com/te/1n1.htm

What Is A Grantor Retained Interest Trust ("GRAT")?

1. Introduction

A grantor retained annuity trust ("GRAT") is a trust to which a donor transfers property, retaining the right to receive annual payments from the trust for a term chosen by the donor. A taxable gift is made as to the present value of the remainder interest in the property. If the grantor survives the fixed term, the entire value of the property escapes estate tax. The value of the grantor's annuity interest is subtracted from the value of the trust property in determining the amount of the taxable gift resulting from the creation of the trust. The transaction is leveraged in the sense that the gift removes a larger amount from the grantor's gross estate for estate tax purposes than is subject to the gift tax. Basically, a GRAT allows property to be transferred to member of the grantor's family at a reduced transfer tax cost.

2. Incentive To Create A GRAT.

With an asset which is expected to outperform the current federal interest rates used to value such gifts, the remainder interest will be undervalued when the trust is created—that is, the present value of the remainder interest for gift tax purposes will be less than the present interest of the property the remaindermen actually receive.

In fact, if the assets are expected to significantly outperform the federal rate, the grantor can create a "zeroed-out" GRAT. A "zeroed-out GRAT" is a GRAT in which the annuity amount is so high that the value of the remainder interest is zero, so that at the time of the transfer to the trust, no gift is made. Thus, the grantor does not have to use up any of his unified credit when he transfer property to the trust.

3. Basic Structure.

What Is A Qualified Personal Residence Trust ("QPRT")?

1. Description.

A Qualified Personal Residence Trust ("QPRT") is an irrevocable trust created by the Grantor for his or her own benefit. The Grantor transfers a primary or secondary residence (the Property) to the trust and retains the continued right to use the Property for the term of the trust. The Grantor selects a term of years the trust will exist. After the trust ends, the Property will pass to the named trust beneficiaries.

2. Operation.

    a. During Term of Trust.

The Grantor will have unlimited access to and use of the Property. Rights include the right to occupy the Property, have guests join them at the Property, receive rentals if the Property is rented to third persons, and sell Property and purchase other substitute Property. The Grantor is responsible for paying all expenses relating to the Property.

    b. Termination of Trust.

i. Expiration of Trust Term. If the term of the trust expires during the Grantor's life, the Property will pass from the trust to the remainder beneficiaries. The terms of the trust can provide that at the end of the term, the Grantor has the right to rent the residence from the remainder beneficiaries at fair market value or to purchase the property from the remainder beneficiaries at fair market value.

ii. Upon Death. If the Grantor fails to survive the term of the trust, the trust will end. The Grantor's interest

A Qualified Personal Residence Trust or "QPRT" is yet another type of Grantor Retained Interest Trust. It too is a gamble of sorts. Basically, the way it works is that the you transfer your residence into a trust and are then allowed to reside in that residence for a specified period of time. If you die before the terms of the trust expires, the value of the home is subject to estate tax. If you outlive the terms of the trust, part of the value of the residence escapes gift and estate tax altogether and you get to buy your own house back.

http://www.rbvdnr.com/te/1n2.htm

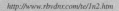

One of the issues faced by anyone hoping to reduce the size of their estate by giving gifts is that once a gift is given you lose any say as to how it is handled. Family Limited Partnerships (FLP's) allow the giver to reap all the tax benefits that go hand-in-hand with generosity while still reserving the right to manage and control the purse strings.

FLPs aren't for everybody. For one thing they are expensive to set up. But for the affluent, they can be a good way to reduce taxes while maintaining financial control.

http://www.rbvdnr.com/te/1.htm

What Is A Family Limited Partnership ("FLP")

1. General Structure.

    a. A general partner controls all decisions and a limited partner typically has no voting rights.

    b. Parents or grandparents ("Senior Generation") contribute assets to a limited partnership and initially hold all the partnership interests ("Interests"). Senior Generation makes the only contributions and is the sole general partner in the limited partnership (although it may also own limited partner units in the limited partnership).

    c. Children or grandchildren ("Junior Generation") do not contribute assets to the partnership or only contribute assets with a nominal value.

    d. The Junior Generation receive limited partner units in the limited partnership as gifts from the Senior Generation. Generally, these are gifts of present interests and are eligible for the $10,000 annual exclusion.

2. Typical Assets To Be Transferred To The Partnership.

    a. Real estate.

    b. Marketable Securities

    c. Stock in closely held C Corporations, not S Corporations, due to limitations on S Corporation shareholders.

    d. Operating businesses.

Each state has discretion as to how it handles the transfer of assets. Some states don't have a death or inheritance tax at all. Whatever the laws in your state, you still have three separate federal taxes to contend with. The first two, the gift tax and estate tax, have been covered. The third tax, the Generation-Skipping Transfer Tax (GSTT), applies to any assets above $1 million that skip a generation (e.g., to grandchildren). The GSTT is an enormous, across-the-board rate of 55 percent and applies *in addition* to applicable estate and gift taxes. Ouch.

http://www.rbvdnr.com/te/1n4.htm

What Is The Generation-Skipping Transfer Tax ("GST")?

1. How The Tax Works.

For practical purposes, the tax covers transfers to grandchildren.

    a. A GST tax is imposed (in addition to the gift or estate tax) on transfers to "skip persons." A skip person is defined as:

        i. A related individual two or more generations below the generation of the transferor.

        ii. An unrelated individual 37-1/2 or more years younger than the transferor.

        iii. A trust if all interests are held by skip persons.

    b. The rate of tax is 55% of the property transferred in excess of the exemptions and exclusions discussed below.

2. Exemptions, Exclusions and Exceptions from GST Tax.

    a. Each donor has a $1 million exemption from the generation-skipping transfer tax.

    b. A gift which qualifies for the gift tax annual exclusion also generally qualifies for generation-skipping transfer exclusion. That is, a gift of less than $10,000 given outright to a grandchild is not subject to GST. On the other hand a gift of less than $10,000 to a trust will be exempt from GST if the trust is for the benefit of only one person.

Liquidity

Liquidity - Will Your Estate Have Enough?

Generally

When an individual dies, his or her estate often suffers high needs for cash due to taxes, administration expenses and the need to support dependant family members. Even if the individual possessed some degree of wealth, often the assets making up the estate cannot be easily converted to needed cash. These concerns are addressed through "liquidity planning."

Liquidity Planning - Examples

- $2 million dollar estate, *all* of which is vacant land. Death taxes are $588,000, and are payable 9 months after death. Where will the cash come from?

- $3 million dollar estate, 50% of which is the family business. Two children, but only one active in the business. the Estate Plan leaves the business to the child active in the business. Death taxes are $1,098,000. The active child gets the business ($1.5 million) and the other child gets $402,000, which is the balance of the estate, net of taxes.

Common Approaches To Liquidity Planning

There are only two ways to deal with liquidity issues: by reducing taxes and expenses which require liquidity and by increasing liquidity

1. Reduce Taxes and Expenses

As opposed to the enviable problems inherent with leaving millions to the grandkids, liquidity is an issue that we must all face. And here's why; When you die, any estate taxes due must be paid within nine months of your death. If a large portion of your estate is tied up, in a large family home for example, this could prove to be a big problem for your heirs. It may mean that much of your estate will need to be sold off at bargain basement prices just so that the taxes could be paid. By planning in advance it is a problem that can be avoided.

http://www.rbvdnr.com/te/1o.htm

One way to give an estate liquidity is through the use of a Life Insurance Trust. Normally, the person being insured pays the premiums on a policy and the proceeds are added to his or her estate. With a life insurance trust the trust becomes the beneficiary and the premiums are paid from gifts made to the trust. Since it's the trust that "owns" the policy and pays the premiums the insurance proceeds aren't subject to estate taxes or the delays of probate. The intended beneficiaries get more of the money and they get it sooner.

http://www.rbvdnr.com/te/1n.htm

Life Insurance Trusts

1. Overview

Many of our clients assign life insurance to an irrevocable trust. Life insurance proceeds, like all other assets, are taxable in the estate of the insured if he owned or had any incidence of ownership of the insurance policy. If, however, the insured assigns the ownership of the policy to a trust which he cannot change and lives at least three years after the date of the assignment, the proceeds should not be included in his taxable estate. The trust could be drafted to provide for a spouse and/or for a child. If the surviving spouse was the beneficiary of the trust, any assets remaining in the trust, would not be included in the surviving spouse's taxable estate. The trust would control the disposition of the assets remaining at the surviving spouse's death and any growth in the assets in the trust would be excluded from the surviving spouse's taxable estate as well. If the insurance death benefit were $1,000,000, the savings by assigning such a policy to an irrevocable trust could be as high as $550,000

2. Detailed Description

Purpose:

An insurance trust is a trust which cannot be revoked or modified, which holds one or more insurance policies. An insurance trust is created to avoid gift and estate tax on policy proceeds (generally, insurance proceeds are already exempt from income tax). The estate tax does not reach the policy proceeds because the trust, and not the insured, "owns" the policy.

Structure:

An insurance trust either receives previously issued insurance policies from the original owner (usually the insured)

Which brings us to broader subject of life insurance and the Web site of the <u>Life and Health Insurance Foundation for Education</u>.

There are about a billion life insurance company Web sites out there these days (allright, *slight* exaggeration), but if you're looking for information that at least *pretends* to be unbiased, this is the best of the bunch. The site is split up into a few sensibly arranged areas. We'll hit the first two. Click on <u>Insurance 101</u> to get a feel for how this stuff works.

http://www.life-line.org

Here's where you're going to learn the basics of life insurance. Under the various subheadings you'll find items of interest such as a buying guide, an article describing the difference between term and permanent (aka whole life) insurance, how to choose a company, and what to look for in an agent. If you're into that kind of thing you'll also find the history of insurance through the ages and, just in case you get confused, a glossary of insurance terms. Explore on your own if you like but for now try clicking on "Estate Planning."

http://www.life-line.org

Under the Estate Planning page you'll find a list of what they consider to be the "Top 10 Pitfalls in Estate Planning." We've covered most of this stuff in the rest of the chapter but you'll want to go through the list just the same and check each item off to make sure that you haven't missed anything important. Oddly enough, one of the Top Pitfalls that isn't to be found on this list is the failure to make sure that you are adequately covered by life insurance. To find that out you'll need to head over to the "Life Calculators" section of the site.

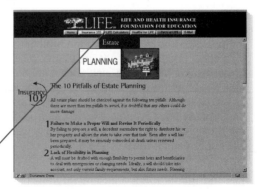

http://www.life-line.org

There are three separate calculators grouped together in this section. The first, the Human Life Value Calculator attempts to impress upon you the financial burden that your death would impose upon those you love. The second, the Disability Income Needs calculator shows you how much you'd need to sustain your current standard of living should you become incapacitated. Last but not least is the Life Insurance Needs Calculator which estimates the amount of life insurance coverage you should be carrying. Try clicking on that one.

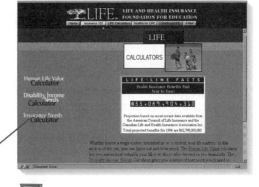

http://www.life-line.org

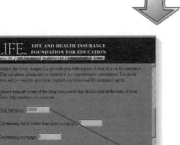

http://www.life-line.org

Unlike the Human Life Value calculator which shows your total earning capacity through your effective wage earning life span, the Insurance Needs calculator estimates how much money your family would need to meet immediate obligations and how much future income would be needed to sustain the household.

You're going to fill in the blanks and click on "Analysis." When you use this calculator note that although the "Final Expenses" field doesn't specify it, this is where you'll include estate taxes and liquidity needs if applicable.

The amount of coverage the calculator recommends is only as accurate as the information you supply is current. As your situation changes your insurance policy should change to reflect your new needs.

If you've just had a baby, *mazel tov*. Now go out and get some more insurance. If your biggest baby has just finished her last year of college, congratulations again. Now maybe you could cut back on those high premiums that you've been paying.

http://www.life-line.org

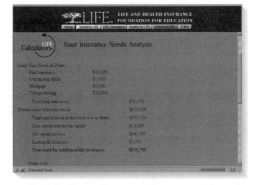

<u>Second to Die Insurance</u> is a relatively low-cost life type of insurance that may be worth looking into, especially if you anticipate leaving a large estate to your spouse. You saw earlier how through the <u>unlimited marital deduction</u> you can leave even a large estate to a spouse without having any estate tax due. But after the death of the surviving spouse the IRS will want it's cut. <u>Insurance InLinea</u> explains how by using second to die insurance you can offset what might otherwise be a heavy tax crunch for your heirs.

http://www.inlinea.com/est2nd.asp

Once you have a good idea about the size and type of insurance policy that you're looking for be sure to shop around before signing on any dotted lines. On the Web site of <u>American Financial Services</u> you can compare the term life plans of over 2,000 "A" rated or better Life Insurance companies in the United States and Canada. Besides being free, one of the nice things about shopping over the Web it is that you don't have to feel obligated to take a policy simply because you feel that you've somehow "wasted" the time of the agent.

http://www.magg.net/~michaels/quote.html

There's no need to feel like you're wasting anybody's time. It's their job. So fill out the form and let them get to work for you. They'll mail you a quote based on the information that you supply.

And don't stop there either. The life insurance industry is pretty competitive. Try one of the <u>other quote services on the Internet</u> and call up a couple of brokers before you sign anything. Show each of them what the other came up with and see if they can do something better for you. It's your life and your money.

http://www.magg.net/~michaels/quote.html

The National Insurance Store bill themselves as "The largest one stop source of life insurance and health insurance companies and agents on the Net" and it may very well be. It's certainly a convenient place to turn to if you're trying to find an insurance agent to call your own or locate the on-line home of an insurance company. Try the Find an Agent link and find a someone that can help you find just the right policy or click on Locate an Insurance Company and research the companies that hold your life in their hands.

National Insurance Store
Key To Your Future

Find an Agent
Obtain a Free Quote
Visit the Educational Section

The largest, one stop source, of LIFE insurance and HEALTH insurance companies and agents, on the Net.

Finding help with life insurance or health insurance problems is easy, fast and in your own area.

Find an Agent

Questions about Insurance

Locate an Insurance Company

Agents - How you can be listed here

http://www.cland.net/~instore/insurance/

Some of North America's finest insurance companies appear here. Others are currently preparing home pages and will be here soon.

Some of the following insurance companies are located on other servers

Use your back button to return to this page.

Aetna Life Insurance and Annuity Company
Aid Association for Lutherans
Alliance Blue Cross Blue Shield (located in Missouri)
American International Companies
Ameritas Life Insurance
American Mutual Life Insurance
Canada Life
Commercial Life Insurance Company
Forethought Life Insurance Company
General American Life
Great American Insurance Group
Great West Life and Assurance Company
Industrial Alliance Life Insurance Company
Kansas City Life Insurance Company
Keyport Life Insurance Company
Indianapolis Life Insurance Company
ITT Hartford
Lincoln Benefit Insurance Company

Some of the life insurance company Home pages offer helpful advice and colorful Web gizmos and gadgets to play around with. Most of them though, in all honesty, are pretty bland. But even the dullest of the bunch will offer, at the very least, financial information about themselves. This may not be your idea of fun but it's something that shouldn't be ignored. After all, you probably want to stick around for a good long time. You'll want to know that your life insurance company will still be there long after you're not.

http://www.cland.net/~instore/insurance/inscomp/company.html

 Top Ten Estate Planning Goof-Ups

We looked at a Top 10 Estate Planning Mistakes list a few pages back. It may seem redundant, but I would suggest you look over the Top Ten Estate Planning Goof-ups that made Randy Carter's list as well.

What's interesting about these two lists is how little they have in common. What that should tell you is that when it comes to estate planning there are enough bloopers, bleeps, and blunders to go around for everybody.

http://www.bullmkt.com/estate.html

Top Ten Estate Planning Goof-ups

by Randy Carver

When beginning to plan for leaving their property to heirs, people are confronted and frightened by the high estate tax rates and rush to utilize sophisticated estate planning techniques to avoid them. Yet, there are some simple moves that can frustrate these elaborate plans and are easily avoided. Here are some of the common mistakes to watch out for.

(1) **Not Funding Your Living Trust.** Many individuals have attempted to install a modern estate plan and use a living trust. Yet, too many fail to transfer the necessary property to the trust, which is like having a conductor without an orchestra.

(2) **Too Much JTWROS Property.** Titling assets under joint-tenancy-with-right-of-survivorship does avoid probate, yet does not avoid estate taxes. Further, improper titling can frustrate an estate plan because property titled JTWROS goes to the surviving joint tenant regardless of what a will says.

(3) **Leaving Too Many Assets to a Surviving Spouse.** Leaving all your property to your spouse does avoid estate taxes at the first death due to the unlimited marital deduction. However, such a plan wastes the first-to-die spouse's unified credit. It may also often be better to pay some estate taxes at the first death at lower marginal rates.

(4) **Not Equalizing Assets Through Gifts Between Spouses.** This is another example of improper titling and wasting the unified credit. Having all property titled in one spouse looks silly when the non-titled spouse dies first and does not pass on any property under her credit.

Taxes

Where Does It All Go?
- The Federal Budget
- The U.S. National Debt Clock
- Tax Factoids: The Flat Tax Home Page
- Angry Taxpayers

Tax Planning Strategies
- Basic Principles Designed to Successfully Minimize Taxes
- Making Hay While The Sun Shines: Tax Deferred Investments
- Tax Calender

State Taxes
- Income Tax Rates by State
- Links to State Tax Agency Home Pages

Preparation Software and Services
- Tax Preparation Software Programs
- All-Purpose Personal Finance Software
- Finding a Local Tax Preparer
- Tax Preparation Services on the Net

Doing It Yourself
- Test Your Tax I.Q.
- Essential Links to Tax Information
- Canadian Tax Sites
- Categorizing Yourself
- Choosing the Right Form
- Tax Brackets
- The Twenty-Five Most Common Tax Preparation Errors

The IRS Step-By-Step
- So This Is Where The Money Goes: The IRS Home Page
  - Publication 17: The IRS's Guide to Preparing Your Return
  - Tax Trails
  - Downloading The Necessary Forms
- Revenue Canada's Income Tax Guides, Forms, and Schedules

Calculating Your Taxes On-Line
- JavaScript 1040EZ
- NetTax '96

Audit's, Abuses, and Excuses
- Interactive Audit Bait Worksheet
- Cruel and Unusual Punishment
- When the Tax Man Cometh!
- Who's Afraid of the Big, Bad Wolf?
- The Humorous Side of Taxes

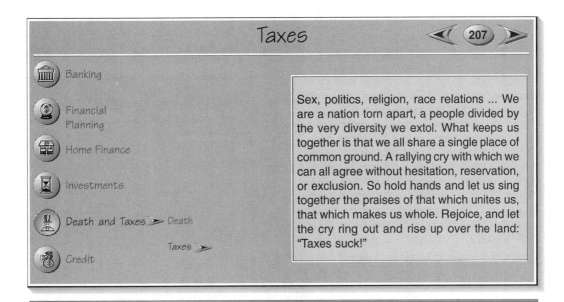

- Banking
- Financial Planning
- Home Finance
- Investments
- Death and Taxes ➤ Death
        Taxes ➤
- Credit

Sex, politics, religion, race relations ... We are a nation torn apart, a people divided by the very diversity we extol. What keeps us together is that we all share a single place of common ground. A rallying cry with which we can all agree without hesitation, reservation, or exclusion. So hold hands and let us sing together the praises of that which unites us, that which makes us whole. Rejoice, and let the cry ring out and rise up over the land: "Taxes suck!"

Where Does It All Go?

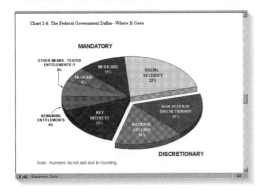

Chart 2-6. The Federal Government Dollar--Where It Goes

Before we open up the can of worms collectively referred to as taxes, it might interest you to know where all those hard-earned tax dollars are heading. There are a few places on the Web where you can find a line-by-tedious-line description of the latest budget, but for a bird's-eye view of the whole mess nothing beats a pie chart.

OMB, the President's Office of Management and Budget includes this savory treat in their Citizen's Guide to the Federal Budget. Pick out your least favorite piece and open wide.

http://www.doc.gov/BudgetFY97/guide2.html

I'm sorry to say so, but even with all this talk going round about balancing the budget, taxes aren't about to disappear any time soon. A balanced budget simply means that the government spends no more than what it takes in. That's a great plan, but it would still leave us with an enormous debt to pay off. Howard Hullen of TIPS has created this scary little program that shows the federal deficit spinning out of control. Pop some Gravol and head on over to compare the numbers shown here to the ones blurring by on your screen.

http://www.toptips.com/debtclock.html

If proponents of the flat tax model ever have their way, chapters like this one will no longer be necessary and tax returns will look like post-cards. In the meanwhile, you'll find some startling tax factoids on The Flat Tax Home page. Did you know, for example, that 293,760 trees are felled yearly to print the Federal Tax Regulations or that Americans devote 5.4 billion hours a year to tax-related paperwork? And that doesn't include the trees that gave their all to bring you this book or the time it's taken you to read it.

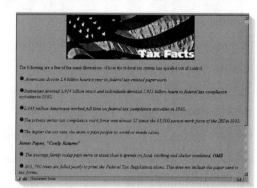

http://flattax.house.gov/taxfacts.htm

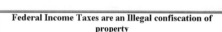

It's no wonder that there are a lot of very angry taxpayers out there. This article on the Wicked Cool site argues that Federal Income Taxes are an Illegal confiscation of property. Compared to some of the angriest tax sites on the Net, this one barely registers as miffed. The most rabid sites call for armed rebellion and a refusal to pay the "illegal" taxes—neither of which are very good ideas unless you intend to file your next return from behind bars. Miffed is OK, but taking out an IRS agent with an AK-47 is generally frowned upon.

http://www.wcool.com/mo96/0326.html

Tax Planning Strategies

Since not paying taxes is not a viable option, the next best thing you can do is minimize them. To that end David Ness of Raymond James & Associates offers some Basic Principles Designed to Successfully Minimize Taxes. Remember as you read what he has to say that these tips will work only as part of a cohesive strategy. Waiting until April the four-teenth to implement them just won't cut it. For to quote a tired old saying "a failure to plan is a plan for failure." It may be trite, but as far as taxes go, it's entirely true.

http://www.rjf.com/tax_plan.htm

Tax Planning: Basic Principles Designed to Successfully Minimize Taxes

by
David Ness
Vice President, Financial Planning
Raymond James & Associates

Taxes. For some investors, avoiding them is an obsession. Others, however, consider tax implications only after a transaction is executed or a financial plan implemented.

There are those who view tax planning as so complex that only the very sophisticated can solve the riddle and others who have concluded that various changes in legislation over the years have essentially eliminated any tax-saving possibilities.

Regardless of how an investor views them, tax implications should be considered with every financial planning decision he or she makes. With the current tax laws, there are opportunities for the savvy to save. Yet, costly traps also exist for the unwary or unsophisticated.

Just as financial planning decisions have tax implications, income tax decisions also have financial planning implications. When crafting a comprehensive financial plan, it is critically important to select those tax-saving strategies most consistent with achieving one's overall goals.

Intelligent tax planning is based on certain fundamental principals. When successfully understood, the principals that follow may help guide individuals to tax-smart decisions.

Taxes act like rust on investment returns.

The first fundamental principal of effective tax planning is to understand how taxes affect investment returns. Analyzing the tax impact of a strategy requires the use of marginal tax rates. Under current laws, there are five marginal tax rates: 15%, 28%,

You like cliches? I've got more of them than you can shake a stick at. How about "it takes money to make money" or " a penny saved is a penny earned" or maybe "don't put off 'till tomorrow what you can do ..." Hmm, scratch that last one. The point, as shown here on The Wealth Creator, is that even with tax-deferred investments, there's no such thing as a free lunch—you *will* have to pay the piper eventually. But by deferring your taxes you get to make hay while the sun shines and cross that bridge when you come to it.

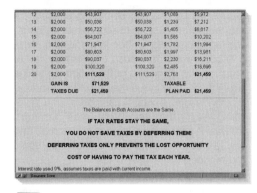

http://www.wealthcreator.com/myth1.html#Top

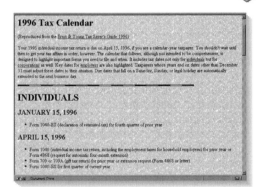

If you're going to be planning for taxes it sometimes helps to have a calendar. We all know that April fifteenth is T-day for most of us, but depending on the forms that you have to fill out you may be on a different schedule. Also, if you've had an extension (or even an extension on an extension) you will need to meet a difference deadline.

Ernst & Young has made a Tax Calender available. It highlights the important forms you need to file and the dates by which you need to file them.

http://www.ey.com/tax/calendar.htm

 ## State Taxes

All of this talk about taxes has so far concentrated strictly on Federal tax. But as many readers know all too well, states can, and often do, collect tax. Each state is different, with some collecting no taxes at all and others with rates as high as 12 percent of annual income. Whichever state you live in, and whatever its rules, the Federation of Tax Administrators Home Page has more information about the state taxes that you can expect to pay. Start by clicking on "State Tax Rates/Structures" and then on "State Individual Income."

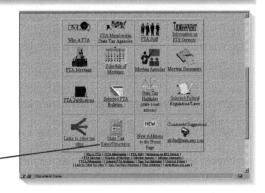

http://sso.org/fta/fta.html

Governments change, political promises are made and are just as often broken. In short, the following is not written in stone (if it were, this book would be *much* heavier) but as of July 1, 1996, residents of the following states are off the hook: Alaska, Florida, Nevada, South Dakota, Texas, Washington, and Wyoming. As for the rest of you, read on. You'll find basic information on each states high and low tax rates, income brackets, and personal exemptions.

http://sso.org/fta/ind_inc.html

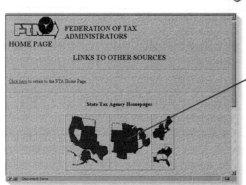

If you want more details, you'll have to return to the FTA Home page and select "Links to other tax sites." From here you begin to narrow the search by clicking on the appropriate chunk of the map and selecting a geographical region. You will then be able to choose states individually. Some states on-line offerings are pretty bare-bones, others have gee-whiz gizmos and on-line doodads that may prove so entertaining that you forget why you're there in the first place; to figure out how much they want to soak you for.

http://sso.org/fta/nestoa.html

Preparation Software and Services

With 50 states plus the District of Columbia each following their own tax agendas, state tax policies are fractured and second party assistance all but nonexistent. In contrast, Federal tax is something that we all have to contend with and there are any number of tax preparation software packages that can help you get a handle on them. Frank McNeil's TaxSites lists the Home pages of virtually every tax software publisher on the Net. Click on a name to learn more about what that program can, and can not, do for you.

http://www.best.com:80/%7Eftmexpat/html/taxsites/software.html

Millions of us do our own taxes, but unless you're some sort of an expert you may be paying more in taxes than you really owe. By using a specialized tax package or a good all-purpose personal finance program like Quicken you'll not only be able to track your taxes but you may even discover hidden deductions that you wouldn't have found yourself. Tax software won't lick the stamp for you or pay the IRS but at the very least it's a good way to keep on top of things and a better way to organize a shoebox full of receipts.

http://www.qfn.com/quicken/whatsnew/living-with-quicken/23-taxgift.html

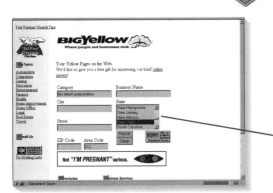

If there's one problem with using a tax program it's that you have to use it. Shelling out $64.95 on software only to find that you have neither the time nor inclination to use it leaves you no closer to getting your taxes done. If that's the case, save your money and put it towards a hiring a tax preparer, BigYellow will even help you find one. Enter the state name, zip, or area code in the space provided and click on "Find It!" for a list of tax preparers in your area. Sure beats pounding the streets with a shoebox full of receipts under your arm.

http://www.bigyellow.com

The ones with stars next to their names are well represented on the Net. You can click on them and go to their Web sites to check out rates and services or leave them some e-mail. The ones without stars are telecommunicationally deprived; they have phone numbers and addresses listed but there's no way to check them out at three in the morning. You'll have to wait until business hours to phone them or gather up all your papers in that shoebox and start wandering down the street.

http://www.bigyellow.com

If finding a tax preparer *through* the Net left you somewhat underwhelmed, you can now try using a tax preparer *on* the Net. With on-line tax preparation services like the Tax Wizard starting to crop up, you may find that the closest tax preparer isn't down the street but on your desk.

You can click on the Tax Preparation Service link to send them the information they need to complete your taxes. Or try clicking on Ask the Wizard and e-mail a particularly thorny tax related question to the wizards.

http://taxwizard.com/

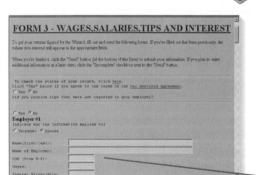

Before using this, or any tax preparation service, you should take the time to find out what the fees are and which services are offered. In the case of an on-line service you should also make sure that the information is on a secure Web site, safe from prying eyes.

If you're ready to go ahead with the Tax Wizard, you will be given an ID number so that you can return later to add or amend information without having to start over from scratch. Then it's just a matter of filling out the forms.

http://taxwizard.com/

 ## Doing It Yourself

Never allow anyone to prepare your return that isn't qualified, including yourself. You don't need to be a C.P.A. to do your own taxes, but you do need to know what your doing.

Money magazine found on the Pathfinder site *(© 1996 Time Inc. New Media. All rights reserved. Reproduction in whole or in part without permission is prohibited. Pathfinder is a registered trademark of Time Inc. New Media.)* has a quick way to Test Your Tax I.Q.

Try your hand at the test before trying your hand on your taxes.

http://pathfinder.com/@@717i1gYAekgnhcva/Money/features/
taxquiz_0295/taxquiz.html

If you got a perfect score on the Tax I.Q. test you don't need these Essential Links to additional tax information, you need to get out more. On the other hand, if you went 0 for 15 on the quiz it's probably not a good idea to do your own taxes without first doing some more research. Claiming ignorance as an excuse for a faulty return doesn't sit well with the IRS.

Use this page as a starting point to further tax information. If you'll be returning often, you may want to bookmark it.

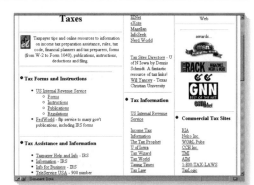

http://www.el.com/ToTheWeb/Taxes/

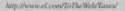

Canadians have fewer on-line tax resources to call their own. This is unfortunate, especially when you consider that on average, Canadians will pay more in taxes than their American counterparts (What, you didn't think that universal health care was free did you?).

Links to most of the biggest and best Canadian tax sites can be found here on the CCH Canadian Web site. The list ain't long, but the sites that you'll find are generally top-notch.

http://www.ca.cch.com/hotlinks/taxlinks.html

Now that you're almost ready to start the process of filling out your return, the question is, where do you start? Not only does the IRS have umpteen different forms to choose from but they ask you to identify yourself on them in one of five ways. They are; Single, Married Filling Jointly, Married Filling Separately, Head of Household, and Qualifying Widow(er) with Dependant Child.

MetLife defines who qualifies for which category and what it all means.

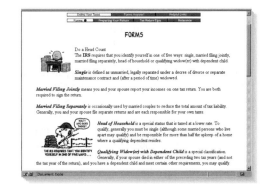

http://www.metlife.com/Lifeadvi/Brochures/Taxes/Docs/tax1.html

Once you know who you are, at least as far as the IRS is concerned, there's still the matter of figuring out which forms and schedules you're going to need to fill out.

Everyone needs to fill out the basic 1040 form but there are a couple of variants on the 1040 theme including the less complicated (and aptly named) EZ version. Depending on the particulars of your financial situation, the basic 1040 may need to be supplemented with a schedule. MetLife lists the most common ones and explains when you would use them.

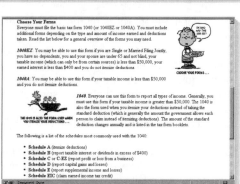

http://www.metlife.com/Lifeadvi/Brochures/Taxes/Docs/tax1.html

Knowing which category you fall under for tax purposes and your approximate taxable income, you can use these tables from Washington University to estimate your tax rate. It's no replacement for a carefully planned return, that will come later, but it should give you a basic idea of what you're in for.

For some unknown reason the Qualifying Widow(er) with Dependent Children category is not found on this list. The other four categories are broken down by taxable income and their corresponding tax rates.

http://alfredo.wustl.edu/mort/96irs.html

The IRS has a funny tendency not to catch tax preparation mistakes that are to their advantage and yet has the uncanny ability to ferret out even the smallest errors when it's in their favor. It's up to you to see to it that you're not cheating yourself and that you've included all the information they need to process your return. So if for no other reason than to avoid the pleasure of filling out a tax return twice, you'll want to take a look at the Ernst & Young list of the Twenty-Five Most Common Tax Preparation Errors before you send it off.

http://www.ey.com/us/tax/25error.htm

And finally we arrive at the Real Deal—the Home page of the U.S. Internal Revenue Service. Stop for a second and take a look at the the attention to detail. Notice how it counts down the number of days left until April fifteenth. Isn't that nice? It's cute, it's funny, it's well organized, useful ... Enjoy it, you paid for it. Congratulations and snide comments aside, the IRS site is the final word on taxes on the net. Literally.

There's lots to see and do here so hold tight and I'll take you for the grand tour.

http://www.irs.ustreas.gov/prod/cover.html

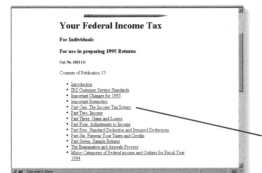

The first stop has to be Publication 17, catalog number 10311G. Too bad the bureaucrats that name these publications don't share their Web designers sense of irreverence. Be that as it may, Publication 17 is still an excellent way for non-accountants to find all the facts they need to know to file their own taxes. It takes you through each part of the return, explaining tax law in a way you can understand. The publication is split up into chapters. Click on any chapter of interest or click on "Introduction" to start at the beginning.

http://www.irs.ustreas.gov/prod/ind_info/pub17/index.html

You can order a printed version of publication 17 from the IRS if you wish but by viewing it on-line you can be environmentally smug in the knowledge that you've helped saved another tree. If I remember my Flat Tax Factoids correctly, that's 1 down 293,759 to go.

It's in this publication that you will find answers to just about any sticky tax question you can throw at it. In the page pictured here for example are instructions on handling medical and dental expenses.

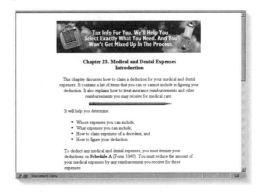

http://www.irs.ustreas.gov/prod/ind_info/pub17/chap23.html

In addition to electronic versions of their standard paper publications, the IRS Web site also includes an interactive feature they call "Tax Trails." It lists the most common tax questions and guides you step-by-step to find the answers.

If everything the IRS did was as straightforward as this you'd see a lot fewer angry taxpayers. Is it a sign of things to come or just a temporary anomaly owing to the fact that bureaucrats haven't had a chance to muck around with it yet? Time will tell.

http://www.irs.ustreas.gov/prod/ind_info/tax_trails/index.html

Once you click on one of the "Tax Trails" listed you are led through a series of yes/no questions. The supplied answer brings you in turn to another question with another yes/no response. And so on, and so on, and so on ... Until at last you arrive at a final reply to your original query.

Precisely because tax law can be so convoluted, an easy-to-use service like this one proves all the more invaluable. I hope it doesn't sound like I'm sucking up to the mighty IRS if I say it again, but, good job.

http://www.irs.ustreas.gov/prod/ind_info/tax_trails/index.html

This next section falls into the category of necessary evil—the form section. It's nice that the IRS has made their forms available over the Net, but as mentioned before, there are so many forms and schedules to choose from it's hard to know which one(s) to pick. If all else fails you can always use last year's returns to guide you.

Once you find what you're looking for just highlight the name, choose a format you can use, and click on "Review Selected Files" to proceed with the download.

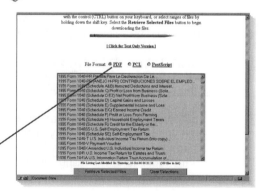

http://www.irs.ustreas.gov/prod/forms_pubs/forms.html

According to the IRS, it takes the average American family about 27 hours to keep records and prepare an itemized Form 1040 with a few additional schedules (yet another fun Flat Tax factoid for you). Downloading the forms in advance gives you a head start on the hours of labor ahead of you.

Depending on the format that you chose to download you will see something like this on your computer. It's an exact duplicate of the one the IRS would have sent you by mail.

http://www.irs.ustreas.gov/prod/forms_pubs/forms.html

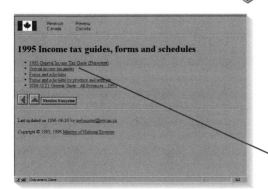

Paying taxes will never be fun but as the IRS Web site proves preparing them doesn't have to be as painful as a root canal.

In contrast to the pizzazz of the IRS, Revenue Canada's site is, how shall we say, utilitarian. You won't find much in the way of gimmicks or interactive features but it too has forms that you can download and it comes in two separate but equally bland multicultural flavors. Choose from the "income tax guide" or the "forms and schedules."

http://www.revcan.ca/menu/EmenuGPA.html

 ## Calculating Your Taxes On-Line

If you have a simple lifestyle, no dependents, itemized deductions, or complicated investments and choose to file the IRS 1040EZ form, Home Pages, Inc., can make the simplified return even simpler.

The program works hand-in-hand with the 1040EZ instruction booklet that comes with the form. Besides showing off the programmer's grasp of the Java language, it's main purpose seems to be that it will help you avoid any unpleasant run-ins with addition and subtraction.

http://www.homepages.com/fun/1040EZ.html

With 15 relatively self-explanatory questions, the EZ form is just that. You will need to refer to the instruction booklet to find the earned income credits you are entitled to and your tax rate. You will also need to have a copy of your W2 form from your employer stating the income that you've made over the year and any taxes that you have already paid in advance. Once you have that information handy, it's a simple matter to fill in the blanks. The program adds and subtracts the numbers leaving you only to copy them over.

http://www.homepages.com/fun/1040EZ.html

Those who qualify for the 1040EZ have their lives made even EZer by the above calculator. Now before you start in with the "that's not fair"s or whine about the complicated 1040 form that you're left to contend with consider the following; in order to qualify for the EZ you must have earned less than $50,000 and claim no dependents. That's right, if you make good coin or have been blessed with children you can't use it. Maybe they're jealous of you. And besides, they don't have a splendiferous program like NetTax '96 to help them.

http://www.nettax.com

NetTax '96 seems to be a labor of love. The author notes that he isn't above accepting non-tax deductible donations for his work but otherwise it's free. Good job too. You can use the program to help you prepare your 1040 or to play around with "what if" scenarios. If you run into trouble, the highlighted terms are linked back to a definition from the IRS.
Start by choosing the tax year and filling in the general information required. Picking "next year ..." allows you to project your taxes in advance.

http://www.nettax.com

Sometime after the New Year's hangovers have cleared but before cupid has reared his little rear you should receive a W2 form from your employer. It details the wages you earned and the taxes and other goodies you had withheld from your pay over the previous year. If you don't get one of these forms, that's something that the IRS would like to discuss with you.

You're going to need to refer to this W2 when preparing your tax return or when filling out the "W2-info" section of NetTax '96.

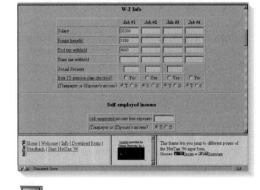

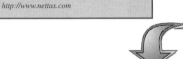
http://www.nettax.com

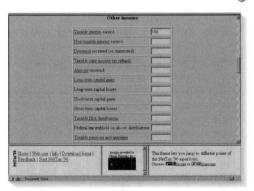

The "Other income" section is where you will enter everything outside of standard wages that you made over the course of the year. This might include alimony, dividends, capital gains, interest earned, and just about anything else you can think of. Alimony and some of the other "other incomes" are fairly cut and dry, but if you're not entirely sure what a "Capital Gain" is but suspect that you may have earned them, remember to click on the term for an in-depth lesson, compliments of the Internal Revenue Service.

http://www.nettax.com

The next two parts to fill out are the "Earned Income Credits" and "Deductions" sections. To oversimplify things a bit, credits are the governments way of defraying the cost of living, notably the cost of living with children. Deductions are good citizen incentives. There are many specialized tax deductions that you won't find on this list but the ones most of us will have to worry about are all here; IRAs, home mortgage interest, charitable donations, state and local taxes, and so on.

http://www.nettax.com

That's pretty much it for NetTax '96 and your 1040. You can now click on the "I'm all done!" button and see what you get. Before you go ahead and do that though, take a second and look over the optional Flat Tax section. Here's where you get to play around and test one of the proposed flat tax plans or make up your own. This section has no bearing on your 1040 calculations whatsoever and you won't find a similar section of your official tax forms, it's just for fun—*if* you get off on that sort of thing.

http://www.nettax.com

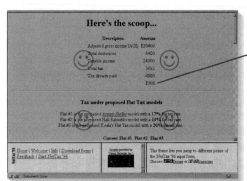

And here, as they say, is the scoop. The last line, it goes without saying, is the bottom line. That's where you find out whether you need to make the check payable to the Internal Revenue Service or The Sharper Image and for how much. That line in particular is filled with technical jargon that not everyone will readily understand, so allow me to translate: If you get a happy face and see the words "Hooray! You get Back ..." flashing next to the number, that's good. A frowny face and a flashing "Oh no! You Owe...", that's ungood.

http://www.nettax.com

Audits, Abuses, and Excuses

Once the taxes are calculated, the forms sent off, and the checks cashed, your tax travails aren't over yet. Until the statute of limitations on a return expires the tax man can always come calling to audit your records. Money magazine (© *1996 Time Inc. New Media. All rights reserved. Reproduction in whole or in part without permission is prohibited. Pathfinder is a registered trademark of Time Inc. New Media.*) has some tips on "How to avoid getting hooked." Look it over and be sure to click on the Interactive Audit Bait Worksheet.

http://pathfinder.com/@ @XhWSqwYAfE0fbITI/money/features/ auditbait_0196/audittext.html

Taxes

Page 221

The Audit Bait Worksheet (Which, by the way, is © 1996 Time Inc. New Media. All rights reserved. Reproduction in whole or in part without permission is prohibited. Pathfinder is a registered trademark of Time Inc. New Media.) ... what was I saying? Oh yeah—it's useful.

Based on the premise that the vast majority of audits are triggered by a high deduction to income ratio, the worksheet will calculate your chances of being audited. Fill in the blanks and click on Am I Audit Bait? for the results.

http://pathfinder.com/@@vj*rHwUATDDa6lzw/cgi-bin/Money/auditbait2.cgi

Worksheet Results

There were plans in the works for the IRS to conduct hundreds of thousands of random audits each year. That plan was scrapped indefinitely but if you find that your itemized deductions come to more than 35 percent of your adjusted gross income you still stand a good chance of being targeted for an audit.

By the way, did I mention that this is © 1996 Time Inc. New Media. All rights reserved. Reproduction in whole or in part without permission is prohibited. Pathfinder is a registered trademark of Time Inc. New Media.

http://pathfinder.com/@@vj*rHwUATDDa6lzw/cgi-bin/Money/auditbait2.cgi

We've all heard horror stories about the IRS, right? Well, in case you haven't, read on. The Zon Association suggests that you brace yourself before delving into example after example of what they consider Cruel and Unusual Punishment Inflicted Upon Innocent Working-class Americans.

If misery loves company and the IRS has made you miserable, you'll certainly find plenty of companionship here. If yours is a story worth telling you can even add your tale of woe to the pile.

http://www.neo-tech.com/irs-class-action/1.html#report1

It's hard when you're in the midst of an audit, but try not to panic. You *do* have rights, and no one, not even the formidable U.S. Internal Revenue Service is allowed to trample on them.

If you find yourself in the unenviable position of having to face an audit be sure to stop by the Tax Prophet® and take a look at their collection of articles including this one, When the Tax Man Cometh! Their prudent advice may help you and, just as importantly, may help put your mind at ease.

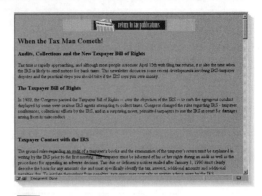

http://www.taxprophet.com/pubs/taxmn_nl.html

Worse then the specter of an audit is the surety that you owe the IRS a lot of money and that there is no way that you will be able to pay it on time. It's not a fun predicament to find yourself in, but then it's not the end of the world either. You can negotiate with the IRS collection division. This article, Who's Afraid of the Big Bad Wolf from the Web site of Don Fitch Accountancy details what you can expect to happen and what you can do about it, from the first delinquent notice to negotiating a final deal.

http://www.paylesstax.com/wolfarticle.html

After all this depressing talk about tax forms, audits, and delinquent payments, a little bit of levity seems in order. Jay Starkman's Only Taxes might just do the trick with their Best of TaxLetter, The Humorous Side of Taxes. The stories range from the best excuses to the most original use of a deduction. One of my favorites is the one about the guy serving trial as a delinquent taxpayer. The accused, speaking in his own defense, informed the judge that he was *not* a delinquent taxpayer. A taxpayer pays taxes, and he never did.

http://www.mindspring.com/~starkman/bestof.htm

Credit 101

What Are We Talking About Here?

- Glossary of Credit, Financial and Legal Terms
- How Americans Spend Their Money
- When Should I Use Credit?
- Saving Money on Credit Cards
- The Various Credit Schemes

The Real Cost of Credit

- Principle and Interest Charges Over The Life of a Loan
- After-Tax Comparison of Home Equity and Consumer Loans
- The Loan Wizard Payment Calculator

Things Every Borrower Should Know

- Money Rates
- Annual Percentage Rates
- The Truth in Lending Act
- Understanding the Fine Print

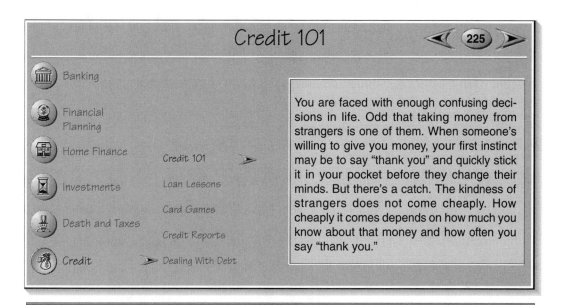

Banking

Financial
Planning

Home Finance   Credit 101 ➤

Investments   Loan Lessons

                     Card Games

Death and Taxes   Credit Reports

Credit   ➤ Dealing With Debt

You are faced with enough confusing decisions in life. Odd that taking money from strangers is one of them. When someone's willing to give you money, your first instinct may be to say "thank you" and quickly stick it in your pocket before they change their minds. But there's a catch. The kindness of strangers does not come cheaply. How cheaply it comes depends on how much you know about that money and how often you say "thank you."

What Are We Talking About Here?

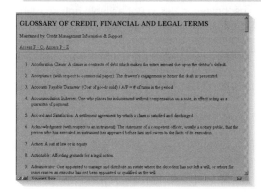

As adults, we're supposed to understand grown-up stuff like APRs, prime rates, and grace periods. No one ever explains this stuff, mind you, but we're supposed to know it just the same. Presumably, we should all wake up one morning and by some magical feat of maturity find that we can suddenly comprehend bankerspeak. If that morning has come and gone and you still don't have a clue what an "APR" is, you will find that Credit Management Information & Support is less a Web site than a rite of passage.

http://www.teleport.com/~richh/glossary.html

The definition of credit is hardly as enigmatic as some of the more obscure credit related terms, but neither is it as precise. Take a look at this graph on the Household Finance site entitled How Americans Spend Their Money. From mortgages to music, each time you consume a piece of this pie and pay for it later you are using credit. How much credit you have, and how wisely you use it, defines how much of the pie you get. Hungry for more? Scroll down the page and click the Contents button.

http://www.hfc.com/money/p1.html

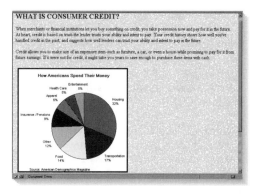

You are given a list of credit-related articles that together give you a general overview of credit in all its myriad and mysterious forms. Clicking on any of the article titles brings up that article. You can navigate between articles by choosing the forward or back buttons at the bottom of each screen or by choosing the contents button which brings you back to this list.

Try clicking on <u>When Should I Use Credit</u>.

http://www.hfc.com:80/money/toc.html

It would be nice if we could afford to pay for all of our purchases from savings. For most of us, however, this is not a viable option. Using credit without abusing it can quickly become a juggling act between getting what we want (or need) and living within our means. This article shows some of the pros and cons of purchasing on credit and spells out your responsibilities as a credit user.

— Click the forward button to continue.

http://www.hfc.com/money/p2.html

With the notable exceptions of mortgages and auto loans, this table lists the most common forms of credit, when each is applicable, and to what end. Charge and credit cards, installment plans, home equity loans, cash advances, and personal lines of credit are all covered.

Once again, you will find the forward button at the bottom of the screen. You know what to do with it.

http://www.hfc.com:80/money/p3.html

Back in the age when bell-bottoms ruled the runways and disco ruled the night, the question was whether or not you needed a credit card. With credit cards a ubiquitous fact of life in the 90s, the question today is which card do you need. The answer depends on you, the monthly balance that you carry and the importance you place on special services and reward programs. Before you go ahead and click the forward button, stop for a moment, read the article and consider your own spending habits.

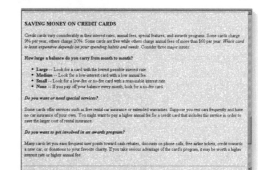

http://www.hfc.com/money/p4.html

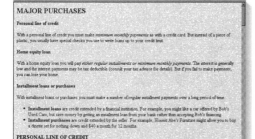

You probably wouldn't buy a home on a credit card, and yet many of us don't hesitate to use that same credit cards as an expensive personal line of credit. Credit cards, personal lines of credit, home equity loans, and installment plans each have their place and purpose. This article will help to put each of the various credit schemes into perspective. Read it to learn the functions that each of the different credit variants is intended to serve as well as the potential pitfalls of each.

http://www.hfc.com/money/p5.html

The Real Cost of Credit

This graph shows how some merchants weigh the principle and interest charges over the life of an installment loan. More generally, it also serves to illustrate the way in which many lenders front-load interest charges thereby guaranteeing the profitability of a loan regardless of how quickly it's paid off.

If you like, click the forward button at the bottom of each page and continue to read on at your own pace.

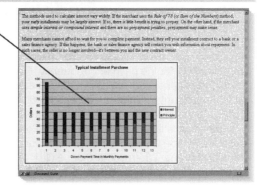

http://www.hfc.com/money/p5.html

We will be using the interactive calculators from FinanCenter later on to calculate credit card costs. For now, just take a look at their After-Tax Comparison of Home Equity Loans and Consumer Loans. What you get is a bird's-eye view of some of the costs associated with different types of credit. While mileage on a loan will vary, the bottom line is clear; not only are different types of credit intended to serve different functions, but in using the wrong credit for the job you may end up cheating yourself.

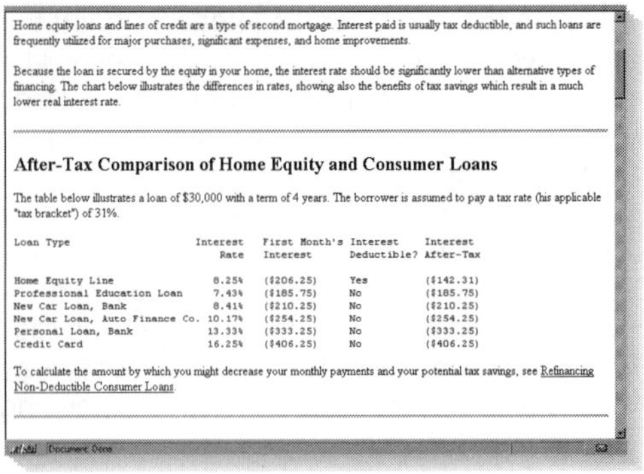
Home equity loans and lines of credit are a type of second mortgage. Interest paid is usually tax deductible, and such loans are frequently utilized for major purchases, significant expenses, and home improvements.

Because the loan is secured by the equity in your home, the interest rate should be significantly lower than alternative types of financing. The chart below illustrates the differences in rates, showing also the benefits of tax savings which result in a much lower real interest rate.

After-Tax Comparison of Home Equity and Consumer Loans

The table below illustrates a loan of $30,000 with a term of 4 years. The borrower is assumed to pay a tax rate (his applicable "tax bracket") of 31%.

Loan Type	Interest Rate	First Month's Interest	Interest Deductible?	Interest After-Tax
Home Equity Line	8.25%	($206.25)	Yes	($142.31)
Professional Education Loan	7.43%	($185.75)	No	($185.75)
New Car Loan, Bank	8.41%	($210.25)	No	($210.25)
New Car Loan, Auto Finance Co.	10.17%	($254.25)	No	($254.25)
Personal Loan, Bank	13.33%	($333.25)	No	($333.25)
Credit Card	16.25%	($406.25)	No	($406.25)

To calculate the amount by which you might decrease your monthly payments and your potential tax savings, see Refinancing Non-Deductible Consumer Loans.

Document: Done

http://www.financenter.com/autoloan/helinfo.htm

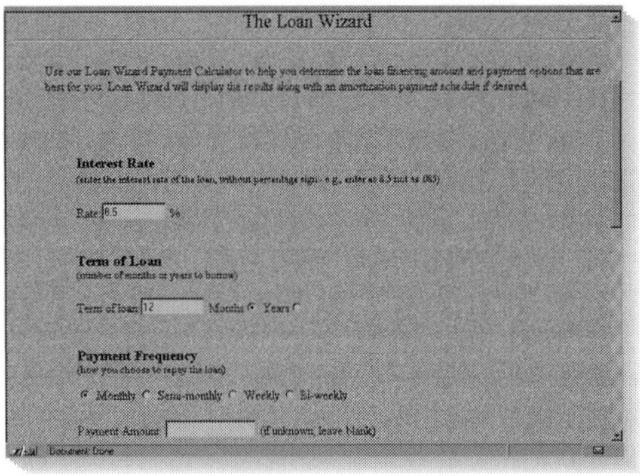

Regardless of the kind of credit you use, you need to know how much it's going to cost you, both at the end of the month and at the end of the loan. To find out, use this Loan Wizard Payment Calculator from the Community Credit Union.

Since all loans are based on the same basic amortization formula you can use this calculator with any loan. Or, you can use it to compare one loan against another to see which one makes the most sense for you.

http://www.communitycu.org/OnlineServ/Calculators/C2A.html

You will need to fill in the interest rate, term of the loan, payment frequency, and amount being borrowed. For calculating the cost of using a credit card, fill in "12 months" for the term and "monthly" for the payment frequency. For loans that requires a down payment, you can fill in the amount as either a percentage or a dollar figure. Choosing to show the amortization schedule will show you how much of the payments made are applied to principle and interest charges. When you are done click on Submit.

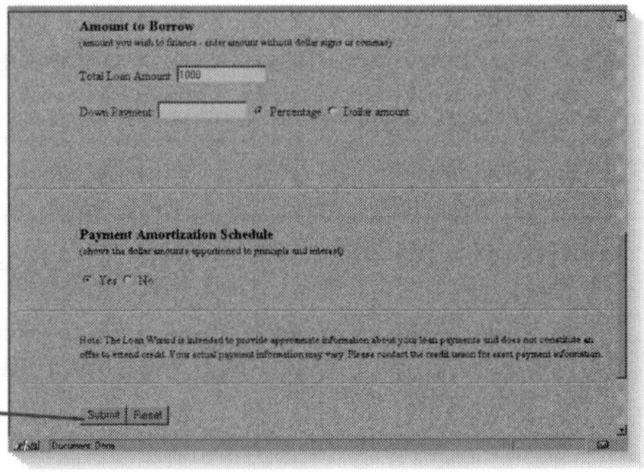

http://www.communitycu.org/OnlineServ/Calculators/C2A.html

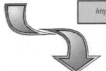

The results screen shows your monthly payments, the interest charged, and the total amount paid. Use your browser's <u>back button</u> to put in new numbers and try out different credit scenarios before signing on the dotted line.

Compare what it costs to install storm windows on a credit card versus a personal loan or see if a home equity loan is a better deal for financing a car than a dealer.

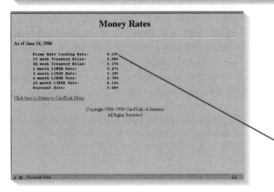

http://www.communitycu.org/OnlineServ/Calculators/C2A.html

Things Every Borrower Should Know

When you deal with credit and loans you will inevitably bump into the term "prime rate," often shortened to simply "prime" as in "prime plus 5." The reason that it's always prime plus X is that lenders traditionally reserve this prime rate for their largest institutional customers. The interest rate that these prime customers pay, and therefore, the interest you will pay based on it, fluctuates daily. Here, at the <u>Card Trak</u> Web site, you will find the prime rate du jour.

http://www.ramresearch.com/moneyrates/moneyrates.html?

The other term that you will be confronted with when you look into credit in any of it's many forms is "APR" or Annual Percentage Rate. <u>The Real Estate Information Network</u> has a more detailed definition of the term, but basically the APR is a standardized way to compare apples to apples when dealing with any type of loan. It takes into account the periodic (or yearly) interest rate and all applicable fees to show how much borrowing will really cost you.

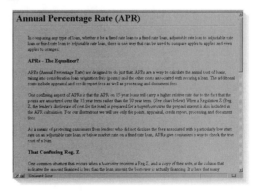

http://www.reinfonet.com/fxdapr.html

While an <u>APR</u> shows the cost of a loan in the form of a percentage rate, it is only on the loan agreement where you will see the final cost of that loan. <u>The Truth In Lending Act</u> requires lenders to spell out all of the terms and costs involved in writing, before you sign. Read these documents carefully, they're usually the only place where you will get to see, in dollars and cents, exactly what you're getting yourself into.

http://www.mortgagemart.com/jmregz.html

What You Should Know When Making A Loan

SHOULD A PERSON DOCUMENT A LOAN TO A FRIEND IN WRITING?

Yes. When you loan a significant amount of money to a friend you should write up what is called a promissory note, which is basically a statement in which your friend agrees to pay you back according to the terms of the agreement. Also, if your friend is offering something as collateral (an asset that you can take if he or she fails to repay the loan), then you should have a written security agreement. The security agreement should state that you can take possession of the collateral if your friend defaults (fails to pay you back).

Both the promissory note and the security agreement should include the following information:

- your name and address
- your friend's name and address
- the amount of the loan
- the purpose of the loan
- the duration of the loan and a promise to pay according to a set schedule
- the amount of interest to be charged and how it will be assessed
- a description of any collateral securing the loan
- the actions you can take to collect the debt in the event of a default

If the offered collateral is personal property, you may want to make what is known as a UCC filing, usually with the office of your state's secretary of state. There may be a fee (generally between $5 and $50), but the filing can

In addition to spelling out what the loan is going to cost you, every loan agreement must include the amount being borrowed, the duration and schedule of payment and (heaven forbid) the consequences of failure to repay the loan.

At the <u>American Lawyer Media</u> site you will find a detailed explanation of all the small print in your loan agreement. Although the print may be small, it is only in understanding it that you get the big picture.

http://www.courttv.com/legalhelp/survival/money/88.html

Loan Lessons

The World's Oldest Lending Institutions
- Borrowing From Family
- Pawnbrokers

Home Equity Loans
- FinanCenter's Home Equity Info Page
- Home Equity Worksheet

Borrowing for College
- Financial Aid Calculator
- Frequently Asked Questions About Student Loans
- Subsidized Federal Stafford Loans

Cars: Loans, Leases, and Killer Deals
- One-Minute LoanAbility Test
- How to Get the New Car, Truck or Minivan You Really Want
- Banks Near You
- Monthly Payment Loan Calculator
- The Fit My Budget Calculator
- What to Do When the Lease Bug Bites
- Loan vs. Lease Calculator
- Auto-By-Tel: Getting a Great Deal the Easy Way

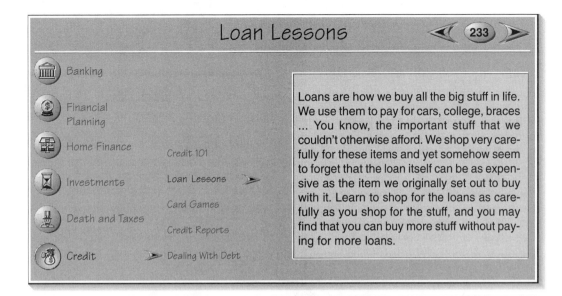

Banking
Financial Planning
Home Finance
Investments
Death and Taxes
Credit
Credit 101
Loan Lessons
Card Games
Credit Reports
Dealing With Debt

Loans are how we buy all the big stuff in life. We use them to pay for cars, college, braces ... You know, the important stuff that we couldn't otherwise afford. We shop very carefully for these items and yet somehow seem to forget that the loan itself can be as expensive as the item we originally set out to buy with it. Learn to shop for the loans as carefully as you shop for the stuff, and you may find that you can buy more stuff without paying for more loans.

The World's Oldest Lending Institutions

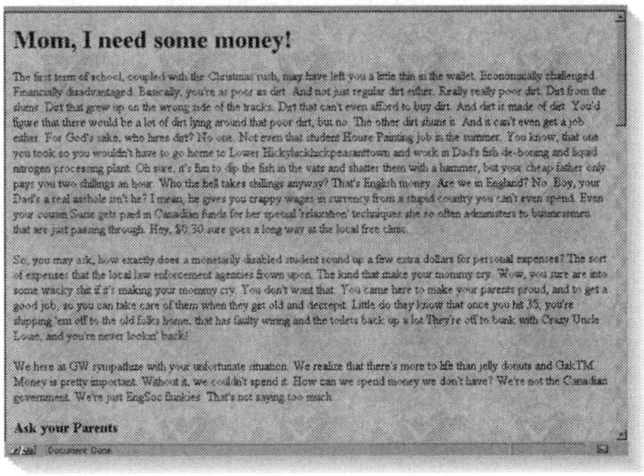
Mom, I need some money!

The first term of school, coupled with the Christmas rush, may have left you a little thin in the wallet. Economically challenged. Financially disadvantaged. Basically, you're as poor as dirt. And not just regular dirt either. Really really poor dirt. Dirt from the slums. Dirt that grew up on the wrong side of the tracks. Dirt that can't even afford to buy dirt. And dirt is made of dirt. You'd figure that there would be a lot of dirt lying around that poor dirt, but no. The other dirt shuns it. And it can't even get a job either. For God's sake, who hires dirt? No one. Not even that student House Painting job in the summer. You know, that one you took so you wouldn't have to go home to Lower Hickylackbackpeasanttown and work in Dad's fish de-boning and liquid nitrogen processing plant. Oh sure, it's fun to dip the fish in the vats and shatter them with a hammer, but your cheap father only pays you two shillings an hour. Who the hell takes shillings anyway? That's English money. Are we in England? No. Boy, your Dad's a real asshole isn't he? I mean, he gives you crappy wages in currency from a stupid country you can't even spend. Even your cousin Suzie gets paid in Canadian funds for her special 'relaxation' techniques she so often administers to businessmen that are just passing through. Hey, $0.30 sure goes a long way at the local free clinic.

So, you may ask, how exactly does a monetarily disabled student round up a few extra dollars for personal expenses? The sort of expenses that the local law enforcement agencies frown upon. The kind that make your mommy cry. Wow, you sure are into some wacky shit if it's making your mommy cry. You don't want that. You came here to make your parents proud, and to get a good job, so you can take care of them when they get old and decrepit. Little do they know that once you hit 35, you're shipping 'em off to the old folks home, that has faulty wiring and the toilets back up a lot. They're off to bunk with Crazy Uncle Louie, and you're never lookin' back!

We here at GW sympathize with your unfortunate situation. We realize that there's more to life than jelly donuts and OakTM. Money is pretty important. Without it, we couldn't spend it. How can we spend money we don't have? We're not the Canadian government. We're just EngSoc flunkies. That's not saying too much.

Ask your Parents

Document Done

When you were younger Mom, I need some money! might have seemed like a perfectly reasonable loan application. But if you find yourself instructing your children to "go tell Grandma that Daddy needs a new mortgage," you might be pushing your luck. Borrowing from friends and family certainly has its unique advantages, but having Granny threaten to bust your kneecaps unless you come up with the dough brings the point home quickly—there's got to be another way.

http://engsoc.queensu.ca/services/gw/issues/issue15/page4.htm

With tens of millions of branches around the globe and more opening daily, The Bank of Dad, est. circa 12,000 B.C, is undoubtedly the oldest, largest lending institution on the planet Earth. After that, pawnbrokers run a close second. While not as sarcastically funny as the aforementioned piece on scamming cash off your parental units, this article from the National Pawnbrokers Association Web site does answer every question you could conceivably ask about the world's second oldest source of loans.

http://www.pic.net/business/npa/npa8.html

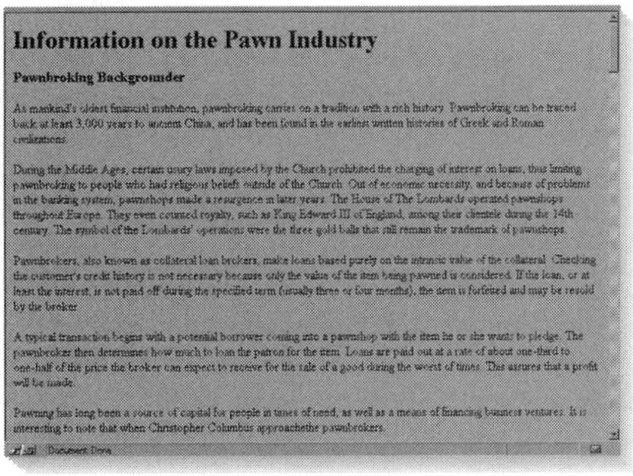
Information on the Pawn Industry

Pawnbroking Backgrounder

As mankind's oldest financial institution, pawnbroking carries on a tradition with a rich history. Pawnbroking can be traced back at least 3,000 years to ancient China, and has been found in the earliest written histories of Greek and Roman civilizations.

During the Middle Ages, certain usury laws imposed by the Church prohibited the charging of interest on loans, thus limiting pawnbroking to people who had religious beliefs outside of the Church. Out of economic necessity, and because of problems in the banking system, pawnshops made a resurgence in later years. The House of The Lombards operated pawnshops throughout Europe. They even counted royalty, such as King Edward III of England, among their clientele during the 14th century. The symbol of the Lombards' operations were the three gold balls that still remain the trademark of pawnshops.

Pawnbrokers, also known as collateral loan brokers, make loans based purely on the intrinsic value of the collateral. Checking the customer's credit history is not necessary because only the value of the item being pawned is considered. If the loan, or at least the interest, is not paid off during the specified term (usually three or four months), the item is forfeited and may be resold by the broker.

A typical transaction begins with a potential borrower coming into a pawnshop with the item he or she wants to pledge. The pawnbroker then determines how much to loan the patron for the item. Loans are paid out at a rate of about one-third to one-half of the price the broker can expect to receive for the sale of a good during the worst of times. This assures that a profit will be made.

Pawning has long been a source of capital for people in times of need, as well as a means of financing business ventures. It is interesting to note that when Christopher Columbus approachethe pawnbrokers.

Document Done

If after raiding your parents pocket change and pawning your cubic zirconia cuff links you still find yourself $62,784 short of what you need to buy that recreational vehicle you had your eye on, where do you turn? For many homeowners, the answer is a home equity loan.

Explore the home equity info pages of Finan-Center and you may discover a way to finance that RV yet. You can scroll down the page or click on any of these links to begin.

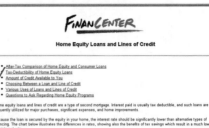

http://www.financenter.com/homeloan/helinfo.htm

Chances are you've seen the commercials on TV for home equity loans. You know, the ones that go "Bad credit? No Credit? No problem! If you're a home owner ..." And there's the catch. In order to qualify for a home equity loan you first need a home in which to have equity. No home, no loan.

The reason that lenders can give you a home equity loan even if you have bad credit is that they have little to lose. But default on the loan and you sure do—your house.

http://www.financenter.com/homeloan/helinfo.htm

Home equity loans do have their advantages. On the plus side are the relatively low interest rates that come with the lender's relatively low risks. That and the fact that home equity loans are up to 100 percent tax deductible can make them a bargain compared with other types of financing. Also worth noting is that unlike an item specific loan, like a mortgage or an auto loan, lenders of home equity loans don't really care where you spend the money, just as long as you make the payments.

http://www.financenter.com/homeloan/helinfo.htm

While there are plenty of good reasons to take out a home equity loan there are also hard questions you'll want to ask any lender before signing on the dotted line. All the more so because your home is riding on that line.

FinanCenter has a list of those questions to ask. Print this list out to use as a guide when evaluating the various loan programs out there.

Questions to Ask Regarding Home Equity Programs

Because terms of withdrawal and repayment vary greatly and may be as important to you as your interest rate, comparison shopping of home equity products is recommended. The following questions you may ask a lender will serve as an evaluation tool and guide in evaluating home equity loan programs:

- Is a home equity line of credit most suitable for my needs, or would another kind of loan be more appropriate?
- What is the initial rate of interest? Is it fixed or variable? If it is variable, on what index is it based? How often can the rate change? Is there a cap or maximum increase in interest rate?
- Is there a minimum loan amount required to qualify for a loan at the rate I am seeking?
- What fees must I pay at the time of application and closing? Is there an annual fee? Are there any withdrawal fees? Any charges for checks?
- What payment options are available? For my own convenience, can my payments be automatically drafted from my checking or savings account?
- Is there a minimum withdrawal? A deadline by which the first withdrawal must be made?
- What will my minimum monthly payment be for each $10,000 in credit, and how much of the minimum payment will go to principal?
- If interest rates go up, will my minimum monthly payment go up with a variable rate loan? What increase in rate would cause my payment to go up?
- Are there circumstances under which my outstanding debt can increase if I only make the minimum payment? (Also

http://www.financenter.com/homeloan/helinfo.htm

Home Equity Worksheet

Your home is probably your single largest investment. And each month you make a mortgage payment, some of those funds are available to you as equity in your home. What's more, if you've been in your home for a while and it's worth more now than when you purchased it, that difference is also available as equity.

Simply put, the equity is the "cash value" of your home. It's the difference between the current value of your home and the amount you owe on your mortgage(s). With help from The Money Store, you can access this equity *without* having to sell your home. Best of all, this money you receive can be used for home improvements, bill consolidation, purchase a new car or any other reasons -- *it's up to you!*

To find out how much equity you have in your home, just complete the following:

Enter value and hit TAB to move to next worksheet entry

	Estimated value of your home if you were to sell it today. Consult a real estate agent or find out the purchase price of similar homes in your neighborhood to determine your home's value.	$ 100000
2	Total amount(s) you owe on your home.	Value
	Add together your: First mortgage	$ 40000
	Second mortgage	$
	Home equity line of credit	$ 1500

How much you can borrow with a home equity loan depends on how much of your home isn't borrowed already. In other words, you can only borrow against the equity that you've built in the house, not the amount still owing on your mortgage.

The Money Store has a Home Equity Worksheet that you can use to calculate how much of your house is really yours. You can then use that amount to borrow more and own less.

http://www.themoneystore.com/hmeqws.html

Put in the estimated value of your home and all of the amounts still owing on the property then press the "Calculate your home equity" button. What you will get is the total cash value in your home expressed as a dollar amount and a loan-to-value percentage.

The rule of thumb is that you need at least a 20 percent loan-to-value ratio before a lender will grant you a loan. Look hard enough though and you may find a lender willing to thumb their nose at that particular rule.

http://www.themoneystore.com/hmeqws.html

are available to you as equity in your home. What's more, if you've been in your home for a while and it's worth more now than when you purchased it, that difference is also available as equity.

Simply put, the equity is the "cash value" of your home. It's the difference between the current value of your home and the amount you owe on your mortgage(s). With help from The Money Store, you can access this equity *without* having to sell your home. Best of all, this money you receive can be used for home improvements, bill consolidation, purchase a new car or any other reasons -- *it's up to you!*

To find out how much equity you have in your home, just complete the following:

Enter value and hit TAB to move to next worksheet entry

	Estimated value of your home if you were to sell it today. Consult a real estate agent or find out the purchase price of similar homes in your neighborhood to determine your home's value.	$ 100000
2	Total amount(s) you owe on your home.	Value
	Add together your: First mortgage	$ 40000
	Second mortgage	$
	Home equity line of credit	$ 1500
	Home improvement loan	$
3	Calculate your home equity	Reset

Funding a college education is one of the most expensive, most confusing things you will ever have to deal with. Anyone able to just figure out the convoluted calculations involved ought to earn three credits towards a Ph.D. in cryptology.

The various worksheets found on the Web pages of the College Board on-line helps. Sort of. A word of warning before you go and click on the Expected Family Contribution link, this ain't gonna be pretty.

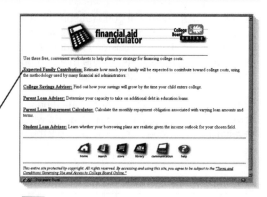

http://www.collegeboard.org/html/calculator000.html

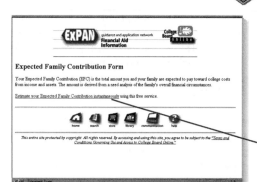

So far, so good. You are given a definition of what is meant by expected family contribution (or, in typical bureaucratic fashion, an EFC). Basically, an EFC is how much the student and his/her family can be reasonably expected to pay towards college expenses. The lower the family's income is the more financial aid available. Poverty does have its advantages.

Click on Estimate your Expected Family Contribution Instantaneously, but don't get your hopes up. Instantaneous it is not.

http://www.collegeboard.org/expan/html/efc.html

It starts off simply enough. Fill in your age and home state and continue on down the page to complete either of the two sections below. One is for students that are financially independent, the other for students still receiving support from their families.

Fill in the appropriate section and click on the Federal Methodology Worksheet button at the bottom of the page.

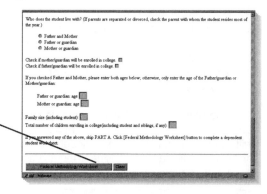

http://www.collegeboard.org/efc/bin/efc-init.cgi

OK, here's where the fun starts. Before you can even begin to fill out this worksheet you need to do some homework. You're going to need to know things like your annual income tax, how much you have in savings and investments, how much equity you have in your home, your yearly medical/dental bills and so on ad nauseam. Count on a minimum of half an hour to complete these worksheets. The process isn't entirely incomprehensible, but it isn't what anyone could call intuitive either.

http://www.collegeboard.org/efc/bin/efc.cgi

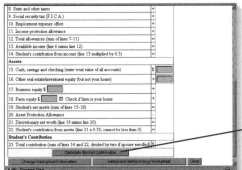

The worksheet comes in four parts, federal methodology worksheets for both parents and students and institutional methodology worksheets for both parents and students. Financially independent students need not complete the parent versions.

With each worksheet, fill in the applicable blanks and click on the "Calculate Student/ Parent Contribution" button to subtotal the numbers. Then click the appropriate button to take you on to the next worksheet.

http://www.collegeboard.org/efc/bin/efc.cgi

After completing all of the individual worksheets, you will be given a total figure that schools can use to estimate how much you can cough up for college. This amount is subtracted from school costs to determine financial aid eligibility. Unfortunately, the pittance that most students end up receiving in financial aid grants, together with the meager reserves so often saved for college, leaves many students with a gap between what they need, and what they have. A gap that can only be bridged with student loans.

http://www.collegeboard.org/efc/bin/efc.cgi

Now that you have an idea what you are expected to contribute towards college expenses,
you're probably thinking to yourself, "Oh well,
maybe if I keep flipping burgers at <u>McDonalds</u>
I'll eventually be promoted to Keeper of the
Secret Sauce." No, you're thinking, "How much
do I have to save between now and the time I
have to pay for all this hiyer edgeacation?" Son,
I'm glad you asked that question. Just click on
<u>College Savings Advisor</u> and prepare to be
amazed.

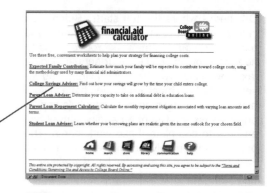

http://www.collegeboard.org/html/calculator000.html

This calculator is not nearly as confusing as
the last. All you need to know is how much
you have socked away for college as of this
moment, how much you can set aside each
month, a low-ball estimate of the return (i.e.,
interest rate) you can expect to see on those
savings and how long until you have to come
up with the goods. Enter these numbers and
press the "Send data" button for the results. If
the amount you get isn't enough you still have
some choices; save more, borrow more or wait
longer.

http://www.collegeboard.org/css/html/save.html

Take a step <u>back</u> when you're through to return to the list of calculators. This time choose
the <u>Parent Loan Advisor</u> where you will be able
calculate how much you can really afford to
borrow in student loans.

Same as the other calculators, fill in the
amounts for income and debt and click the
"Send data" button for the results. One thing
of note here is the debt load figure. While you
might personally be willing to take on more risk,
lenders probably will not.

http://www.collegeboard.org/css/html/pardebt.html

Click the back button once more and it's déjà vu all over again. One last calculator before leaving the ever gracious College Board, the Parent Loan Repayment Calculator.

The standard term for student loans is 10 years, replace this number if your loan is different. Likewise for the interest rate and amounts borrowed for each year in college. Click on "Send data" when done for a rundown on the total amount borrowed, the total interest paid and the total total paid.

http://www.collegeboard.org/css/html/parpay.html

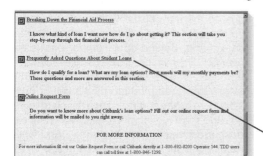

Interactive calculations are kind of cool, but they don't tell the whole story. CitiBank's Web site helps to fill in some of the blanks with their student loan pages.

The diverse student loan resources compiled on this page combine to form a comprehensive primer for would-be scholars and their proud parents. There's lots to look at here and the Frequently Asked Questions About Student Loans is a good place to begin.

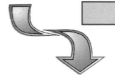

http://www.citibank.com/student/

As the name implies, here are the most common questions asked about the loan process in Q & A format and, of course, the equally common answers; How do you qualify, when will you get the money ... That sort of thing.

All of the underlined terms are linked to a more detailed explanation of that term. Clicking on the Subsidized Federal Stafford Loan, for example, calls up a description of that particular loan program.

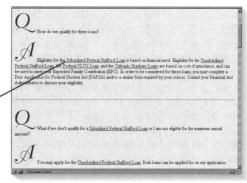

http://www.citibank.com/student/qna.htm

Higher education is a major expense in life, and the expenses get higher with each passing year.

You will attend a school for four long years, but you'll be paying for that school ten years longer still. All the more reason then to consider your financial matters as carefully as you consider the ivy covered halls of your alma mater.

Subsidized Federal Stafford Loans

Program Description

This is a long-term, low-interest loan designed to provide students with additional funds for college.

Subsidized means the interest on the loan is paid by the government while the student is in school.

You must repay this aid.

Eligibility

- Full- or half-time undergraduate students.
- Need Analysis required.
- Application and promissory note required.
- Student borrower must be a U.S. citizen or have a Permanent Resident Alien Card.

Annual Aggregate Loan Limits

- Year 1 --$2,625
- Year 2 -- $3,500
- Years 3, 4, 5 -- $5,500

http://www.citibank.com/student/substaff.htm

Cars: Loans, Leases, and Killer Deals

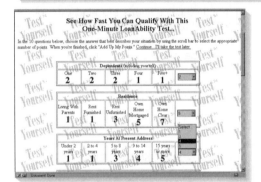

See How Fast You Can Qualify With This One-Minute LoanAbility Test...

In the 10 questions below, choose the answer that best describes your situation by using the scroll bar to select the appropriate number of points. When you're finished, click "Add Up My Points." Continue. I'll take the test later.

Dependents (including yourself)

One	Two	Three	Four	Five+
2	2	2	1	1

Residence

Living With Parents	Rent Furnished	Rent Unfurnished	Own Home Mortgaged	Own Home Clear
1	1	3	5	7

Years At Present Address

Under 2 years	2 to 4 years	5 to 8 years	9 to 14 years	15 years or more
1	1	3	4	5

Just to the right of the white picket fence in your sweet American dream you see a double-car garage. Behind door number one is the ever popular, ever practical cherry red convertible. And Vanna, what do we have for our sleepy contestant behind door number two? Why, it's a luxury sedan ... Then the alarm goes off, and reality jolts you awake like a shot of double espresso. Hold the sugar. And while rubbing the gunk from the corner of your eyes, you wonder, "What kind of clunker can I really afford?"

Http://www.banksite.com/dcartest.htm

Well good morning! And welcome to the BankSITE™ Auto LoanAbility Test™. No doubt you know what to do here, but at the risk of stating the obvious; next to each question is a drop down list, click on it and select your answer. Before you go ahead and click the "Add Up My Points" button, take a second to read the disclaimer below it. BankSITE™ makes a point of noting that this test does not include all of the factors lenders use in approving a loan. Absolutely true, but it's a good indication of what you can expect.

Years With Previous Employer

Under 1 years	1 to 3 years	4 to 6 years	7 to 10 years	Over 10 years
1	1	2	4	6

Percent Of Monthly Income Remaining After Expenses

Less Than 10%	10% to 15%	16% to 25%	26% to 33%	Over 33%
1	2	3	4	5

Bonus Points (add up all that apply - maximum 3 points)

Checking Account	Savings Account	IRA With Bank	CDs With Bank	Loan With Bank
1	1	1	1	1

Retake Test   Add Up My Points!

This chart is for your information only. It does not include all of the factors considered by financial institutions in evaluating a loan request such as your payments history and your ability to meet your monthly obligations. Financial institutions reserve the right of final loan approval.
©1996 The Forms Group, All Rights Reserved

http://www.banksite.com/dcartest.htm

You are given a test score that falls into one of the price categories on the <u>Vehicle BuyAbility Guide</u>. Beside each category is a list of vehicles in that price range. BankSITE™ notes that "if you've got your heart set on something a little bigger or more luxurious than what your total score indicates, you can apply for it anyway". To which I would add, "and if you don't need such a big, luxurious car, *don't* apply for it anyway."

When you're ready, click on <u>How to Get the New Car, Truck or Minivan You Really Want</u>.

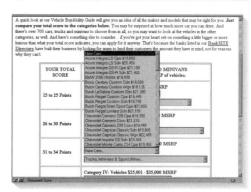

http://www.banksite.com/dcar1.htm

One of the suggestions here is that you shop for the best deal on the loan as aggressively as you shop for the best deal on the car. Usually, this means separating the financing from the purchase. Besides potentially saving you money on interest charges, walking in to a dealership with a preapproved loan also strengthens your negotiating position.

BankSITE™ offers a directory of <u>banks near you</u> that you can help you in your search for good deals on low interest car loans.

http://banksite.com/dcar2.htm

Not every bank on the Net is listed here, let alone the holdout banks not yet on the Net. Still, it's a good place to begin your search. At the very least, the banks that are here should serve as a ruler by which you can measure the interest rates of the banks that aren't.

Click anywhere on the map or use the drop down list to select a state and press the "Go To" button. You can then stop by the Cyberspace branch of any bank on the list and see what they have to offer.

http://www.banksite.com/cgi-bin/cmapusa

It's nice to know how much of a loan lenders will let you drive away with, but with car loans, monthly payments aren't an option, they're standard equipment.

MotorCity has all the accessories you'll need to make sure you don't get taken for a ride. Click on their Monthly Payment Calculator and find out how much that shiny new car will cost you at the end of the month, each and every month, 'till the loan payments end and the car's lost it's shine.

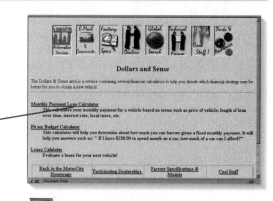

http://www.motorcity.com/site/MC/Finance.html

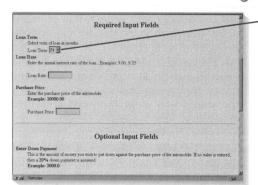

Click the down arrow to choose a term length of 24, 36, 48, or 60 months. There are exceptions, but most new car loans will fall somewhere into this two to five year spread. Continue down the page and fill in the required interest rate and purchase price numbers. The down payment, trade-in, and sales tax fields are optional. Note that if the down payment field is left blank, the calculator assumes a 20 percent down payment—not necessarily a correct assumption. When you're finished, click on the "Submit" button.

http://www.motorcity.com/site/MC/AutoLoan.html

You are given a breakdown of your car loan. Hmm, "breakdown" probably isn't a word that you want to hear while car shopping. Let's try that one again: You are given a *summation* of your car loan. Yes, much better.

Down at the bottom of this summation is the calculated monthly car payment. To see how a different term length affects this number, click on your Web browser's back button, select a new term length and resubmit.

http://www.motorcity.com/cgi-bin/autoloan

MotorCity
Loan Calculation

Purchase Price: $10000.00
Trade-in: $ 1500.00
Taxable Amount: $ 8500.00

Sales Tax: $ 510.00
Down Payment: $ 2000.00
Total: $ 7010.00

Amount Borrowed: $ 7010.00
Term of Loan: 24.00 months
Loan Interest Rate: 9.20%
Loan-to-Value Ratio: 70.10%

Loan Payments: $ 320.89

The above calculations are for comparison shopping only, see your local dealer for exact terms and conditions.

Banks have a funny way of lending you exactly as much as they feel you can afford to pay back. But having just enough to squeak in the monthly car payments won't do you much good if there's nothing left over for gas. In the end, only you can decide how much you are willing to shell out each month for a car. You can use MotorCity's Fit My Budget Calculator to start with a set amount, how much you're willing to spend each month, and work backwards to figure out how much car that would get you.

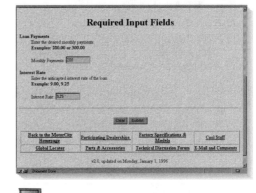

http://www.motorcity.com/site/MC/FutureValue.html

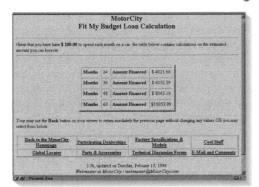

Fill in the amount that you are willing and able to spend each month, the interest rate and submit.

You are shown a table with various term lengths and the amounts that could be financed given your parameters. The longer that you are willing to make these payments, the more you can finance and still stay within budget. On the other hand, the longer you pay and the more you finance, the less you have in your budget for later.

http://www.motorcity.com/cgi-bin/futurevalue

An increasingly popular alternative to the whole car buying concept is auto leasing. And though leasing now accounts for some 30 percent of new car sales, there's more to consider than just what the seven previous car shoppers chose before you got on line at the dealership. Or, as your mother might have put it, "Would you jump off a bridge just because your *friends* did?"

The Greater Toronto Internet Auto Centre (GTIAC) has these words of wisdom.

http://www.listthem.com/gtiac/ontheroad/lease4.html

What to Do When the Lease Bug Bites

The lease bug is surely on the loose, accounting for 29% of all new car sales. The more you know about life in the leasing jungle, the less likely you are to get stung, next time you're car shopping.

But first a disclaimer: I've never owned or leased a new car ... and probably never will. I like cheap, well maintained used cars -- and I only buy ones I can finance with cash.

Since you might make a different decision, here are the facts of leasing life -- how to get the most for the least:

1. **Never, never, never!** Never make your decision based only on the monthly payment. Make sure you know the bottom line, total cost for each option you're considering. Invariably, a salesperson's first question will be "How much can you afford a month?" Your best response: "How low can you go on the purchase price?" Your worst answer, something like: "$300 a month."

2. **Buy first.** Always price shop as if you were going to buy. Only after you've agreed to a bottom line price, should you break the news that you might consider leasing. And in case you didn't hear me before, never, never, never answer the "How much can you afford a month?" question. Once they have that number, all they have to do is "reel you in."

3. **Small Print = Warning.** That tiny type on the bottom of your TV screen ... under the flashing $199/month ... will up your actual cost. In fact, even if you disregard the fine print, and forget about sales tax, registration, and insurance --- which all come to a pretty penny on a new car --- there's still income tax to factor in.

If you're in the 28% tax bracket, you'll need to gross about $520 every month to make a typical $375 lease payment. And that

Leasing is undoubtedly a smart decision for some, but it's not the right decision for everyone. And whether you choose to buy or lease, it's a decision that you're going to have to live with, and pay for, for years to come.

GTIAC has some pointers you should read before coming to any final decisions on the loan/lease question. Down at the bottom of the page is a list of links to these articles. Click, read, and choose wisely.

http://www.listthem.com/gtiac/ontheroad/lease4.html

Sure, the unmitigated pride that comes with ownership is nice. And driving off in a brand spanking new leased car every couple of years would give anyone the warm fuzzies, but how do you calculate a warm fuzzy? Invariably, the lease/loan debate comes down to a question of economics. And that is something you can calculate, to the penny.

Use this Loan Vs. Lease Calculator from WebPoint and see for yourself which of the two options makes better cents.

http://www.webpoint.com/lovle.htm

There are variables not covered here worth consideration, wear and tear charges, for example, and income tax issues. So while this isn't a true apples-to-apples comparison, at least it puts loans and leases in the same food group.

Fill in the blanks and click on the "Calculate" button. If you find any of the terms used confusing just click on the offending term for a definition.

http://www.webpoint.com/lovle.htm

The two key areas to look at here are the Monthly Payment and Total Cost lines. Not shown here but also worth considering is the fact that after the terms of the loan are fulfilled you are left with a car. After the terms of the lease are fulfilled you are left with a severe transportational handicap.

With so many considerations and so little time 'till next year's models roll off the assembly line, you'll want to look at the numbers but hedge on the side of a hunch.

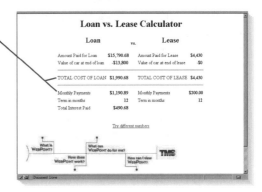

http://www.webpoint.com/cgi-bin/lovle.cgi

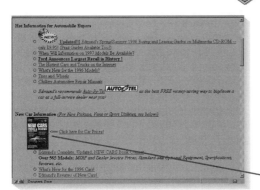

Pay cash if you have it. Pick a lease or a loan if you need to. However you choose to pay for it, it is the car itself that has always been the ultimate objective. Once the question of finances has been resolved, there is still the little matter of choosing your wheels. Edmund's Web site, from the same people that bring you Edmund's Auto Guides, can help save your sole when it's time to kick some tires.

Poke around and click on the picture for new car prices or the link below it for used.

http://www.edmunds.com/

Shopping for a car is exciting stuff. Here's your chance to look around, burn off some of that excess nervous energy, and peek in on the offerings of just about every car manufacturer on the planet (sorry Yugo enthusiasts, it would seem that the war has claimed yet another casualty).

Choose a carmaker then go ahead, pick a car, any car.

http://www.edmunds.com/edweb/manufact.html

Next to the model name of each car on the list is the manufacturer's suggested retail price. You'll rarely pay full sticker price, but it will give you an idea of what you're getting yourself into. Clicking on any of the models brings up an information page like this one for the Chrysler Cirrus LX.

Each vehicle spec sheet comes complete with a detailed review (Edmund's didn't like the mushy backseat of the Cirrus) and all the info any "how many horses," Mario Andretti wanna-be, could possibly ask for.

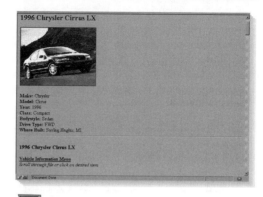

http://www.edmunds.com/edweb/cars/Chrysler/126.97.html

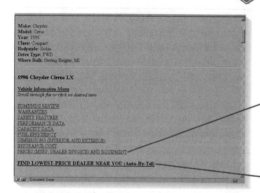

Car dealers, like everyone else, need to make a profit. How much of a profit they make depends on how good you are at negotiating and how much you know about the dealer's costs, the dealer's *real* costs. Forget the sticker price, click on the "Prices ..." link and find out what the dealer paid on the car's invoice and how much more they skim off the top in holdbacks and bonuses from the manufacturer.

Or avoid the hassle of haggling altogether and click on Find Lowest Priced Dealer.

http://www.edmunds.com/edweb/cars/Chrysler/126.97.html

If you are serious about buying a car and you don't want to bother with the whole negotiation rigmarole only to wonder afterward if you really got the best deal, use this free quoting service from Auto-By-Tel. It comes highly, highly recommended. And I'm not being paid to say this.

Here's how it works: Dealers pay Auto-By-Tel a fee to be part of the program. You fill out this form on the Net and Auto-By-Tel turns around and gets the dealers bottomline, no bull, best price on your behalf.

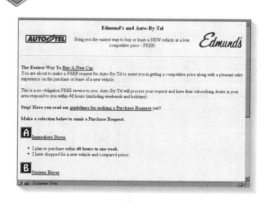

http://www.edmunds.com/edweb/abt/abt.html

The only catch, if you can call it that, is that you shouldn't fill out this form if you're still looking. Do your homework first. Decide on the car, the options you want, and the color, then come back. Waste their time and the dealers will start to walk away from the program, Auto-By-Tel quickly goes out of business, car buyers everywhere begin to panic, the world's economy collapses, anarchy in the streets ... You get the picture.

When you are ready to buy, fill this form out and click on "Continue".

http://www.edmunds.com/edweb/abt/abt.html

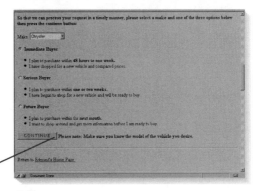

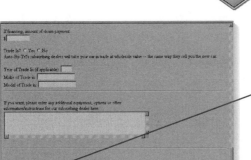

A few notes and caveats: First of all, the service is free. Second, this offer is not available in Guam. But if you live in the United States or Canada, go right ahead and fill in the info they need to get started. Click the "Send Request" button and within 48 hours a car dealer will call with a no haggling required, bottom-line price. If you don't like the price, you don't buy the car. No muss, no fuss.

You know, Dude, it's gnarly stuff like this that makes me proud to say "I surf the Net."

http://www.edmunds.com/edweb/abt/form1.html

Card Games

The Devil's in the Details

- Market Share and Total Number of Credit Cards in Force
- The American Dream Credit Card Info Index
  - Bank Cards, Travel and Entertainment Cards and House Cards
  - Good and Bad Deals in Credit Cards
  - Fixed and Variable Rate Cards
  - Annual Fees
  - Grace Periods
  - Discounts and Rebates
- The Different Ways That Card Issuers Compute Your Balance

Card Shopping

- Determine Your Credit Limit Potential
- How to Build a Credit History and Establish Credit
- The Credit Card Comparison Calculator
- Finding the Card That Meets Your Needs
- Secured, Rebate, Frequent Flyer and Canadian Credit Card Lists
- Applying for a Card On-Line

Credit, But at a Price

- The True Cost of Credit (Or Why Paying the Minimum is a Bad Idea)
- Visa's Interactive Credit Card Statement

Fraud, Scams, and Secrets

- Your Rights as a Credit Card User
- Credit and Charge Card Fraud
- Consumer Rights at the Cash Register
- 12 Credit Card Secrets Banks Don't Want You to Know

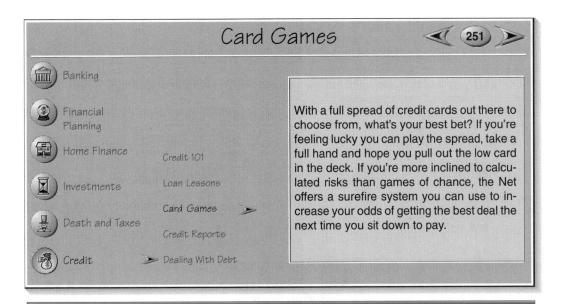

Banking

Financial Planning

Home Finance

Credit 101

Investments

Loan Lessons

Card Games

Death and Taxes

Credit Reports

Credit

Dealing With Debt

With a full spread of credit cards out there to choose from, what's your best bet? If you're feeling lucky you can play the spread, take a full hand and hope you pull out the low card in the deck. If you're more inclined to calculated risks than games of chance, the Net offers a surefire system you can use to increase your odds of getting the best deal the next time you sit down to pay.

The Devil's in the Details

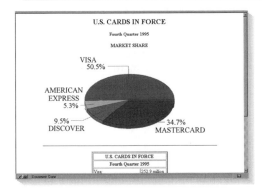

U.S. CARDS IN FORCE
Fourth Quarter 1995
MARKET SHARE

VISA 50.5%
AMERICAN EXPRESS 5.3%
9.5% DISCOVER
34.7% MASTERCARD

U.S. CARDS IN FORCE	
Fourth Quarter 1995	
Visa	252.9 million

With over half a billion cards in use and hundreds of billions of dollars in earnings, credit cards are big business.

Credit card companies want a spot in your wallet and they spend millions on advertising to get there. You know the names of all the players and you can call up their catchy slogans faster than your own mother's maiden name. But do you really want to choose a credit card because it has a hummable jingle or a cute catch phrase?

http://www.ramresearch.com/carddata/4us_cards.html

You may very well never leave home without it, but what is all of that plastic, and why, exactly, do you take it with you everywhere you want to be? We may refer to all of the plastic in our wallets collectively as credit cards, but as you'll see in this article on the American Dream Web site, not all credit cards are credit cards at all. Cards can fall into any number of categories; bank cards, travel & entertainment cards, and house cards. Each type has its own benefits and drawbacks and each is explained here.

http://www.amdream.com/credit/cardsetc.htm

Credit Card Info Index

- What kinds of cards are there?
- What is an affinity card?
- Is MasterCard better than Visa, or vice versa? What about American Express, Diners Club, etc?
- Why does my neighbor's MasterCard or Visa have different rates and fees from mine?
- What is a secured card?
- What is a guaranteed card?
- What is an unsecured card?
- What is a debit card?
- How does an ATM card differ from a debit card?
- Where can I find information about telephone credit cards?
- What is a PIN?

What kinds of cards are there?

- "bank cards," issued by banks Visa, MasterCard, and Discover.
- "travel and entertainment (T&E) cards" like American Express and Diners Club.
- "house cards" that are good only at the stores of one chain. Sears is the biggest one of these, followed by the oil companies and phone companies and on down to your local department store.

T&E cards and national house cards like Sears have the same terms and conditions wherever you apply (return to Index)

<u>American Dream</u> is also home to the exhaustive (and exhausting) hyper-document <u>Good and Bad Deals in Credit Cards</u>. In its electronic pages you will find straightforward answers to a wide range of credit card questions.

Jump to any section of the document by clicking on that subject's title. At the very least, you'll want to be sure to read the first couple of pages that cover <u>interest rates</u>, <u>annual fees</u>, <u>grace periods</u>, and <u>rebates</u>.

http://www.amdream.com/credit/goodnbad.htm

The interest rate that you pay on your credit cards can be based on either a <u>fixed or variable rate</u>. Most credit cards are based on a variable rate (also called an adjustable or floating rate). Variable rate cards have the advantage of a lower initial rate than their fixed rate counterparts but are more prone to the vagaries of the economy. Fixed rate cards, on the other hand, may have a slightly higher interest rate but you'll be sure not to have any unpleasant surprises on your monthly statement.

http://www.amdream.com/credit/goodnbad.htm#Do I want a fixed-rate or floating-rate (variable-rate) card?

As the piece goes on to explain, <u>annual fees</u> are quite aptly named. These fees can range anywhere from $18 all the way on up to $40 for some gold cards. They are often waived for the first year as an enticement for you to join. Thereafter, renewal fees will be automatically charged to your account on the anniversary of the day that you first became a customer. Some present, huh? What few people know, is that some credit card companies will waive these annual fees. Sometimes, all you have to do is ask.

http://www.amdream.com/credit/goodnbad.htm#How do annual fees work?

A <u>grace period</u> is the time between when a purchase is first made and when the credit card company starts charging interest on that purchase. How long of a grace period you have and how those grace periods are applied vary from card to card. Some cards, particularly cards with low interest rates, have no grace period at all.

Understanding grace periods and using them effectively can save you big bucks.

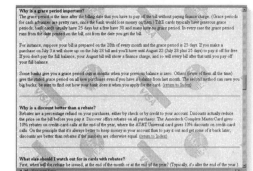

http://www.amdream.com/credit/goodnbad.htm#Why is a grace period important?

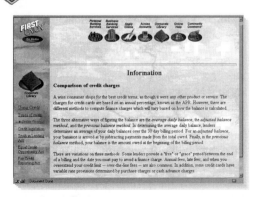

Some card companies prominently advertise special perks for cardholders. Frequent flyer miles, reduced rate cars, cash back deals, and other such <u>discounts and rebates</u> are common bells and whistles in the credit card industry. Whether or not you should be lured to bite this rebate depends on how much these perks will cost you in increased interest rates and how much you will take advantage of the program. Five percent off a <u>GM</u> truck doesn't do you much good if you're planning to buy a <u>Toyota</u>.

http://www.amdream.com/credit/goodnbad.htm#Why is a discount better than a rebate?

The method used by a credit card issuer to determine a card's monthly balance can significantly affect the finance charges assessed on it. The three standard methods used to calculate credit card balances are <u>average daily balance, adjusted balance, and previous balance</u>. Depending on which of the methods is used, two cards with identical balances and interest rates can be assessed different finance charges. Turn to this article from <u>FirstUnion</u> for all the dirt.

http://www.firstunion.com/2/library/econews/articles/credit/credcomp.html

Credit cards give you the flexibility to buy what you want when you want it. Credit cards with higher spending limits give you the flexibility to buy more of what you want more often.

Whether your going to be applying for a credit card for the first time or you already have a stack of them but want one with a higher spending limit, this LoanAbility Test™ from BankSITE™ will help you to determine your credit limit potential.

http://www.banksite.com/ecctest.htm

The calculator consists of ten questions that are typical of the sorts of things that any self-respecting credit card company will need to know before extending you credit. To the right of each question is a drop down list. Use this list to select your answer.

Once you've completed the test, click on the "Add Up My Points" button at the bottom of the screen. You will be given an overall score which you can then use to determine your chances of getting that gold card.

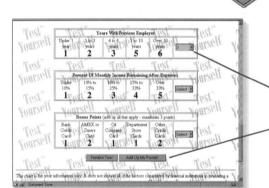

http://www.banksite.com/ecctest.htm

Even if you scored well on this test, don't pat yourself on the back and run to fill out a flurry of credit card applications just yet.

Stop for a moment and consider the possibility that in calculating your potential for credit you also inadvertently calculated your potential for financial trouble. Hate to be a bummer, but at a time when personal debt is at an all-time high in this country, it might be wise to rethink your reasons for wanting more credit in the first place.

http://www.banksite.com/ecc1.htm

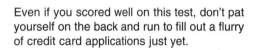

Credit Card Potential Chart

Total Points	What Your Score Means...
If You Scored 15 to 17 Points	You could qualify for a credit card limit up to $ 1,000
If You Scored 18 to 21 Points	You could qualify for a credit card limit up to $ 2,000
If You Scored 22 to 27 Points	You could qualify for a credit card limit up to $ 3,000
If You Scored 28 to 32 Points	You could qualify for a credit card limit up to $ 5,000
If You Scored Over 32 Points	You could qualify for a credit card limit up over $ 5,000

With a higher credit limit, you'll have more flexibility for purchases, vacations, and cash advances... and you may be able to consolidate other credit card balances and save on interest as well. And since you pay nothing for credit you don't use, it makes sense to apply for the highest credit card line possible.

The above chart is for your information only. Even if you scored less than 15 points, speak to a loan officer at a bank listed in our BankSITE Directory about your particular situation. You'll find that these institutions always look for ways to approve loan requests, not for reasons why they can't.

If you didn't score very well on the LoanAbility Calculator don't despair. (Re)building a good credit history is important but it's not impossible.

The Federal Trade Commission has advice for establishing credit if you're just starting out and for reestablishing credit if you're starting out all over again.

http://consumerlawpage.com/nographics/brochure/84.shtml

How to Build A Credit History and Establish Credit

Building a good credit history is important. If you have no reported credit history, it may take time to establish your first credit account. This problem affects young people just beginning careers as well as older people who have never used credit. It also affects divorced or widowed women who shared credit accounts that were reported only in the husband's name. If you do not know what is in your credit file, check with your local credit bureau. Most cities have two or three credit bureaus, which are listed under "Credit" or "Credit Reporting Agencies" in the Yellow Pages. For a small fee, they will tell you what information is in your file and may give you a copy of your credit report.

If you have had credit before under a different name or in a different location and it is not reported in your file, ask the credit bureau to include it. If you shared accounts with a former spouse, ask the credit bureau to list these accounts under your name as well. Although credit bureaus are not required to add new accounts to your file, many will do so for a small fee. Finally, if you presently share in the use of a credit account with your spouse, ask the creditor to report it under both names.

Creditors are not required to report any account history information to credit bureaus. If a creditor does report on an account, however, and if both spouses are permitted to use the account or are contractually liable for its repayment, under the Equal Credit Opportunity Act you can require the creditor to report the information under both names. When contacting your creditor or credit bureau, do so in writing and include relevant information, such as account numbers, to help speed the process. As with all important business communications, keep a copy of what you send.

If you do not have a credit history, you should begin to build one. If you have a steady income and have lived in the same area for at least a year, try applying for credit with a local business, such as a department store. Or you might borrow a small amount from your credit union or the bank where you have checking and savings accounts. A local bank or department store may approve your credit application even if you do not meet the standards of larger creditors. Before you apply for credit, ask whether the creditor reports credit history information to credit bureaus serving your area. Most creditors do, but some do not. If possible, you should try to get credit that will be reported. This builds your credit history.

If you are rejected for credit, find out why. There may be reasons other than lack of credit history. Your income may not meet

---

When it comes time to apply for a credit card you will be bombarded by a Chinese menu of choices. FinanCenter has the credit card bill of fare covered. Whether you haven't yet acquired a taste for credit or the benefits of a gold card leave you frothing at the mouth, there's a little bit of something here for everyone.

Once you've had your fill, you can click on either the Compare APR and annual fees or Compare rewards or rebates offered links.

http://www.financenter.com/credit/cselect.htm

Contents:
- Types of Cards Available
- Selecting a Card

Types of Cards Available

Debit Card
A card which directly accesses the cardholder's account, providing payment for a transaction in like fashion to writing a check. No credit is extended to the cardholder; no debt is incurred.

Gold Card
A credit card providing above average benefits, including travel services, rental car insurance, and insurance for items purchased. Please see Gold Cards for further information.

Rebate/Reward Card
A credit card which supplies benefits based upon the card's usage. Benefits are usually in the form of services, such as air line tickets, discounts on future purchases, or cash refunds and are based upon a percentage of the purchase amounts charged.

Secured Card
A credit card for which the cardholder has made a security deposit, frequently in the form a savings deposit, to ensure payment of the outstanding balance should the cardholder default. Designed for those who lack credit or have damaged credit.

In keeping with the ongoing edible motif, you can use this credit card calculator to compare apples to apples or even apples to oranges.

Shop around and come back here to see which card is really the best deal. The credit card comparison calculator works to level the playing field even when cards might seem too dissimilar to be directly compared, such as when one card offers rewards and the other does not.

http://www.smartcalc.com/cgi-bin/smartcalc/CRE7.cgi/FinanCenter

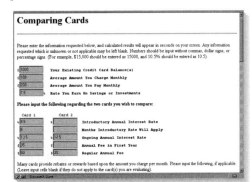

Comparing Cards

Please enter the information requested below, and calculated results will appear in seconds on your screen. Any information requested which is unknown or not applicable may be left blank. Numbers should be input without commas, dollar signs, or percentage signs. (For example, $15,000 should be entered as 15000, and 10.5% should be entered as 10.5).

1000 — Your Existing Credit Card Balance(s)
100 — Average Amount You Charge Monthly
200 — Average Amount You Pay Monthly
7.5 — Rate You Earn On Savings or Investments

Please input the following regarding the two cards you wish to compare:

Card 1 / Card 2
9.8 — Introductory Annual Interest Rate
6 — Months Introductory Rate Will Apply
13.5 / 12.5 — Ongoing Annual Interest Rate
95 — Annual Fee in First Year
60 — Regular Annual Fee

Many cards provide rebates or rewards based upon the amount you charge per month. Please input the following, if applicable. (Leave input cells blank if they do not apply to the card(s) you are evaluating).

You're going to have to find out all that you can about any cards that you want to compare. Just knowing a card's <u>APR</u> won't cut it. In order to accurately compare two cards you will need to fill in things like how long an introductory rate will apply, when you will receive any rebates, and the number of points required to claim a reward.

Fill in all of the applicable blanks and click on the "Compute Results" button at the bottom of the screen.

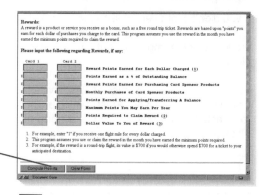

http://www.smartcalc.com/cgi-bin/smartcalc/CRE7.cgi/FinanCenter

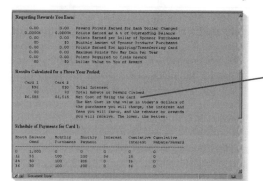

You will be given a rundown on the two cards being compared. The key part of the results screen is to be found in the "Results Calculated for a Three Year Period" section. Look at the line that reads "Net cost of using the card." This number takes into account the estimated value of the purchases you might charge, the interest and fees you would incur on them, and any rebates or rewards you would receive. The lower this bottom line is, the better it is for your bottom line.

http://www.smartcalc.com/cgi-bin/smartcalc/CRE7.cgi/FinanCenter

There are better ways to find and compare credit cards that meet your particular needs than just waiting for card issuers to send you junk mail that you actually want for a change. <u>CardTrak</u> is one of several services out there that surveys the best credit card deals, categorizes them by group, and offers the lists to consumers. But unlike most other lists, CardTrak's lists of cards is easily accessible on the Web and, more important when what you're trying to do is save money in the first place, it's free.

http://www.ramresearch.com/ct_main.html

From CardTrak's main menu you can select any of the numerous credit card surveys offered. You will find lists of some of the best credit card deals going, particularly on <u>Visa</u> and <u>MasterCard</u>, in each of the following categories: Low Rate Standard Cards, No Annual Fee Standard Cards, Low Rate Gold Cards, No Annual Fee Gold Cards, Secured Cards, Rebate Cards, Affinity Cards, Credit Union Cards, and the enigmatic "Other" Cards.

http://www.ramresearch.com/ct_main.html

If you rarely carry a balance on your cards from month to month, then the interest rate is probably less important to you than the fees and the length of the grace periods that cards offer. If that sounds like you, try either the <u>standard</u> or <u>gold no annual fee lists</u>. If, on the other hand, you tend to carry a balance from one month to the next, then the fees will be less significant to you than the interest rate. In that case, take a look at the <u>standard</u> and <u>gold low interest lists</u>, as befits the credit limit you're interested in.

http://www.ramresearch.com/ct_main.html

With secured cards, you deposit money into a bank account as collateral against your credit line, thereby reducing the risk to the card issuer. As such, becoming approved for any of the cards on the <u>secured card list</u> is possible even if you have no credit history or have had credit problems in the past.

The <u>list of rebate cards</u> includes cards that offer rebates on fees, products, or services. If you are looking to take advantage of any of these rebate programs look no further.

http://www.ramresearch.com/ct_main.html

Thousand of organizations offer affinity cards. These organizations get a small percentage of the profits generated by the use of their cards. If your intent is to make a contribution to a worthy cause by using one of these "kick-back" cards, you're generally better off to make a tax deductible donation directly to the organization instead. If you just want to see how your affinity card stacks up against the competition, this somewhat random list of affinity cards is as good a place as any to check.

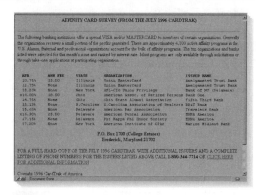

http://www.ramresearch.com/ct_main.html

Credit Unions are not allowed to offer cards to nonmembers, but on the whole offer lower interest rates than bank issuers. The cards found on the credit union card list can be a good deal, if you're a member.

The "other" credit cards list is everything other than Visa and MasterCard. These "others" include American Express, Discover, Diner's Club, Optima, and Bravo. Here is where you will be able to find the APR (if applicable) and annual fee for each.

http://www.ramresearch.com/ct_main.html

The Credit Card Network is another Web site that offers lists of good deals on low interest rate credit cards. There is a charge of $9.95 for this list, but if it helps you to find a good deal on a card, it could be money well spent. Also available from The Credit Card Network are lists of secured, rebate, frequent flyer, and Canadian "best deals." These four lists are free, sort of—you will have to fill out a survey to get to them. Even so, well worth the small effort. Especially for our friends in The Great White North.

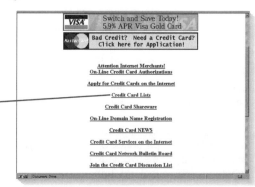

http://www.creditnet.com/

You will find these credit card lists easily enough by clicking on the link that says Credit Card Lists. The directions are straightforward and the four free lists can be downloaded into your computer in numerous formats or viewed directly over the Web.

Also of special interest on this site is an extensive list of on-line credit card applications. Get to it by clicking on Apply for Credit Cards on the Internet.

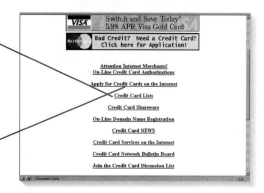

http://www.creditnet.com/

This list of links to on-line credit card applications is hardly complete, but then given the ever changing, ever expanding nature of the Net, show me an Internet list that is. Many of the credit card issuers that offer Web based application forms are covered here, including most of the big names in the industry. There's a good chance the credit card company that you're interested in is listed here as well. When you find the one you're looking for click on the link to begin the application process.

http://www.creditnet.com/ccn-cardlinks.html

When you apply for a credit card on-line, just as in real life, you will need to supply certain specific information before you can be considered for approval. This credit card application from FirstUnion is typical of the sort of things you will be required to fill out.

Besides the obvious, name, address, and so on, you will be asked to supply employment and income information and specifics about your finances, including any loans, debts, and bank accounts.

http://www.firstunion.com/apply/

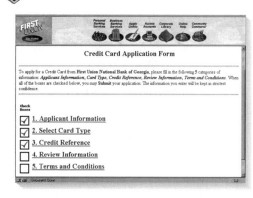

You may not group the various plastic cards you have accumulated in the same league as a mortgage, but in the eyes of law anyway, credit cards do qualify as a loan and are subject to certain rules and regulations designed to protect the consumer. The Truth in Lending Act requires all lenders to spell out all of the terms and conditions of a loan before it is made.

Read these terms and conditions carefully, they contain everything you need to know but didn't know you need to ask.

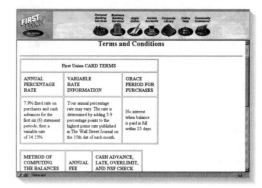

http://www.firstunion.com/apply/

Credit, But at a Price

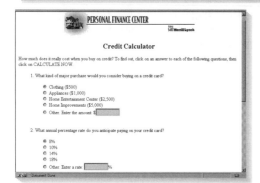

Credit cards have a way of burning a hole in your pocket. With them, you may be tempted to buy things on credit that you wouldn't dream about buying from savings, reasoning, perhaps, that while you don't have the money to get that surround sound mega-entertainment center right now, you can afford to pay for it little by little.

Merril Lynch has a Credit Calculator that you can use to see just how much that new toy will really cost.

http://www.ml.com/personal/liabil/credcalc.html

In calculating the overall cost of a credit card purchase, you must consider not only the interest rate that will be applied to an item but also how long it will take to pay it off.

Fill in the appropriate numbers for the amount borrowed, the interest rate paid and the monthly payments made and click the "Calculate Now" button for the results.

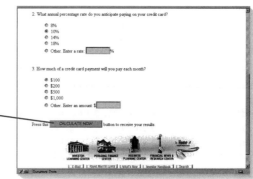

http://www.ml.com/personal/liabil/credcalc.html

What you find may shock you. In paying only the minimum amount due listed on your monthly card statement, you don't just keep the credit card company happy, you keep them very happy. Paying the minimum due each month on a $1,000 purchase can rack up in the neighborhood of $500 in interest charges and take over a year to pay off.

Remember, the minimum amount due is merely a suggestion. Paying a little more now will cost you much less later.

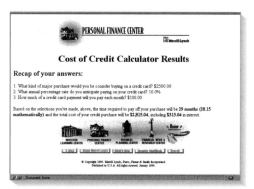

http://www4.merrill-lynch.ml.com/cgi-bin/costcred.exe

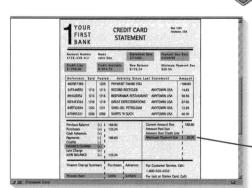

If the only thing you ever look at on your monthly card statement is the minimum payment due line, it may be because the rest of the statement is so confusing. There is a method to this madness, however, and deciphering this confusion of numbers and entries doesn't have to drive you insane.

Visa has an interactive example of a typical credit card statement for you to explore. Click on any of the highlighted areas for an in-depth explanation of its significance.

http://www.visa.com/cgi-bin/vee/ff/tips/bill/statement.html?2+0

Fraud, Scams, and Secrets

Beyond merely the purchase of happiness, credit card users are endowed with certain unalienable rights. You have the right to receive prompt credit for payment, the right to dispute billing errors, the right not to pay for unauthorized charges, and the right to withhold payment for faulty merchandise.

The FTC has a declaration of these credit card rights and information on places to turn to when your credit card company does not hold these rights to be self-evident.

http://www.webcom.com/~lewrose/brochures/cc.html

The Federal Trade Commission also publishes this guide to credit card fraud. It, and over 100 other consumer "scam" brochures issued by the FTC are available on the Arent Fox law firm Web site.

Designed to help you to help yourself, the brochure spells out the sorts of skulduggery to watch out for, the precautions you can take to avoid being taken and what to do if you're duped.

http://www.webcom.com/~lewrose/brochures/ccfraud.html

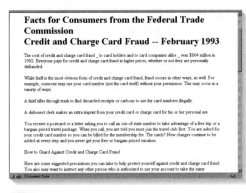

Sometimes your rights are trampled under foot by store merchants who don't even realize they're stepping on your toes. Many states, and most credit card companies, have laws and regulations in place that are designed to protect both your privacy and your purchase price.

At the Bankcard Holders of America Web site you can learn your rights at the till and print out a copy of BHA's Consumer Action Card to pull out of your wallet and show unwary merchants that you mean business.

http://www.epn.com/bha/rights.htm

Perhaps the worst kind of credit card scam is the one that's perfectly legal. Caveat emptor is treated as a business practice by some unscrupulous credit card issuers, a practice made perfect by hiding it between the lines of your monthly card statement for all to see. Shortened due dates, retroactive rate hikes, and interest backdating are some of the 12 Credit Card Secrets Banks Don't Want You To Know About.
Discover their dirty little secrets here and let the banker beware.

http://www.consumer.com/consumer/CREDITC.html

Credit Reports

Who's Watching You and What Do They See?
- The Better Business Bureau: Money and Investments
  - Tips on Credit Reporting
  - Credit Reporting Agencies
- VCR (Victims of Credit Reporting)
  - VCR's Take on the Credit Reporting Agencies
- The Three Major Credit Bureaus
  - Trans Union Corporation
  - Equifax
    - Ordering a Copy of Your Credit Report From Equifax
  - Experian (Formerly TRW)
    - Credit 101: The Basics of Consumer Credit Reports
    - What Information is on a Credit Report?
    - Ordering a Copy of Your Credit Report From Experian
    - A Sample Credit Report
    - Revolving Showcase: Divorce and Credit

Repairing Your Credit
- How to Fix Your Credit
- Are Credit Repair Agencies Legitimate?
- The On-Line Credit Repair Kit

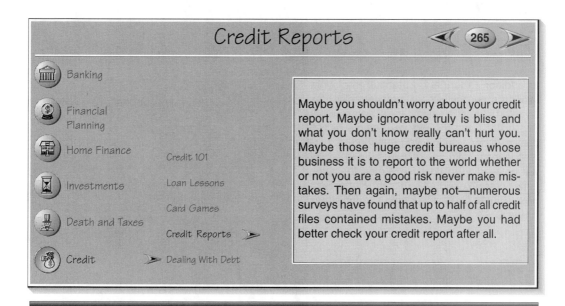

Banking

Financial Planning

Home Finance

Investments

Death and Taxes

Credit

Credit 101

Loan Lessons

Card Games

Credit Reports ➤

➤ Dealing With Debt

Maybe you shouldn't worry about your credit report. Maybe ignorance truly is bliss and what you don't know really can't hurt you. Maybe those huge credit bureaus whose business it is to report to the world whether or not you are a good risk never make mistakes. Then again, maybe not—numerous surveys have found that up to half of all credit files contained mistakes. Maybe you had better check your credit report after all.

 # Who's Watching You and What Do They See?

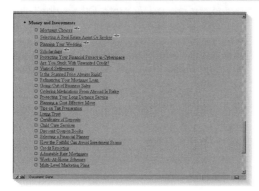

You may or may not have heard of something called a credit bureau before, but one thing is for sure, credit bureaus have most certainly heard of you. Odd that while they keep track of your every financial move most of us have only the faintest clue about who they are and what they do. Go on-line with the Better Business Bureau to learn more about these mighty credit bureaus and what they have to say about you. Log in, scroll down to the "Money and Investments" section and click on Credit Reporting.

http://www.bbb.org/library/searchBySubject.html

The idea of some company tracking your finances and peddling your credit history might feel like an invasion of your privacy, but before someone is going to loan you a big chunk of change they'll want to know if you're good for it. Lenders turn to credit bureaus to find out. Trans Union, Equifax, and Experian (formerly known as TRW) are the three major credit bureaus. Each keeps an independent, and often discrepant, version of your past credit history on file, so it's important to know what each one of them has to say on the subject.

http://www.bbb.org/library/tipcred.html

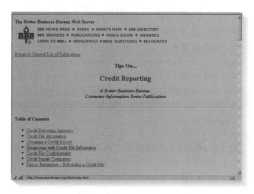

In addition to lenders, potential employers, landlords, and insurance underwriters all have a vested interest in your financial history. When that history, and the picture it paints of you, comes under scrutiny, you may find yourself wondering what kinds of things these people will be reading in your file. When the questions come up, you can turn to the Better Business Bureau Credit Reporting tips for honest answers.

http://www.bbb.org/library/tipcred.html#agency

Many people don't like the 300 pound gorillas of the credit reporting industry because they invade our privacy for profit. Others don't like them because they possess the pernicious combination of extraordinary power and ordinary human error. The folks at VCR (Victims of Credit Reporting) just plain old don't like them at all.

Whatever you personally think of credit bureaus, you've got to admire the chutzpah it took to create this pull no punches site.

http://pages.prodigy.com/ID/vcr/vcr.html

VCR has all sorts of articles on credit bureaus and credit repair firms. None are very flattering, to say the least. For example, click on The Players. At the risk of being sued, I won't reprint here how VCR defines the acronym TRW, but you just *know* these folks aren't going to be getting any Xmas cards from the credit bureaus this year.

As a last line of defense, VCR includes the e-mail address for the members of the U.S. House of Representatives and Senate.

http://pages.prodigy.com/ID/vcr/play.html

Critical perspective on the credit reporting industry is all very interesting, but what really matters to you is what is in your credit file. To find out, you'll have to pay a visit to each of the three major credit bureaus that keep those files on you.

First stop, <u>Trans Union</u>. A newcomer to the Net, the Trans Union Web site was still very much under construction when we paid them a visit. Try them now or phone them at 1-800-851-2674 for a copy of your report.

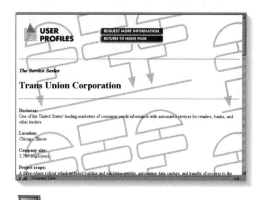

http://www.sapling.com/trs.html#top

Next up is <u>Equifax</u>. Unfortunately, their Web site has also been something of a hit-and-miss affair. Sometimes it's up and working and sometimes it isn't. When it is working you will find information on obtaining a copy of your credit report by clicking on the <u>Order Your Credit Profile!</u> link.

http://www.equifax.com/consumer/consumer.html

The fee Equifax charges for obtaining a copy of your report is about as stable as their Web site; sometimes there is a fee and sometimes there isn't. Depends on how good of a mood the company is in that day.

After receiving your request, Equifax promises to send out a copy of your report within 72 hours. Once you've had a chance to look it over, you can call one of their "information consultants" with any questions you have.

http://www.equifax.com/consumer/order/info.html

Last stop on the credit bureau express; Experian, the new name for the agency formerly known as TRW (TAFKATRW), largest credit bureau in the known universe. At the top of the page you can read all the gory details, how they keep track of "more than 190 million credit-active consumers" and how they process 43 million pieces of information about those consumers each day. Amazing—I can't even keep track of my two children.

Click here, on Consumer Credit Pavillion.

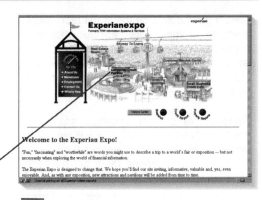

http://www.trw.com/iss/iss.html

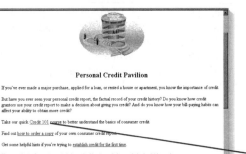

I'm sure that my third grade teacher, Mrs. Divine, would agree that my math skills leave much to be desired. Not one to let a little thing like incompetence stand in my way, I sharpened up old No. 2 and used TAFKATRW's astounding numbers to calculate that the bureau took note of your financial dealings an average of nearly seven times last month. Here's your chance to see what *they're* up to.

Scroll past the PR blurb and click on Credit 101 for a list of the most frequently asked questions.

http://www.experian.com/personal.html

Some of the most common credit report questions are covered here, running the gamut from what is, and isn't, found in your credit report to questions about how credit granting decisions are made. Clicking on any item brings up that topic's section in the larger document.

This stuff may not seem interesting to you, but it's of interest to anyone considering extending your credit. So click on What information is on a consumer credit report? and learn what everyone else will be learning about you.

http://www.experian.com/personal/index.html

The <u>Fair Credit Reporting Act</u> was enacted by Congress to protect your rights as a credit-active consumer. The information on this Web page is a direct result. It states who's allowed to look at your credit history and for what reasons, how long negative information is allowed to remain on your file and what you can do to dispute any inaccurate information that you find. Of course, you won't find any inaccuracies unless you look. And to do that you'll want to click on <u>how to order your Experian consumer credit report</u> at the top of the page.

http://www.experian.com/personal/index.html#information

What information is on a consumer credit report

The typical consumer credit report includes four types of information:

- Identifying information: your name, nicknames, current and previous addresses, Social Security number, year of birth, and current and previous employers. (On your copy of your Experian credit report, but not the version provided to others, your spouse's name may appear.) This information comes from your credit application, so its accuracy depends on your filling out the forms clearly, completely and consistently each time you apply for credit.

- Credit information: specific information about each account such as the date opened, credit limit or loan amount, balance, monthly payment and payment pattern during the past several years. The report also states whether anyone else besides you (your spouse or cosigner, for example) is responsible for paying the account. This information comes from companies that do business with you.

- Public record information: federal district bankruptcy records; state and county court records, tax liens and monetary judgments; and, in some states, overdue child support. This information comes from public records.

- Inquiries: the names of those who obtained a copy of your credit report for any reason. (On your copy of your Experian credit report, addresses are included.) This information comes from the credit reporting agency, and it remains up to two years, consistent with federal law.

Your Experian credit report does *not* contain — and Experian does *not* collect — data about race, religious preference, medical history, personal lifestyle, political preference, medical history, friends, criminal record or any other information unrelated to credit.

How long information stays on a consumer credit report

Federal law specifies how long negative information may remain on your credit report.

How to request a copy of your consumer credit report

Sorry, but security and privacy concerns prevent us from accepting e-mail requests for consumer credit reports at this time.

All requests for consumer credit reports must be made in writing.

Experian provides two ways for you to obtain a copy of your credit report:

- <u>at no charge, whenever</u> you have been denied credit, employment or rental housing based at least in part on your credit report

- <u>for a fee</u>, which varies by state, if you have not been denied credit

A <u>sample consumer credit report</u> is available for viewing.

A copy of your credit report is free if you've been denied credit, employment or rental housing in the last 60 days or, for a small fee, whenever you want (like before a potential employer sees it).

Even if you do have to pay for it, it's a good idea to check your credit report for mistakes from time to time and as the need arises. Follow the appropriate link and you will find all the information you need to get a copy of your report for your own records.

http://www.experian.com/product/consumer/index.html

Privacy and security issues are cited as the reasons for your not being able to request a copy of your credit report directly over the Net. So until the day arrives when we can prove identity over the Net, you can get the instructions on the Web site but you'll still have to send away for the report the old fashioned way. <u>Print</u> out the form, fill it in, sign on the dotted line, and send it off with your check or money order (sorry, no credit cards accepted). You should recieve a copy of your report in the mail—you know, eventually.

Experian National Consumer Assistance Center
P.O. Box 949
Allen, TX 75013-0949

Experian will mail your report within four days of receiving your request.

Your full name (including generation, such as Jr., Sr., III)   _____
Current address   _____
City, state, zip   _____

If you've lived at this address less than five years, please list your previous addresses for a five-year period.

Previous address #1   _____
City, state, zip   _____
Previous address #2   _____
City, state, zip   _____

Spouse's first name (if married)   _____
Your Social Security number   _____
Your date of birth   _____
Your signature   _____

We ask for this information to ensure that the credit report we compile for you is as complete and accurate as

http://www.experian.com/product/consumer/fee.html

Getting a copy of your credit report is relatively painless compared to deciphering it. Be sure to check out the sample credit report.

The reports supplied by each credit reporting agency will look somewhat different, but they all contain the same basic information. Credit reports show things like the highwater mark for credit you have charged, how long and how often payments have been past due and a list of everyone that has inquired into your credit history.

http://www.experian.com/personal/sample.html

Divorce is messy no matter how you slice it, and a neat separation of credit responsibilities is no exception. There are things you can do to help make as clean a financial break as possible. Experian's Revolving Showcase has some helpful suggestions to that end.

When all is said and done though, the only thing that will put an end to a fiscal union is time; it takes 7 years for most credit records to fade, 10 years for bankruptcies. Long after the relationship is forgotten, you will still have the memories of debt to hold on to.

http://www.experian.com/crossroads.html

Repairing Your Credit

In looking over your credit report don't be too surprised to find inaccurate, misleading, or out-and-out incorrect information. If you find a bona fide blemish, the best suggestion is to keep your nose clean from here on in and rest assured that the negative information will disappear in time. If, on the other hand, your spotty file is the result of someone else's sloppy mistakes you should follow the step-by-step instruction on How to Fix Your Credit from American Dream.

http://www.amdream.com/credit/fixcredt.htm

You don't need to have a degree in law to follow this advice and you certainly don't need to pay for some "credit repair" agency to take you to the cleaners. These agencies don't do anything for you that you can't do for yourself with less hassle. Click on the Are "credit repair" Agencies Legitimate? article before shelling out big bucks to anyone that promises to "fix" your records. Everything you'll need to fix your credit report yourself can be found in the Credit Repair Kit and followed for the price of a few stamps.

http://www.amdream.com/credit/fixcredt.htm#Are credit repair agencies legitimate?

The on-line Credit Repair Kit holds your hand and walks you through the various steps needed to correct the mistakes on your credit report as quickly and painlessly as (legally) possible. If you find yourself in the unenviable position of having to clear your financial name, this repair kit should be your first stop. With any luck, it will also be your last.

Do yourself a favor and print out the entire section for you to refer back to later on.

http://www.amdream.com/credit/fix2crdt.htm

The kit includes instructions and several effective form letters of complaint, each one more emphatic than the last. These letters ought to get the bureau's attention, but if that doesn't work you'll find instructions on contacting the FTC and your state government. Credit bureaus know what the inside of a courthouse looks like all too well and tend to be leery of getting dragged into court. Again. It's nice to know that when all else fails you can always call in the cavalry.

http://www.amdream.com/credit/fix2crdt.htm#sample_letter_3

Dealing With Debt

Debt Reduction Plans That Work
- Warning Signs and Evasive Maneuvers
- The Debt-To-Income Worksheet
- What Bill Collectors Can and Can Not Do
- Watch Out For These Scams: Credit "Doctors"
- Software Assistance: The Debt Analyzer
- Bill Consolidation Worksheet
- Debt Counselors of America
  - The Debt Forum
  - Debt Sucks

Last Resorts
- Frequently Asked Bankruptcy Questions
- ABBC Certified Bankruptcy Attorneys Listed by State

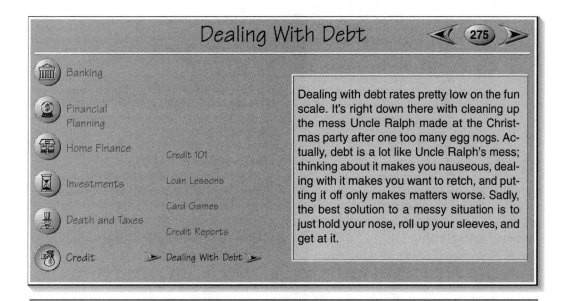

Banking

Financial
Planning

Home Finance   Credit 101

Investments   Loan Lessons

                            Card Games

Death and Taxes   Credit Reports

Credit   ➤ Dealing With Debt ➤

Dealing with debt rates pretty low on the fun scale. It's right down there with cleaning up the mess Uncle Ralph made at the Christmas party after one too many egg nogs. Actually, debt is a lot like Uncle Ralph's mess; thinking about it makes you nauseous, dealing with it makes you want to retch, and putting it off only makes matters worse. Sadly, the best solution to a messy situation is to just hold your nose, roll up your sleeves, and get at it.

Debt Reduction Plans That Work

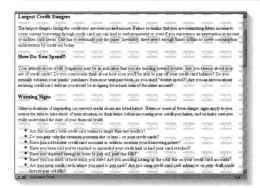

If you pretend you're not at home when there's a knock at the door or screen your phone calls for fear of bill collectors, you can skip to the back of the chapter. If things aren't quite that bad yet but you're afraid they may be getting worse, take this quick credit abuse test on the Bankcard Holders of America. If you can answer yes to two or more of these warning signs you might be heading towards fiscal meltdown.

http://www.epn.com/bha/out-debt.htm

Don't skip this site just because you think failing the test is a forgone conclusion. You won't find anyone wagging their fingers and calling you naughty here. What you will find are solutions, and admitting the fact that you have a debt problem is the first step towards finding those solutions.

Before you can even begin to consider throwing up your hands in surrender and declaring bankruptcy, you owe it to yourself to try the debt reduction plans outlined here.

http://www.epn.com/bha/out-debt.htm

Prioritize payments.

Put the most money toward your highest interest rate debt. Contact creditors to try to set up a new payment schedule. A new affordable repayment plan can result in a lessening of the financial burden when forces outside your control rob you of pay-back power (unemployment, divorce, death in the family, etc.). Serious devotion to repayment once a life crisis has passed can mean the difference between rescheduling your debt and nasty collection proceedings. See BHA's DEBT ZAPPER!

Debt consolidation

Debt consolidation may make dollars and sense in your situation. Rolling all debts into one large note with a single monthly payment (in lieu of numerous payments at 18-24% interest rates) has saved many a credit abuser. This will only work if you close off the credit accounts you've consolidated. If you continue to use them, you'll only be in worse shape. One benefit of a consolidation loan - and staying current on its monthly payment - is that your credit record will not be ruined by repeated late payments, late charges, and dunning notices from several small accounts.

In the worst case, if you've abused your credit privileges beyond hope of repayment under your current income circumstances, the law does allow a last resort - personal bankruptcy. Under the U.S. Bankruptcy Act of 1978, you can file a petition for a straight bankruptcy or seek protection under Chapter 13. Chapter 13 is more favorable to the debtor. Under the protection and supervision of a bankruptcy court, old debts are regularly paid off with your future income while basic assets are protected from claims.

A straight bankruptcy would be more appropriate when you don't enjoy a regular income but you wish to discharge all your debts. Current law provides that certain debtor assets - $7,500 equity in a home, $1,200 equity in a car or truck, $200 per item in household goods, up to $400 worth of any other property, $750 worth of trade tools, books, etc., $500 worth of personal jewelry, social security payments, unemployment compensation, etc.- are retained and protected from credit claims. Court filing fees, trustee fees, and legal bills, however, can add to the cost of filing for bankruptcy. And reports on your bankruptcy are carried in credit bureau files for up to 10 years. Thus, if you've tried budgeting, increasing your income, or consolidating your debt and all these methods proved inadequate to deal with your credit overextension, bankruptcy can be an

Lenders and consultants take a more systematic approach to debt assessment than simply asking how much month is left at the end of the money. In order to determine the severity of your situation they will use a <u>debt-to-income worksheet</u> like this one from the Web pages of <u>Educaid</u>.

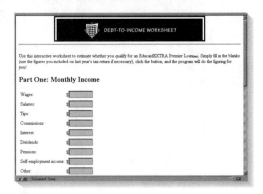

Fill in the amounts for any income sources that you have and all of the monthly payments you must make and click the "Calculate your debt-income ratio" button.

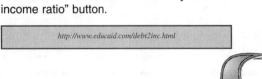

http://www.educaid.com/debt2inc.html

The debt-to-income ratio number given is a good indication of how large a problem you have to contend with. Measure your numbers against the 30 percent required by most banks before they can grant you a mortgage. How close your numbers are to that figure should give you a good indication of where you stand. Above 43 percent and, as one banker succinctly put it, "I wouldn't give Mother Teressa a mortgage if she brought along a character reference from the Pope himself." God bless her soul.

http://www.educaid.com/cgi-bin/debt2inc.pl

When debt becomes serious, bill collectors come calling. Sometimes the harassment of bill collectors becomes so unbearable that people with otherwise solvable financial problems declare bankruptcy just to stop the abuse. It doesn't have to be like that. Just because you owe someone money doesn't mean you lose your rights. <u>The Fair Debt Collection Act</u>, recapped here by the <u>FTC</u>, draws the line between what collectors can and can not do to collect and what you can do when that line is crossed.

http://consumerlawpage.com/nographics/brochure/36.shtml

The lure of a quick fix is strongest when you are at your weakest. Credit "Doctors," the parasites of the industry, know this and take advantage of it. At best, they charge an arm and a leg to do what you can do yourself. At worst, they take their pound of flesh and leave you with nothing but a headache.

Homefair has all the dirt on these quacks and explains why using one is a prescription for financial disaster at a time when you can least afford it.

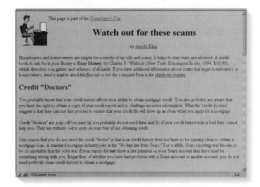

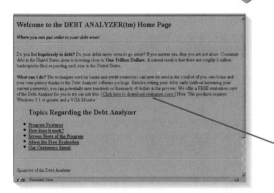

One of the best ways of solving a debt problem is by stopping it before it's gone too far. This little program called the Debt Analyzer can be found on the Net, downloaded for free and taken for a test drive for 21 days before you have to either purchase it or give it up. By that time you should know for sure if it's worth the money anyway.

Click here to download the test drive version of the program. Sorry Mac fans, this one requires Windows 3.1 or higher.

There's nothing that this software can do for you that you couldn't do for yourself with a couple of pencils and a load of patience. Whether you use a pencil or a program, you will attack the debt problem in one of two ways; by prioritizing your debts by interest rates, highest first, and paying them off or by consolidating all your debts into one loan at a lower interest rate and paying it off. The important part is that you make a plan, you stick to that plan, and you don't take on any additional debt while you're at it.

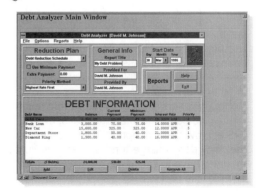

Most debt worries come from having run up the bills on high interest credit cards. Loan consolidation helps solve this problem by taking those high-priced credit card bills and lumping them together into one larger loan, presumably at a lower interest rate. You save money on interest charges and have just one monthly bill to contend with.

Use this Bill Consolidation Worksheet from The Money Store Web site to calculate how much you'll need to cover all your debts.

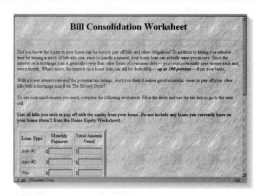

http://www.themoneystore.com/billcon.html

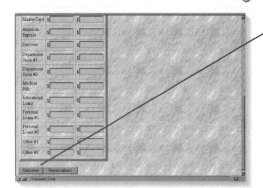

Fill in the blanks and click the "Calculate" button at the bottom of the screen for a summary of the results.

Loan consolidation can make a lot of sense, but if you use it to clear the balances of your credit cards and then go on to charge those cards up to the hilt again you end up in worse shape that when you started. With a consolidation loan you can either defeat your debt or defeat your purpose.

http://www.themoneystore.com/billcon.html

When you're up to your assets in alligators the last thing you want is for someone to hand you a crock. Getting the no-nonsense, no bull counselling of a professional can be the difference between the lifeline you need and just another line.

Debt Counselors of America® has a reputation for helping people in financial straits. They're IRS approved and nonprofit. That's not to say that they don't charge for their services, just that they have to spend the profits they make on cute little cartoons.

http://www.dca.org/home.htm

Past the cartoon is this list of links for you to explore. You'll find testimonials, common questions and answers, and a list of the programs offered. From "cash poor" to "in over your head broke," DC of A has designed a program to meet every degree of indebtedness. Click on any of the program titles to look over the all important details.

If, more than anything else, what you need is some advice, stop by the Debt Forum to browse through the messages or post your own question.

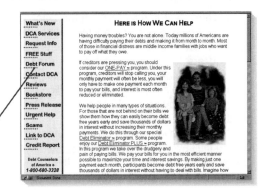

http://www.dca.org/toc.htm

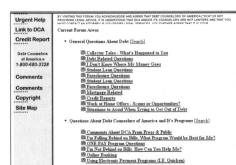

The postings in the debt forum are organized into categories such as student loans, foreclosures, and horror stories starring debt collectors.

Browse around, there's a good chance your question has already been asked by someone else in a similiar situation. If you don't see anything applicable, or if you just want to have your question answered personally by one of the staff debt counsellors, you can register yourself and ask away.

http://www.dca.org/forum.htm

Not to be missed on the Debt Counselors of America® site is the Money Savers and Free Stuff area. You will find coupons, publications, deals on phone rates, and free software. Above all, you'll find the instructions for ordering this fashionable DEBT SUCKS bumper sticker.

The sticker is free but for a small, tax-deductible donation you can help support the good work of a nonprofit help organization and the starving cartoonist they employ.

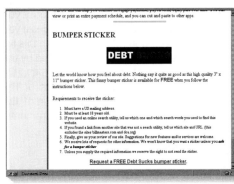

http://www.dca.org/free.htm#BUMPER

If you've made it this far through the Dealing With Debt chapter it's probably because you have already tried everything else there is to try and are left considering some drastic choices. If it makes you feel any better, you are not alone. There are over two million personal bankruptcy cases either pending or currently in the courts right now.

You'll want to talk to a lawyer, but for now you turn to the Law Offices of Warren E. Agin and begin exploring your options on their Frequently Asked Bankruptcy Questions page.

http://www.agin.com/bkfaq/

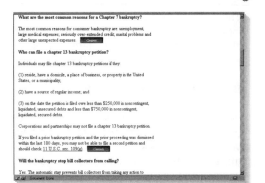

These Web pages don't have any confusing lawyerly gibberish, just straight answers, in English. They explain the various types of bankruptcy and which type would be best (if "best" is the right word) in your particular case. You'll find answers to all the pressing questions. Questions like "Will I lose my house?", "Do I lose everything?", "How long will this affect me?", "Can I sell my assets to my family?"... All the stuff that's been keeping you awake at night. It's here.

http://www.agin.com/bkfaq/faq4.html#Q3

When the time comes to call an attorney you can always flip through the yellow pages if you have to. But you don't. The lawyers on this list are organized by state and are certified by the American Bankruptcy Board of Certification. Click on the state name for a list of the attorney's in your area that have met the ABBC's stringent standards and requirements.

Oh, and good luck.

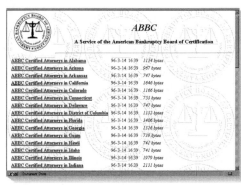

http://www.abiworld.org/abbc/con/index.html

Banking: E-Money

American Banking Systems
http://www.absbank.com/

If you are a merchant interested in hosting your product on the web, this site is a must see. They feature on-line payment systems for credit cards, checks, and more.

Credit Card Network
http://www.creditnet.com/

A good site to check out for information on credit cards before you get one from your bank.

CyberCash, Inc.
http://www.cybercash.com/cybercash/financial/bankfin.html

Links to sites supporting CyberCash. This is your starting block for information on the new world of electronic money.

DigiCash
http://www.digicash.com/ecash/about.html

This location hosts the FAQ for E-Cash. There is lots of information here about the entire electronic cash services

InfoFINANCE
http://www.siam.net/metro/finance/finance.cgi?file=press15.ff

This vendor develops interactive financial applications to banks and financial institutions throughout the Asia Pacific Region. Lots of services are provided here like calculators and branch locators.

Intell-a-Check
http://www.icheck.com/

Intell-a-Check lets you pay for products by check "OVER THE PHONE" and if you are the merchant, it lets you print out the phoned check which you can then take straight to your bank and deposit.

Inter Coin
http://www.intercoin.com/

If you are interested in the idea of E-Money, but are concerned that most providers set a ten dollar minimum purchase, then do some browsing on this site.

Mondex International Limited
http://www.mondex.com/index.html

Mondex uses a smart card to store electronic cash, which can be used to pay for goods and services in the same way as cash, but with some key benefits over traditional cash.

NetChex
http://www.netchex.com/

NetChex offers consumers a "user-friendly" and secure way of writing an electronic check on the Internet to a business or to any other entity they may choose.

On-line Check Systems
http://www.onlinecheck.com/

This site offers the same electronic check idea as others, but has an on-line demo that you can use to try the service for yourself.

TelPay
http://www.telpay.ca

Canada's largest on-line bill payment service group. Now you can pay your bills over the Net.

WC3
http://www.w3.org/pub/WWW/Payments/

Articles and discussions on various electronic payment methods.

Banking: Banking Services

Bay Bank
http://www.baybank.com/products/calculators/index.html

Like the above site, Bay Bank has calculators on-line to help you find out if you can prequalify for a loan, what your closing costs are, refinancing, and more.

CorpFiNet
http://www.corpfinet.com/

Extremely comprehensive lists of any items related to personal finance. They have an easy-to-use search engine to locate banks in a specific location or across the world.

Creative Investment Research
http://www2.ari.net/cirm/

This site lists provides general investment information and information on minority and women-owned brokerage firms, banks, and thrifts.

Credit Union Magazine
http://www.cuna.org/page10.htm

Credit Unions also need research. Credit Union Magazine has news and articles pertinent to anyone interested in placing their savings in a Credit Union.

Duncan Resource Group, Inc.
http://www.corpfinet.com/

Another great link site to banks, investments, and more. Worth checking out.

Hypertech Media
http://hypertechmedia.com/Interest.html

If you ever need to calculate compound interest for payoffs from fixed interest investment accounts, this site has a nice little Java calculator for just that purpose.

IFBG Göttingen
http://www.gwdg.de/~ifbg/bank_usa.html

A very good link site to banks and lots of financial services. You can find investments, electronic banking services, currency, and more here.

InterSoft Solutions, Inc.
http://www.FinanceHub.com/finance/invbanks.html

Are you interested in finding banks specifically oriented towards "investments?" If you are, hop, skip, and crawl your way to this site.

Motor City
http://www.motorcity.com

You need that new car, but don't know whether to lease, loan, or if you can even afford it on your budget. Motor City has on-line calculators for all three of those questions.

Mycrowynn Corp.
http://www.mycrowynn.com/apr/

For those people who need an APR or loan amortization calculator, this site has both on-line.

On-line Banking Report
http://www.netbanker.com/resources/bankdir.html

Good link site to most of the major bank and credit union directories in the world. If the bank you want isn't listed here, it should be.

Qualisteam
http://www.qualisteam.com/aconf.html

This site has links to almost 800 banks around the world. Perfect for checking the value of your Swiss Bank account.

The FinanceHub
http://www.catalog.com/intersof/finance/obanks.html

Another site with links to banks around the world.

The Money Page
http://www.moneypage.com/banks/

Do you want to look up the latest news and reference material? This link site has its feelers tapped into lots of information.

The World Bank Group
http://www.worldbank.org/

The World Bank lends money to developing countries-not individuals. So unless you happen to own your own country, you won't be able to get a loan here. There is however a wealth of information on banking that is of value to individuals.

Ultradata
http://www.udweb.com/other.htm

Do you prefer a credit union to a bank? Take a look at all the credit union links on this site.

Westpac Banking Corporation
http://www.westpac.com.au/deposit.html

Westpac has a deposit calculator that allows you to see how long it would take you to achieve some sort of goal, like a house, a boat, or a holiday depending on how much you save per month.

Banking: On-Line Banking

American Banker
http://www.americanbanker.com/

Ready for inside news on topics pertinent to the banking industry. American Banker has articles and reviews just waiting for you.

Angelfire Communications.
http://www.angelfire.com/pg1/bloans/

Want some tips on how to do business with banks? Look no further.

Apollo Trust Company
http://bankswith.apollotrust.com/

Rated as one of the better banks on the Internet. Take an on-line tour of some of their services and features.

Bank of America
http://www.bankamerica.com/

This is a very well written web site. Good on-line features coupled with interesting graphics make this bank a common link point from many services. The feature that really sets it apart is the ability to build your own bank. Log on to the site and see for yourself.

Bank One
http://www.bankone.com./

Electronic banking for the corporate world. This site is great for the basement-managed businesses that are more interested in making money than spending hours doing "paper" paperwork.

Bank Rate CD Scanner
http://vanbc.wimsey.com/~emandel/question.html

The search for the best CD rates has just gotten easier. Let the Bank Rate CD Scanner and the WWW find the best deals for you.

Bank Rate Monitor
http://www.bankrate.com/index.htm

News, tips, rates and PC banking. What more could anyone want from an on-line banking service provider?

BanxQuote
http://www.banx.com/

Featuring on-line banking, deposits, and loans, quoted by leading banks in each market. You'll also find state-by-state, regional, and national composite benchmarks, as well as useful links and snapshot profiles of the banking institutions.

BayBank
http://www.baybank.com/

Want to locate an ATM, or just do some on-line banking? Try this bank out.

Canada Trust
http://www.canadatrust.com/

Use CT Connect to manage your accounts in a secure fashion. Then try the WWW to view your accounts, find ABMs anywhere in Canada, check stock quotes, rates and fund prices.

Credit Union Times
http://www.cutimes.com/

Credit Union Times carries paid advertising and provides timely and unbiased news coverage of credit unions and the related financial services industry.

Direct Debit
http://www.directdebit.co.uk/

This is a very trendy site from the U.K that discusses on-line banking and how the electronic age has changed the way you do everything. They even start you off by asking if you are in your pajamas yet. Seems to me, that phrase has been used before.

Electronic Banking Resource Center
http://www2.cob.ohio-state.edu/~richards/banking.htm

This site provides a centralized source of information on electronic banking and electronic money. It provides links to news, Internet banks, and electronic money.

Global Network Navigator, Inc.
http://gnn.com/gnn/meta/finance/res/mri.html

Each business day GNN updates the "Highest Nationwide Bank Rates." Bookmark this site for quick reviews of current rates.

Information, Inc.
http://www.webplus.net/infoinc/finnews.html

The newsletter from this site issue contains 20 to 25 summaries focusing on banks and bank regulation, financial instruments, economic trends, domestic and foreign financial news, and other issues.

Intuit
http://www.intuit.com/

Quicken is one of the leaders in PC financial software and lots of banks now support direct uploads and downloads of your Quicken ac-

counts. This site is a must view if you have any interest in personal interactive financial planning.

Microsoft
http://www.microsoft.com/moneyzone/

Like its largest competitor, Microsoft also sports a web site dedicated to their personal finance software. There are lots of articles and interactive guides on home banking, personal finance and investing. Do you ever wonder if Bill uses MS Money to keep track of all those zeros in his bank accounts?

Money On-line
http://pathfinder.com/@@@ttbawYAS0feFMyf/money/

Daily news and links to the best web sites and newsgroups containing articles on banking, investing, and money.

Net Guide
http://www.courant.com/enter/ng_1207.htm

Interesting article on the future of on-line banking with links to the hottest bank sites.

On-line Resources & Communications
http://www.orcc.com/banking.htm

Great site to see the kind of '90s features that today's banks will offer to their clients.

Prime Rate
http://www.primerate.com/

One of the better examples of on-line services offered by banks today.

RDK Enterprise
http://www.rdkenterprise.com/

Now that you have all of this on-line money and on-line bank accounts, what can you use it for. Well, how about shopping at an on-line mall.

Salem Five
http://www.salemfive.com/

With Salem Five, now you can bank from around the corner and around the world! On-line calculators, home banking, and a great interactive demo of how on-line banking works makes this a great site to visit wearing your pajamas.

Security First Network Bank
http://www.sfnb.com/

Right from the start, this bank site gets your attention with a hot linked picture of the inside of a bank. Visit the customer service center to open a new account or go straight to the on-line teller. The best part is that to date, no one has invented virtual lines to wait in.

The Daily Reporter
http://www.sddt.com/~columbus/Files/9511012.html

This site has an article describing why local banks are pursuing on-line banking.

The New York Times
http://www.nytimes.com/partners/banking/index.html

The New York Times Banking Center features daily quotes on on-line banking, deposits and loans, offered by financial institutions in each market.

The Wall Street Journal
http://interactive2.wsj.com/bin/login?Tag=/&URI=/banx/banx.htm

Probably one of the premier financial newspapers in the world. You must be a member to have full access, but once set up, there is lots of information that makes this an invaluable research tool in any person's financial toolkit.

Wells Fargo Bank
http://wellsfargo.com/

Wells Fargo Bank was one of the first Internet aware banks and it shows. Like the other major Internet banks it has on-line calculators, PC banking demonstrations, on-line bill payment, and more.

Banking: Further Exploration

Alta Vista
http://www.altavista.digital.com/cgi-bin/ query?pg=q&what=web&fmt=.&q=bank

Type in "Bank" in the search field.

Excite Netsearch
http://www.excite.com/Reviews/Business/Electronic_Commerce/ index.html?CCt

Section to search is "Business," subsection "Electronic Commerce."

Lycos, Inc.
http://a2z.lycos.com/Business_and_Investing/ Banks__Banking_and_Financial_Institutions/

Section to search is "Business and Investing," subsection "Banks, Banking & Financial Institutions."

Magellan
http://magellan.mckinley.com/ browser.cgi?unb=Business_and_Economics&sub=Banking_and_Insurance&f=0&/

Section to search is "Business and Economics," subsection "Banking and Insurance."

Yahoo!
http://www.yahoo.com/Business_and_Economy/Companies/ Financial_Services/Banking/

Section to search is "Business and Economy," subsection "Companies," subsection "Financial Services," subsection "Banks."

Banking Related Newsgroups
Note: You must have a news reader installed to take part in newsgroups

news:clari.biz.industry.banking

Post questions and read on-line discussions about banking.

Financial Planning: What You Have

Center for Financial Well-Being
http://www.ns.net/cash/

This site features an nice magazine style layout and lots of articles and guest speakers to help you start planning your financial future.

CNNfn
http://www.cnnfn.com/

This is another of those "must view" sites that should be a requirement for anyone who has any sort of financial aspirations.

Debt Free
http://dfnewsletter.com/crownteam/Debt Free

The Debt Free Newsletter is a "no nonsense" monthly publication packed full of debt reduction strategies and ideas to help you increase your income.

Finacenter
http://www.financenter.com/

This is another one of the premier sites on the web for issues dealing with finance. They have calculators for everything and brief, concise descriptions of what everything is.

FinanceNet
http://www.financenet.gov/sales.htm

A "one-stop-shop" for information on the sale of all manner of public assets. Covers everything from real property and loans to planes,

boats, cars, jewelry, and just about anything else that a Federal, state, local or International government will be offering for sale to the general public electronically.

Financial Consultant
http://haven.ios.com/~toadman/finance.html

A great link site to financial planners, investor services, newsletters, and more.

Financial Independence
http://personal.riverusers.com/~jwdiana/

This site has an 800 number that you can call to receive tips on achieving financial independence.

GNN Personal Finance Center
http://www.gnn.com/gnn/meta/finance/

GNN is one of the best financial sites on the web. Articles, hot links, calculators, this site has it all and it's a great place to start your research on what you have.

Grady Cash
http://www.ns.net/cash/selftest/selftest.html

This site has a neat little Java utility to identify what your spending habits are and which of the seven spending profiles you fall into.

Household Budget Management
http://www.netxpress.com/users/hadap/budget.html

Great tips on managing your budget, defining what a budget is, and, of course, the mandatory links to other sites.

Julie's Frugal Tips
http://www.brightok.net/~neilmayo/

This site has links to all many sites that feature quick tips for those looking to save just that little extra every week.

MoneyWeb
http://www.demon.co.uk/moneyweb/index.html

This is probably the most comprehensive financial planning site in the United Kingdom. It features tons of articles, links and more.

Ohio State
http://www.hec.ohio-state.edu/hanna/index.htm

Ohio State hosts the "Financial Counseling and Planning Journal" a yearly guide whose purpose is to disseminate scholarly research related to financial counseling and planning education.

Prosperity Partners, Inc.
http://www.note.com/note/pp/jackpot.html

What do you do with all your money if you ever won a lottery? This site has some answers and advice for you. Of course, the hard part is winning that lottery in the first place.

The Dollar Stretcher
http://www.stretcher.com/dollar/index.htm

A weekly column on family finance and how to stretch that buck.

Tight-Wadding
http://pages.prodigy.com/Tightwadding-frugal-living/

Newsletters, newsgroups, hotlinks; this site gives financial planning tips and information to anyone interested in being a "tight-wad."

University of Minnesota
http://cfanews.co.net/

Are you interested in a newsletter that will help you deal with your everyday financial problems. Of course you are!

Your Life
http://www.yourlife.com/

Your Life has topics like, It's Only Money, When Every Penny Counts, Family Affairs, and more on line. These topics are fun and informative.

Financial Planning: What You Need

Angelfire Communications
http://www.angelfire.com/pages2/bobbyp/index.html

Power planning for everyday life is the idea behind this site. This site links to federal articles on your rights as a financial consumer.

Bonehead Finance
http://ourworld.compuserve.com/homepages/Bonehead_Finance/

Budget plan basics, retirement planning, reference material, and a glossary make this a site worth taking a look at.

Fielder Financial Management
http://networth.galt.com/www/home/planning/fielder/

Devoted primarily to helping you manage and plan your financial needs by looking at tax saving methods, this site has some good tips on what you need to do to minimize the impact of the government on your personal finances.

Financial Fitness Centers
http://www.financialfitnessonline.com/

Financial Fitness Centers are private financial resource centers open to members who want to improve their financial fitness. There is a fee for the software and advice.

Guenot & Associates
http://nwiinc.com/JAGuenot/

Guenot & Associates was created for the sole purpose of helping individuals and families achieve their financial goals. They believe that basic financial principles should be understandable and workable for anyone.

Ingham Group
http://www.ingham.com/

Most of the major financial planning strategies for retirement and investments are listed on this site. Helps you plan for the future.

Integrated Financial Concepts, Inc.
http://www.cwis.com/pages/ifc/ifc1.htm

At IFC, their mission is to assist clients in achieving their personal financial goals. They offer a financial planning process that encompasses the design, implementation, and monitoring of a personalized strategy.

International Association for Financial Planning
http://www.iafp.org/

The only industry-wide organization that provides an exchange of knowledge and experience among professionals in all areas of the financial services industry, IAFP has more than 15,000 members.

LifeNet
http://www.lifenet.com/faq.html

LifeNet wants to provide you with sound advice while you plan your financial future. At the LifeNet FAQ, you will find answers to questions you have posed to their on-line discussion group.

Moneysense
http://www.win.net/~moneysense/

A fee-only practice, Moneysense consults on college funding and financial aid and provides other family financial planning services.

Pinnacle Asset Management Group
http://cust.iamerica.net/pamg/

Another company that offers a wealth of financial planning services including estate planning, wills, and insurance.

Primerica Financial Services
http://www.pfsnet.com/

One of the largest groups in the world who provide financial planning advice, PFS is now on-line and helping people just like you to plan for the future.

Retire Web
http://www.retireweb.com/

RetireWeb is a WWW site packed with financial planning information for Canadians of all ages to help them with all stages of retirement: saving for retirement, options at retirement, and post retirement.

The Center for Debt Management
http://members.aol.com/DebtRelief/index.html

Like the name says, this is a web site devoted to understanding your debts and how to actively manage them.

The Financial Advisors Group
http://www.geocities.com/WallStreet/3257/

Boldly slamming any other site that charges Internet fees for financial information, this site has an interactive brochure and lets you get a free insurance quote.

The Pension Professor
http://www.america.net/~davids/

The Pension Professor provides free advice for setting up your pension and getting ready for those retirement years you worked so hard for.

Financial Planning: Making Up the Difference

401k Forum
http://www.401kforum.com/

401k Forum offers one of the most exciting innovations ever to hit the retirement planning marketplace: investment advice for individuals, available on-line.

Altimira
http://www.altamira.com/altamira/rrsp_calc.html

The RRSP calculator will help you determine if your current RRSP savings and future contribution amounts will be adequate to fund your desired retirement lifestyle

American Express
http://www.americanexpress.com/direct/tools/cashflow/docs/summary.html

American Express has a cash flow summary worksheet to help pinpoint your monthly or annual savings plans contributions.

Austin Municipal Federal Credit Union
http://www.amcu.org/onlineserv/retirement.html

Use this retirement wizard calculator to help you determine the amount of money to save each year in order to achieve your financial goals.

DCB&T
http://www.dcbt.com/FinCalc/Savings.html

DCB&T has an on-line "Financial Planning Calculator Investment Savings Planner" calculator to make your investment decisions as easy as possible.

Diversified Financial Services
http://home.navisoft.com/greyhound/mw96/shelton.htm

This site can help you arrange loans, venture capital, startup financing, and more.

Diversified Investment Advisors
http://www.divinvest.com/

DIA has some on-line games to test your retirement savvy and prepare you for investing your savings.

First Trust Corporation.
http://www.drpira.com/

Focusing on DRP IRAs this site will answer your questions if you can't find the answers among the many topics on-line.

Gordon Pape
http://www.gordonpape.com/

This Canadian site has a free newsletter and a goal to help Canadians with information on Canadian mutual funds and RRSPs.

Household Budget Management
http://www.netxpress.com/users/hadap/software.htm

If you are game and willing to try using shareware and freeware programs, this site has links to lots of financial planning information.

Legal & General
http://www.legal-and-general.co.uk/lg/

This U.K. site has topics on pensions, insurance, mortgages, health care and investments. The site is colorful and most of the information is valid even if you live in the United States.

Merrill Lynch
http://www.merrill-lynch.ml.com/personal/taxes/defer.html

How can tax-deferred annuities fit into my retirement planning? Why don't you crawl your way over to Merrill Lynch and see how.

NASA
http://www.jsc.nasa.gov/bu2/inflate.html

This is a calculator for adjusting cost for inflation from one year to another year. This calculator uses the GDP Deflator.

NJ State
http://www.state.nj.us/treasury/taxation/njit8.htm

If you have questions about IRA distributions, read the article from this site. While designed for New Jersey residents, the site is a useful resource for anyone interested in financial planning.

On Ramp Communications
http://www.orci.com/adc/notins.html

Annuities are not now nor have they ever been insurance. This site explains some of the differences and concepts behind annuities.

Piper Jaffray
http://www.piperjaffray.com/cgi-shl/dbml.exe?template=/pj2/retire_first_version.dbm

Are you investing enough for a comfortable retirement? Will your current rate of return enable you to reach your goal? Try the on-line calculator and find out.

Prudential Securities
http://www.prusec.com/wlth_cal.htm

Using the Wealth Accumulation Calculator, you can calculate how much you can save towards a financial goal based upon a certain savings amount per year.

Smith Barney
http://nestegg.iddis.com/smithbarney/iracalc.html

The Smith Barney IRA Calculator is a personalized computer projection used to demonstrate the value of tax-deferred investing available through an Individual Retirement Account (IRA).

Torrid Technologies
http://www.torrid-tech.com/retire/

Torrid technologies developes on-line interactive software for you to use when planning out your retirement. Included are calculators for 401k managment.

Waddell & Reed
http://www.waddell.com/ins_ill.html

This calculator enables you to estimate how much life insurance your family requires to be adequately protected.

Washington Investment Corp.
http://www.rpg401k.com/

Fill out the on-line form and Washingtom Investment Corp. will send you a free, custom tailored retirement and investment plan designed to meets your particular needs.

Financial Planning: Planning for College

Bank of America
http://www.bankamerica.com/tools/stud_budget.html

An on-line budget calculator to help you plan out what your costs for a college education will be. Very enlightening.

College Board On-line
http://www.collegeboard.org/efc/bin/efc-init.cgi

If you are interested in an on-line calculator to show you what your expected family contributions to a student loan would be, check this site out.

CollegeCash
http://www.pressroom.com/~eastland/

This site guarantees to provide (for a fee) at least seven matches for your application with various private sector scholarship moneys.

FTC Consumer Education
http://www.ftc.gov/bcp/conline/pubs/scholarship/index.htm

This site has some articles on scholarship scams and what to watch out for.

Interactive Services Association
http://www.isa.net/college/resources/scholarships/fast-cash/

Interactive Services Association has an on-line application form for financial aid for students.

Mark Kantrowitz
http://www.finaid.org/finaid/calculators/student-loan-advisor-m.html

This Student Loan Advisor provides you with an estimate of the amount of educational debt you can reasonably afford.

Scholarship Resource Network
http://www.rams.com/srn/index.htm

SNR is a software program and database of college financial aid and scholarship information as well as student loan forgiveness programs with a focus on portable scholarship information.

Student Loan Application Hotline
http://www.loanhotline.com/

You can request a student loan application on-line from the "Hotline" and then submit this form as your request for financial aid.

ThinkQuest
http://tqd.advanced.org/

ThinkQuest challenges students from ages 12 to 18 to embark on the "Quest" to move learning from the homeroom to the Home page. Winners share in prizes and awards that can total more than $1 million.

Tuition Management Systems
http://www.afford.com/

To further address the issue of rising student debt, Tuition Management Systems has introduced BorrowSmart. BorrowSmart ensures families only borrow what they must borrow and not a penny more.

U.S. Bank
http://www.usbank.com/slloan/index.html

The application forms for student aid are quite complex. U.S. Bank has information describing the entire application process and follow-up.

U.S. Dept. of Education
http://gcs.ed.gov/

This web page from the federal government has information on grants and contracts and links to other web sites dealing with these issues.

United College Marketing Services
http://www.collegevisa.com/

If you are a student and would like a credit and loan information, take a look at this site.

Financial Planning: Further Exploration

Alta Vista
http://www.altavista.digital.com/cgi-bin/ query?pg=q&what=web&fmt=.&q=financial+plan

Type in "Financial Plan" in the search field.

Excite Netsearch
http://www.excite.com/Reviews/Money_and_Investing/ Personal_Finance/index.html?CCt

Section to search is "Business," subsection "Business News and Directories, Money, Personal Finance."

Lycos, Inc.
http://a2z.lycos.com/Business_and_Investing/ Personal_Finance_and_Taxes/Personal_Financial_Services/

Type in "Financial Plan" in the search field.

Magellan Internet Guide
http://magellan.mckinley.com/ browser.cgi?umb=Business_and_Economics&sub=Finance&f=0&

Section to search is "Business and Economics," subsection "Finance."

Yahoo!
http://www.yahoo.com/Business_and_Economy/Companies/ Financial_Services/

Section to search is "Business and Economy," subsection "Companies, Education, Financial Aid."

Financial Planning Related Newsgroups

Note: You must have a news reader installed to take part in newsgroups

news:soc.college.financial-aid

Interested in items about financial planning for college students? Post those questions here.

Home Finance: Mortgage News

Bloomberg Personal

http://www.bloomberg.com/

A great newspaper that lists trends and financial advice. It sports charts and indices to help you make informed decisions about you mortgage.

Canada News Wire

http://www.newswire.ca

Want to keep track of ALL the mortgage rates with the major Canadian lenders. Give this site a try.

Dept. of Housing and Urban Development

http://www.hud.gov/mortgage.html

Get the straight talk on "Mortgage Loan Sales Programs" right from the source.

Essential Information

http://www.essential.org/EI.html

Billing themselves as providers of "provocative information to the public on important topics neglected by the mass media and policy makers." There are some good articles and interesting items here.

Gateway Equity & Loan Network

http://www.geloan.com/info/newslet.html

This site features regular newsletters from a professional real estate writer.

Global Network Navigator, Inc.

http://gnn.com/gnn/meta/finance/feat/bible/index.html

The mortgage applicant's bible. What else could we possibly say about this site, the description says it all.

Loans on Line

http://www.electriciti.com:80/~insight/

Current market trends and information tips are just a few of the links on this site. They even have a direct link to their local government so you can "talk" to your officials.

Mixstar Mortgage Information Exchange

http://www.mixstar.com/index.htm

Daily benchmark pricing and market commentaries are featured on this site.

Money World Personal Finance

http://www.moneyworld.co.uk/ukpfd/out.htm

Browse articles of relevance to United Kingdom residents or those interested in moving there.

Mortgage Mart

http://www.mortgage-mart.com/defa.html

A very comprehensive glossary of terms for the mortgage industry.

National Mortgage News

http://nmnews.fgray.com/

No real surprises here. The National Mortgage News site contains exactly that . . . National Mortgage News. Go figure! All joking aside, it's worth a look.

Newsletter Library
http://pub.savvy.com/

Request free newsletters from over 11,000 choices.

Salem Five Saving Bank
http://www.salemfive.com/Request.html

Fill out an on-line form and the company will mail you everything you ever wanted to know about mortgages or at your request, they'll have a bank representative contact you by phone.

Security Management Services
http://www.retire-early.com/

Receive quarterly newsletter indicating market trends, investment tips, the nation's highest CD rates, upcoming tax changes, and much more.

TFK Information Systems
http://www.ultranet.com/~tkf/tkf.htm

Monthly on-line newsletter features articles on mortgage refinancing, tips, and tax implications when you consider buying that new home.

Home Finance:
Mortgage Calculators

Canadian Financial Advisory Service
http://cfas.com/

Mortgage calculators and more. This site performs its calculations based on Canadian laws and regulations

Coldwell Bankers
http://nashvillehomes.com/calculate.html

Good calculator for multiple comparisons of monthly payments. You can dry run up to three scenarios at once.

Financial Wizards
http://www.communitycu.org/OnlineServ/Calculators/C2.html

This site also has a "loan wizard," "loan comparison wizard," and "retirement wizard" in addition to the "mortgage wizard" calculator.

Hewlett Packard
http://hpcvbbs.external.hp.com/calculators/hp12c/

This one's way, way out there! A WWW site that tells you how to do mortgage calculations on your HP calculator.

Karl Jeacle's Mortgage Calculator
http://www.broadcom.ie/~kj/java/mortgage.html

Drag sliding bars to change the number of years, principle, interest, and starting date and watch the monthly and total payment change.

MONEY Personal Finance Center
http://www.pathfinder.com/cgi-bin/Money/loancalc.cgi

A calculator with a slightly different twist. Fill in any three of the cost of the house, length of the mortgage in years, interest rate, or monthly payment and the calculator will tell you the value of the missing item.

Mortgage Calculations
http://ibc.wustl.edu/mort/formula.html

For those of you who really want to know what the heck the calculators are doing. Here are the formulas and a brief text description.

Mortgage Freeware - Hugh Chou
http://ibc.wustl.edu/mort/shareware/

Interested in using your PC or Macintosh to do the calculations? Try out some of these programs listed here. Most are freeware or shareware.

The Minnesota Mutual Life Insurance Co.
http://www.minnmutual.com/crystal/lifecalc.html

Calculate the monthly cost to insure your mortgage and enter their on-line sweepstakes for a chance to receive $1,500 toward your next house payment.

Home Finance: Buying and Selling

ACCNet
http://accnet.com/homes/index.html

ACCNet lets you search or list real estate on the Internet. They have a search engine that will let a new home buyer detail concerns like state, city, lot size, house style. ACCNet will then return with a list of homes that match your criteria. As a home seller you can take advantage of their free listing service.

American Relocation Center
http://www.sover.net/~relo/

Lots of information for those considering a move including free relocation packages which detail public school information, prices, maps, community info, and so on.

Amerispec
http://www.agt.net/public/amerspec/seller.html

Fill out the registration form and Amerispec will e-mail you your choice of their monthly "Home Tip", brochures, price lists, business cards and, most important, free information on home inspection.

Better Homes and Gardens
http://www.betterhomesre.com/

Picture Better Homes and Gardens magazine on-line. The site features a search engine to help you find everything you want to know about Better Homes and Gardens properties.

Cyberhomes
http://204.217.192.110:80/

Very cool site. Has the mapping features of the National Association of Realtors PLUS the ability to plot on a map at "Street Level" the homes that meet your search criteria. Site only lacks coverage to be the best of the best.

Home Base Guide Publications
http://www.islandnet.com/~homebase/homepage.html

This on-line publication has tips and links to lots of useful information. Their mission statement is to build a network of informative ideas and to provide an up-to-date publication in the areas of selling, buying, building, owning, and renovating your home.

Home Improvement Net
http://www.homeimprove.com/~plans/

Some simple interior decorating tips can go a long way towards the sale of a home. This site has "floor plans, drawings, and instructive information are offered throughout for your own personal use—free of charge!" They even invite you to register for a "free gift drawing!" Did someone say free?

Home Net
http://www.netprop.com/

Links to real estate directories, mortgage brokers and vendors, and various products and services offered on the Internet. This site will

let you decide which real estate company offers the best services to meet your needs.

Home Scout
http://www.homescout.com/

Send this agent out to do your shopping for you. It browses over 88 different Real Estate Web sites to find homes that meet your search criteria.

Homes and Land Electronic Magazine
http://www.homes.com/Welcome.html

Tons of stuff on-line. Check out some of their software http://www.homes.com/services/software.html designed to make the move process easier.

Homes for Sale on the Internet
http://www.he.net/~bsonder/homes.html

Want to find a home? Search part of the United States, Canada and the United Kingdom for the home that you want.

InterAd Corporation
http://ns.neptune.com/interad/home1.html

This site features a "Hot Property Alert Button." If they don't have the property you're looking for, just click on the Hot Property Alert Button and fill in your address. If they get a listing that matches your request, they'll e-mail you the information.

Living Home
http://www.livinghome.com/

An on-line publication that covers topics from home improvement projects to remodeling and gardening. They even offer a free CD-ROM of their work.

National Association of Home Builders
http://www.nahb.com/pg2.html

The NAHB has information on housing consumers, market facts and figures, tips for builders and a lot more. Worth a look by anyone who is considering selling a home.

National Association of Realtors
http://www.realtor.net/consumer/seller.htm

A one-stop does it all site with links to "pricing your property," "choosing a Realtor," "marketing your home," "evaluating an offer," "maximizing your home investment," and tips on moving. This site is a must view.

On the House
http://www.onthehoU.Se.com/

The California-based Carey Brothers, nationally recognized experts on home building and renovation, are now giving advice on the Internet. Check these guys out for tips and tricks to home repairs to enhance the value of your property.

Properties OnLine
http://propol.com/

Another popular site that lets you browse listings or use their fast search engine to find the home of your dreams. You can even add your home to their database.

Property Line
http://www.vossnet.co.uk/property/

Interested in house in United Kingdom, Spain, Portugal, or France. This site has global listings.

Real Net
http://oeonline.com/realnet.html

You can search on listings of homes, real estate agent profiles, current mortgage rates and

trends, today's showcase homes, and subdivision news.

Rent Net
http://www.rent.net:1000/

For those renters out there jealous of all the listings provided for homebuyers, here is one created just for you. Rent Net provides listings for over 475,000 units in Canada and the United States. The service is free to renters, but owners wishing to list their units must pay. They even offer a "Free Rent Sweepstakes" promotion.

The Property Wave
http://www.worldserver.pipex.com/pwave/

This site bills themselves as "Your Gateway to Global Real Estate." They have listings for Europe, Atlantic, South Mediterranean, the Caribbean, Australia and Oceania, North America, South and Central America and South East Asia. Good if I ever want to buy that castle in Germany.

The UnReal Estate Cartoon
http://mindlink.net/Rick_Carlsen/unreal.htm

It's here because we all need a laugh. Especially after crying over all the money we're about to spend.

Home Finance: Bankers and Brokers

AAA National Mortgage Directories
http://www.dirs.com/mortgage/

This site has an extensive list of mortgage companies categorized by state. It also features a help desk where you can ask a mortgage professional a question.

American Finance Online
http://www.loanshop.com/

Another site that has tons of stuff and handles on-line mortgage applications. No other on-line application site boasts anywhere near the quantity of mortgage calculators found here.

Bank of America
http://www.bofa.com/

This site has come a long way and offers a wealth of services.

Bank of Montreal
http://www.bmo.com/Tango/Mortgage/0.MainMenu

Lots of tips and information. This bank is a great place for Canadians interested in mortgages.

Canadian Mortgage Listings
http://web20.mindlink.net/cml/cml-abt.html

For a small fee this company will list your mortgage loan requirements on the Internet You'll give literally thousands of direct lenders, private investors, and mortgage brokers across Canada the opportunity to see your listing and to call you directly.

City Bank
http://www.citibank.com/mortgage/mortgage.htm

City Bank offers some of the better Internet mortgage services provided by a bank. The site hosts lots of information and even identifies branch locations nearest you.

Consumer Mortgage Info. Network
http://www.human.com/proactive/index.html

Dedicated to providing home buyers with an impartial source of current information for what is arguably the most complex transaction that most people will ever undertake—the financing of a home. A home buyer's qualification

program for residential financing can be downloaded for free.

HomeOwners Finance Center
http://www.homeowners.com/databank.html

One of the highest-rate mortgage sites anywhere. Links, calculators, news, on-line applications, this site has it all.

Mortgage Tech, Inc.
http://www.mtgtech.com/

Billing themselves as "The ONE place to find EVERY Mortgage Broker, Mortgage Lender and Real Estate Finance Company on the Internet," these guys have pointers going everywhere.

National Association of Mortgage Brokers
http://www.compassnet.com/~macbnr/why.html

Curious about what a mortgage broker is? This site has a nice description and also provides the address for the National Association of Mortgage Brokers.

The Money Page
http://www.moneypage.com/mortgage/usalpha.htm

This is a very attractive site that hosts a current list of the major banks that feature mortgages on the Internet. A must have for checking out the banks in the United States.

The Mortgage Loan Page
http://206.86.104.2:80/loans/

The Mortgage Loan Page maintains a National Directory and Database of Mortgage Brokers that can be searched to meet your specific mortgage loan needs.

The Mortgage Money Guide
http://wolfeprop.com/mortga.htm

Another site dedicated to explaining the concepts and ideas behind financing your dream home. Good background reading that should make your interactions with mortgage brokers and bankers a much more pleasant experience.

Home Finance: Further Exploration

Excite Netsearch
http://www.excite.com/Reviews/Money_and_Investing/Real_Estate/

Type in "Real Estate" in the search field.

Lycos, Inc.
http://a2z.lycos.com/Business_and_Investing/Real_Estate/

Section to search is "Business and Investing," subsection "Real Estate."

Magellan Internet Guide
http://magellan.mckinley.com/
browser.cgi?umb=Business_and_Economics&sub=Real_Estate&p=0

Section to search is "Business and Economics," subsection "Real Estate."

Yahoo!
http://www.yahoo.com/Business_and_Economy/Real_Estate/

Section to search is "Business and Economy," subsection "Real Estate."

Home Finance Related Newsgroups
Note: You must have a news reader installed to take part in newsgroups

news:misc.consumers.house

Discussion about owning and maintaining a home is the focus of this newsgroup.

Investments: Introduction to Investments

Atlantic Broadcasting System
http://www.abslive.com/

Rest your eyes and listen to audio feeds of the major investment news of the day.

Bloomberg Personal
http://www.bloomberg.com/bbn/index.html

Track the latest news and topics that touch on investments. Click on hotlinks to the current trends for various investment vehicles.

CNNfn
http://www.cnnfn.com/

The financial network has up to the minute news and articles, links to other investment sites and research topics.

Invest-o-rama
http://www.investorama.com/

A very colorful, fun site that has good basic information on investments for beginners and detailed quote services for the experts.

Investors' Network Publishing
http://www.investorsnet.com/

Investors' Network has articles on all aspects of the investments market place from news to tax liens. There is lots of information here for you.

Microsoft Investor
http://investor.msn.com/Contents.Asp

You can build your own personal portfolio from this site and use it to monitor your investments. There are also news articles and trends on-line.

Mr. Stockbroker's Financial Market
http://www.angelfire.com/free/quote.html

This site promises to try to answer any questions you may have on any aspect of investments.

Smith Barney
http://nestegg.iddis.com/smithbarney/

Moving from the world of free on-line news services to pay services, we find the major difference is the news is not delayed 15 to 30 minutes. If you need the news as it happens with no delays, try here.

Standards & Poors
http://www.stockinfo.standardpoor.com/

Latest news and trends plus up to the minute values of your investment can all be found here. S&P is one of the standards by which investments are measured.

Stock Market Update
http://www.ucc.uconn.edu/~jpa94001/update.html

Links to major news sources, charts, and market analysis make this an all-in-one site.

The Motley Fool
http://www.fool.com/

A great launch point for anyone interested in investments. Easy to understand lessons, comprehensive coverage, and great graphics.

The Wall Street Journal
http://www.wsj.com/

Another subscription-required site, the Wall Street Journal has been the defacto news source for investors in paper format for years. Now the WSJ is on-line and even better ... now where are the comics?

Vanguard Group
http://www.vanguard.com/

Probably the premier site for those new to investing. This site is like having your own personal university and financial advisor in your basement.

Investments: Stocks

1st Global Partners
http://www.1stglobal.com/

This deep discount brokerage features links to other sites, news articles, a search engine, and a special area for reps only.

American Stock Exchange
http://www.amex.com/

The American Stock Exchange provides extraordinary visibility for over 700 companies and is the world's second largest auction-marketplace.

Auditrack
http://auditrack.com/

Before you try your new trading strategy live, try it using Auditrack's full-service simulated brokerage operation.

Chaos On-line
http://www.webmarketgame.com/

Buy stocks in different web pages. The price of stock changes by how many hits a page has. This game is free and there will be prizes.

Charles Schwab
http://www.schwab.com/

Try their on-line web trading demo, then move on to the big leagues and do research, trading and other functions.

Dendritics
http://www.dendritics.com/a-calcs.htm

Dendritics has a really useful collection of gemstone and metalworking calculations and formulas on their web site.

DynaMind
http://www.DynaMind-LLC.com/services/utilities/currency.cgi

DynaMind has an on-line currency calculator. The rates used are the New York foreign exchange selling rates as quoted at 3 P.M. EST by Dow Jones Telerate Inc. and other sources.

E*TRADE Securities
http://www.etrade.com/html/visitor_center/game.htm

E*TRADE's "Stock Market and Stock and Options Games" will let you try the stock market with $100,000 in "game money."

IMex
http://www.imex-fx.com/

IMEX has some good articles for anyone interested in investing in currency.

Levitt & Levitt
http://www.levitt-levitt.com/

A deep discount brokerage firm that has lots of support for users wanting to open accounts.

Nasdaq
http://www.nasdaq.com/

Nasdaq's comprehensive new Web site has current numerical and graphical index data, free stock quotations, and more.

New York Stock Exchange
http://www.nyse.com/

The NYSE has publications that can assist the neophyte stock investor. They also have live data and a visitors center.

OptionVue Systems Inc.
http://www.optionvue.com/cgi-shl/probcalc.pl

This on-line probability calculator provides the probability of a stock being above, below, or between two price targets which you specify.

Oslo Børs
http://nettvik.no/finansen/oslobors/engelsk/exchanen.htm

This site features links to the international exchanges. Really handy if you want to check the market in Prague.

Pacific Brokerage Services
http://www.tradepbs.com/

This site features a 30 second delayed market quotation service and lets you do transactions for $11 per trade.

The R.J. Forbes Group
http://www.rjforbes.com/

Live Dow Jones Industrials from PCQUOTE—click "Reload" if quote does not appear.

The Toronto Stock Exchange
http://www.telenium.ca/TSE/

The TSE is Canada's largest exchange and provides stock quotes that are linked to the traded companies home pages.

Investments: Bonds

Bond Services
http://www.bondservices.co.uk/

Another good place to start your discovery of what bonds are, how to choose them wisely and how the can benefit you as an investment vehicle.

Bonds On-line
http://www.bonds-online.com/

Bonds On-line is a greater starting point for anyone new to the bond market. They have the "Bond Professor," research, and, of course, bonds.

Cutter & Co. Brokerage
http://www.stocktrader.com/summary.html

Get the latest treasury yield curve and other bond index information from this site.

Daiwa Institute of Research
http://www.dir.co.jp/InfoManage/datarsc.html

The Daiwa bond index is based on a world-standard method. It covers all categories of Japanese publicly-issued coupon bonds.

Federal Reserve Bank of NY
http://www.ny.frb.org/pihome/svg_bnds/sb_val.html

An on-line calculator to compute the redemption values for a savings bond.

Michael Lissack
http://lissack.com/

This site bills itself as "A place for gathering thoughts on the continually brewing and always interesting Municipal Bond Market Scandals."

MonelyLine Corp.
http://www.moneyline.com/

This site claims to be the first "Internet service to provide real-time information on capital markets." They cover U.S. Treasury bonds, notes and bills, agencies, money markets, corporate bonds, emerging markets, and other fixed income securities.

TradeHistory
http://www.tradehistory.com/

TradeHistory has a good little search engine to find a bond using a maturity, description or security type. It's worth a look.

Investments: Mutual Funds

Affinty
http://www.mutualfundinvesting.com/

A Canadian fund dealer offering the best funds on the Canadian market.

Dreyfus
http://www.dreyfus.com/funds/

The Dreyfus On-line Information Center can help you get a clearer sense of the direction to take to match your investment dollars to your investment objectives.

Fabian Investment Services
http://www.fabian.com/

Get a free report here about bear markets and how to avoid them. There is also news and a section called the "secrets of successful investors."

FundLink
http://www.webcom.com/~fundlink/

A mutual fund research center that helps you track performance, get quotes, do on-line research, and find a broker.

Great Pacific Management
http://www.greatpacific.com/

Another Canadian site that helps you find and track mutual funds, rrsps, insurance and other tax-assisted investments.

Internet Closed End Fund Investor
http://www.icefi.com/

Closed end funds are similar to mutual funds. This site covers the differences and explains why these may be a better option for your style of investments.

INVESTools
http://www.investools.com/cgi-bin/Library/mscf.pl

Morningstar has a great search engine to find just the right fund. You can then print the PDF reports and use them to wallpaper that basement office.

Money and Investing
http://users.aol.com/meadowscd/money.htm

Quotes on major market indexes and mutual funds total return charts. They have an on-line search engine to ease the process.

Mutual Fund Letter
http://www.MutLetter.com/

This site features...you guessed it, a mutual fund newsletter.

Mutual Funds On-line
http://www.mfmag.com/fhtm_a.htm

A fund calculator for subscribers that tells you how your funds are doing. At the time of this writing the calculator and registration were free.

Newspage
http://www.newspage.com/NEWSPAGE/cgi-bin/walk.cgi/NEWSPAGE/ info/d10/d3/d4/

Are you ready for the latest breaking news in the fund market. Browse this site to see if there are any articles that may help you capitalize on your investments.

Strong Funds On-line
http://www.strong-funds.com/java/welcome.htm

Right on the home page of this site splashed in red is the text "Avoid these 10 retirement planning dont's". Needless to say, this is a good learning center.

TD Bank
http://www.tdbank.ca/tdbank/mutual/calc/

The Toronto Dominion Bank has a couple of investment calculators on-line to help you plan for your nest egg.

The Mutual Funds Home Page
http://www.brill.com/

News, links, articles and of course quote services. This site lives up to its name as the "Mutual Funds Home Page".

USA Today
http://www.dbc.com/cgi-bin/htx.exe/forms/mark.html?SOURCE=/BLQ/ USAWWW

Track the news and articles concerning today's hottest performing mutual funds. Then track the Forex rates and closed end funds.

Investments: Further Exploration

Excite Netsearch
http://www.excite.com/Reviews/Money_and_Investing/Investments/ index.html?CCt

Section to search is "Business," subsection "Investments."

Lycos, Inc.
http://a2z.lycos.com/Business_and_Investing/ Investing_and_Investments/

Type in "Investments" or "Stocks" or "Bonds" in the search field.

Magellan Internet Guide
http://magellan.mckinley.com/ browser.cgi?urub=Business_and_Economics&sub=Investment_and_Personal_Finance&f=0&

Section to search is "Business and Economics," subsection "Investment and Personal Finance."

Yahoo!
http://www.yahoo.com/Business_and_Economy/ Markets_and_Investments/

Section to search is "Business and Economy," subsection "Markets and Investments."

Investing Related Newsgroups
Note: You must have a news reader installed to take part in newsgroups.

news:alt.invest.penny-stocks

Post questions and read on-line discussions about penny stocks.

news:misc.invest

General discussion about investments is the focus of this group.

news:misc.invest.canada

This newsgroup is about Canadian investments.

news:misc.invest.funds

If you are interested in investment funds, try this newsgroup.

news:misc.invest.futures

The futures market and all of the news pertaining to it is featured here.

news:misc.invest.real-estate

Real estate is yet another investment vehicle. This newsgroup discusses it.

news:misc.invest.stocks

Questions about stocks? Just want to learn the basics. Post your queries to this newsgroup.

news:misc.invest.technical

Investment in technology is the focus of this group.

Death and Taxes: Death

AccuQuote.com
http://www.accuquote.com/

Free e-mail form now makes it possible to quickly compare the prices and features of over 800 top-rated life insurance products. You can also find on-line calculators and a FAQ section.

American Academy of Estate Planning Attorneys
http://www.aaepa.com/

The American Academy of Estate Planning Attorneys is a national membership organization that is "dedicated to helping consumers receive the best in estate planning legal services."

American Risk and Insurance Association
http://www.aria.org/

ARIA bills themselves as "the premier professional association of insurance scholars and other thoughtful insurance and risk management professionals." They have links to other research and teaching sites on the web.

Brentmark Software, Inc.
http://www.brentmark.com/

This site features software that specializes in estate planning, excise taxes, and other related topics. Contact them to arrange a free demonstration copy of their software calculators.

David P.M. Scollnik
http://balducci.math.ucalgary.ca/ari.aotw.html

If you are interested in Canadian Actuaries on the Web, try the hotlinks from this site to jump the actuary of your choice.

FinAid
http://www.finaid.org/finaid/calculators/insurance.html

This Life Insurance Needs Calculator computes an estimate of the amount of life insurance you should carry.

GO! Online Communications
http://www.wearca.com/wear_2.html

Billed as containing "22 of the Best Estate Planning Tips," this site is worth a quick look by those who just need a gentle reminder of some basic estate planning strategies.

Insurance & Risk Management Central
http://www.irmcentral.com/

If you are shopping for personal insurance, drop by this site to check out the advice col-

umn, research agents and brokers, and find agents in your area.

Insurance OnNet
http://pages.prodigy.com/MO/insurance/select_agent.html

With all of the agents on the Web, it is important to find tips on how to select an insurance agent or licensed insurance broker.

inter@ctive insurance innovations inc.
http://www.netrunner.net/insurance/

This site claims to be "designed to provide fast, economical and unbiased answers to your Personal, Business and Financial Insurance and Risk Management questions."

Layne T. Rushforth
http://coyote.accessnv.com/rushfort/advintro.html

A good, step by step site that takes you through the process of estate planning. This site also links to other sites and newsgroups that are pertinent to estate planning.

Life Quote of America
http://lifequote.com/

Tips of the month, a needs calculator, annuity price comparison chart, and, of course, a life insurance quote comparison can all be found on this site.

Lifenet
http://lifenet.com/abestate.html

This site has articles on how to plan your estate, avoiding probate, wills and the differences between them and it also has some interactive calculators to help you along.

Mark J. Welch
http://www.ca-probate.com/attylist.htm

Mark Welch has one of the better sites on the Internet for estate planning. The above link

goes to a regularly updated web page that has links to all known attorneys who practice estate law and maintain a web presence. The lawyers and firms are listed by state.

Markle Stuckey Hardesty & Bott
http://www.hooked.net/cpa/estate/advisor.htm

Who are you going to contact to help you with your estate planning? This site has an article that helps to answer this question.

Myers Internet Services
http://www.dirs.com/insure/

For a national database of insurance agents, the best buys in insurance or visitors medical insurance, give this site a look.

Stephen Elias for Nolo Press
http://www.nolo.com/nn44.html

If you have ever seen those ads on TV or in the papers about "free" estate planning and wondered if there really is such a thing or if the whole thing is one big scam, read the article on this site.

Term Firm
http://www.termfirm.com/

With nearly 1800 life insurance companies to choose from, shopping for the best deal on term insurance could take you a lifetime. Term Firm claims they can do it for you in about a day. Try a free no-obligation quote from them.

The Insurance Help Guide
http://burgoyne.com/pages/rickv/

The Insurance Help Guide is here to help those who have questions about their insurance claims and the claims handling process. This is a free service, but is not designed to dispense legal advice.

University of Nebraska
http://ianrwww.unl.edu/ianr/pubs/NEBFACTS/NF233.HTM

If all of these insurance and estate planning terms are confusing, check out the University of Nebraska's glossary of estate planning terms.

Waddell & Reed
http://www.waddell.com/ins_ill.htm

This calculator enables you to estimate how much life insurance your family requires to be adequately protected. The site also permits you to get a free financial plan sent to you.

WebTrust.com
http://www.webtrust.com/estate/

This site has some good articles and question to help you get started on estate planning. They also feature a search engine to help you quickly obtain more information on estate planning.

Death and Taxes: Taxes

Cable News Network
http://www.cnn.com/EVENTS/1996/tax_day/index.html

On-line filing services, links to sites with tax tips and stories to help you plan the tax season make this a good starting site.

Cross Border Tax and Transactions
http://www.crossborder.com/

If you do business, invest or trade internationally, you need to monitor business, legal and tax developments. This site provides in-

formation that you need whether you are interested in opportunities in Canada, the United States or elsewhere in the world.

Daniel J. Coles, EA
http://www.ezone.com/taxman/

This site features a search engine for federal and state tax forms.

ITT Hartford
http://www.itthartford.com/corporate/life/est_calc1.html

Are you interested in seeing how much money you may have to pay for your estate taxes? If you are, then try the on-line estate tax calculator to estimate the government's share.

Maxwell Technologies
http://www.scubed.com/tax/tax.html

This site features "Taxing Times 1997, an electronic compendium of information related to the upcoming task of filling out and filing your Income Tax forms for 1996."

Merrill Lynch
http://www.merrill-lynch.ml.com/personal/taxes/

Merrill Lynch has a lot of tax tips on-line. Crawl your way to their site and check them out.

NACTP
http://www.nactp.org/

The NACTP includes in its membership approximately 65 member companies that represent tax preparation software companies, electronic filing processors, tax form publishers, and tax processing service bureaus.

Nest Egg
http://nestegg.iddis.com/nestegg/nestind/taxes.html

Nest Egg links to lots of tax related articles and summaries. There is also a PDF down-

load engine that permits you to download the latest tax forms.

Roger A. Kahan
http://www.rak-1.com/

Interested in "Tax Tips and Facts?" Check out the newsletter, which features articles like "Timing of Income and Expense."

Rotfleisch & Samulovitch
http://www.pathcom.com/~davidr/

This Canadian site has links to other tax sites, a top ten tax tidbit section, weekly tax tips, and information on Canadian Income Tax.

Tax Analysts
http://www.tax.org/

Free tips, a tax newsletter, and a tax calendar can all be found on the Tax Analysts home page. They also have a "Tax Snapshot" which is a small pertinent glimpse of how taxes effect you.

TaxLite
http://www.netaccess.on.ca/~gordonco/taxlite.html

Another Canadian site, this company offers a rather innovative idea, preparation of your tax form on-line.

Taxsites
http://www2.best.com/~ftmexpat/html/

A very good link site to anything dealing with taxes. This site makes a good starting point for people who want more information on taxes.

Death and Taxes: Further Exploration

Excite Netsearch
http://www.excite.com/Reviews/Politics_and_Law/Taxes/ index.html?CCtType in "Taxes" in the search field.

Type in "Taxes" in the search field.

Excite Netsearch
http://www.excite.com/Reviews/Money_and_Investing/Insurance/ index.html?CCt

Type in "Insurance" in the search field.

Lycos, Inc.
http://a2z.lycos.com/cgi-bin/pursuit?cat=a2z&query=taxes&x=36&y=6

Type in "Taxes" in the search field.

Lycos, Inc.
http://www.lycos.com/cgi-bin/ pursuit?cat=lycos&query=estate+planning&x=37&y=5

Type in "Estate Planning" in the search field.

Magellan Internet Guide
http://searcher.mckinley.com/ searcher.cgi?query=taxes&onlyrr=1&q.x=45&q.y=19

Section to search is "Business and Economics," subsection "Taxes."

Magellan Internet Guide
http://searcher.mckinley.com/ searcher.cgi?query=estate+planning&onlyrr=1&q.x=48&q.y=8

Type in "Estate Planning" in the search field.

Yahoo!
http://www.yahoo.com/Business_and_Economy/Taxes/

Section to search is "Business and Economy," subsection "Taxes."

Yahoo!
http://search.yahoo.com/bin/search?p=estate+planning

Type in "Estate Planning" in the search field.

Death and Taxes Related Newsgroups
Note: You must have a news reader installed to take part in newsgroups

mail:clari.biz.industry.insurance

Post questions and read on-line discussions about insurance.

mail:can.taxes

If you are interested in discussion about Canadian taxes, check out this newsgroups.

mail:misc.taxes

Commentary and FAQ about taxes are the primary focus of this newsgroup.

mail:misc.taxes.moderated

If you are interested in a "moderated" tax newsgroup, try the articles and discussions held on-line in this group.

Credit: Credit 101

Credit Card Network
http://www.creditnet.com/news/

Credit card industry news and articles ... this site has it all. Start your tour of credit with a look at the current credit news.

Credit Card Network
http://www.creditnet.com/shareware/ccnshare.html

Credit Card Network has assembled these fine shareware software programs for your enjoyment. There are Windows, DOS, and Mac programs listed here.

Merrill Lynch
http://www.merrill-lynch.ml.com/personal/liabil/credcalc.html

How much does it really cost when you buy on credit? Fill out the answers to a few simple questions and let the calculator show you the real costs.

RHT, Inc. (Prime Rate)
http://www.primerate.com/10crds1.htm

Understanding credit cards. This site has some good articles and links to help you understand the credit card process.

Scotia Bank
http://www.scotiabank.ca/croption.htm

Questions to help you prepare for the first time you apply for credit. A little thought up front can make a world of difference when applying for that credit.

TradeWave Corporation
http://lmc.einet.net/galaxy/Business-and-Commerce/Consumer-Products-and-Services/Finance/Credit-and-Debt.html

Good link site to credit oriented companies.

U.S. Small Business Administration
http://www.sbaonline.sba.gov/gopher/Business-Development/Business-Initiatives-Education-Training/Finance-Plan/fin2.txt

Good site with lots of articles describing credit especially in relation to small businesses.

United College Marketing Services
http://www.collegevisa.com/html/css-1.html

Good introduction to credit with special focus from a college student's perspective. If you are a student, make sure you stop by for a look.

Credit: Loan Lessons

America Online, Inc.
http://webcrawler.com/select/persfin.22.html

Links to credit card fraud and FTC consumer brochures.

CreditNet
http://www.geocities.com/WallStreet/4935/journal.html

Some tips on collecting on loans owed to you.

CYBERplex Interactive Media
http://www.cyberplex.com/hotline/Tips.html

Treat your credit cards like cash—10 tips to help you protect yourself.

Joke of the Week
http://www.wuacc.edu/acc/coordi/archives.dir/joke-week.dir/loan.html

The oldest loan joke in the book.

Kent Credit Union
http://www.kentcu.com/loanrate.html

Debt analysis calculator, loan payment calculator, and others. This site features lots of interactive stuff to help you help yourself.

Ram Research Group
http://www.ramresearch.com/cardtrak/holiday.html

Tips for using your credit over the holiday season. Remember, coal is cheap and fits easily into stockings.

Sallie Mae
http://sinetva1.slma.com/consumer/getloan/

Another popular requirement for a loan is for education. Here is how to prepare. This site includes calculators to help you get started.

Steve Lake
http://http2.brunel.ac.uk:8080/~hcsrsml/credit.htm

Download a freeware credit calculator. At this price you don't even need to calculate its impact on your debt load.

The Home Spot
http://www.homespot.com/r4main2l.htm

The loan process. This site takes you through the basics of getting that personal loan.

Tribune Media Service
http://www.tms.tribune.com/rjt_newcars/bestloan.htm

Want to learn how to get the best deal on a car loan? Try this site for tips on getting the loan that will let you get the car of your dreams.

U.S. Postal Inspection Service
http://www.usps.gov/websites/depart/inspect/credit.htm

Want some advice on phony credit card schemes and con artists? If anyone knows fraud, it's the U.S. Postal Service.

Credit: Card Games

American Express
http://www.americanexpress.com/student/

On-line resource for college students looking for answers and of course ... money.

Arent Fox
http://www.webcom.com/~lewrose/brochures/cc.html

Choosing and using credit cards—very good article on the basics with tables to help demonstrate costs involved in credit cards.

Credit Card Network
http://www.creditnet.com/ccn-cardlinks.html

Link site to most credit card suppliers on the net.

CYBERplex Interactive Media
http://www.cyberplex.com/hotline/

A company that provides a hotline to help subscribers when your cards are stolen or lost. The idea is great, but the delivery needs a bit of polish.

First Card
http://www.firstcard.com:80/

This site bills itself as the premier issuer of gold credit cards in the world. If you are interested in the power of the gold, start surfing here.

FMR Corp.
http://www.fid-inv.com/brokerage/card/card_calc.html

Comparison calculator for up to three different cards. Check the rates and yearly fees to see which is the best deal for you.

In Jersey
http://www.injersey.com/msgboard/Living/Finance/CreditCards/subject.html

Are you confused or puzzled by the entire credit card process. Post your messages to the Credit Cards Message Board and see if they can shed some light on your problems.

MasterCard
http://www.mastercard.com/hmv/

Holiday savings and other special offers to help you get a break on your debt load. Mastercard has some good material on their site.

PC Service Source, Inc.
http://pcservice.com/product/credapp.html

Apply for credit using a PDF credit form that you can download right from the Net. Print it out, fill it in and send it back with your credit request.

Travelers Bank
http://partner.qfn.com/directory/travelers_bank/

Want a card that can be fully integrated into your Quicken Program? Give this card supplier a try and watch how easy the electronic age can make the credit process.

Credit: Credit Reports

Continuum
http://titsoc.soc.titech.ac.jp/titsoc/higuchi-lab/icm/personal.html

What about a personal credit supplier. They may not check you references in the normal manner, but to avoid nasty surprises later, this site lists some typical guidelines

Dydacomp
http://www.mailordercentral.com/sms/credref.htm

Interested in checking the credit history of over 10 million businesses. This company sells a CD with this information on it.

Fair Isaac Co.
http://www.nccredit.com/underscores.html

Scoring system used by the big three credit bureaus to ensure that your credit rating is consistent with each bureau.

MoneyWorld UK Limited
http://www.moneyworld.co.uk/glossary/gl00139.htm

A list of the credit bureaus in the United Kingdom.

NCFE
http://ncfe.org/credit.html

A good article about credit repair and links to "credit puzzle games."

The Collins'
http://www.gate.net/~dcollins/credit.html

Getting ready to buy that new Net ready P.C.? First check your credit report.

Credit: Dealing with Debt

Aetna
http://www.aetna.com/financial/investment/mw060396.htm

Market watch newsletter has a brief article on the rising debt load.

American Consumer Credit Counseling
http://www.consumercredit.com/

A non-profit organization devoted to helping you to manage your personal debt.

American Express, Inc.
http://www.americanexpress.com/student/moneypit/credit/control/control.html

An on-line interactive test to demonstrate how credit can increase or reduce your spending power. Give it a try.

E-Houston Credit Union
http://udweb.com/ehouston/debtch~1.htm

Want a calculator to quickly figure out your debt loads? Simple and efficient, give this calculator a try.

FindLaw
http://www.findlaw.com/01topics/03bankruptcy/index.html

Articles and more on the U.S. Bankruptcy laws. This site is quite comprehensive, but is somewhat dry reading material.

Lexington Law Firms
http://www.inconnect.com/~UniSol/Lex/

The secrets of credit repair according to a law firm, FREE! Normally, most of us go into debt to get advice from lawyers.

Nolo Press
http://www.nolo.com/nn217.html

Three strategies for dealing with debt. Each strategy links to an article that explains the risks and consequences of your choice.

PAWWS Financial Network
http://pawws.secapl.com/1stSrc_phtml/finance/debtcalc.shtml

This site has a debt consolidation calculator to help you see if a consolidated loan makes sense for you. List up to five loans and their interest rates in your comparison.

Princeton Business Journal
http://www.pacpub.com/pbj/news/3-19-96/bbar2.html

If you are interested in tips for avoiding bankruptcy and reestablishing personal credit, link up with this site.

Protecting Your Credit
http://www.webknx.com:80/JC850/

Free credit reference guide with quick answers for common credit questions.

U.S. Dept. of Housing and Urban Affairs
http://www.hud.gov/local/sea/seadmcr.html

Information on restitution recovery from the U.S. government.

University of Alberta Students' Union
http://www.su.ualberta.ca/ser/sfaic/Debt.html

Dealing with debt on a temporarily reduced income. Even if your income has changed, your debt load probably hasn't and the worse thing you can do is ignore it. Check out the advice here.

Wealth Quest International, Inc.
http://www.hotsites.net/debtfree/personal.html

What are the warning signs of debt? This site lists some of the common signs of coming disaster. Hopefully you can catch them in time to save yourself from financial woe.

Credit: Further Exploration

Excite Netsearch
http://www.excite.com/Reviews/Money_and_Investing/ Personal_Finance/Credit/index.html

Section to search is "Business", subsection "Money", subsection "Personal Finance", subsection "Credit."

Magellan
http://magellan.mckinley.com/ browser.cgi?umb=Business_and_Economics&sub=Banking_and_Insurance&f=0&

Section to search is "Business and Economics", subsection "Banking and Insurance"

Yahoo!
http://www.yahoo.com/Business_and_Economy/Electronic_Commerce/

Section to search is "Business and Economy," subsection "Electronic Commerce."

Credit Related Newsgroups
Note: You must have a news reader installed to take part in newsgroups

mail:misc.business.credit

Post questions and read on-line discussions about credit.

mail:misc.consumers

Post questions and read on-line discussions about your consumer rights and what you can do when those rights have been trampled.